Mentoring
in
Academic
Medicine

Books in the ACP Teaching Medicine Series

Theory and Practice of Teaching Medicine
Jack Ende, MD, MACP
Editor

Methods for Teaching Medicine
Kelley M. Skeff, MD, PhD, MACP
Georgette A. Stratos, PhD
Editors

Teaching in Your Office, A Guide to Instructing Medical Students and Residents, Second Edition
Patrick C. Alguire, MD, FACP
Dawn E. DeWitt, MD, MSc, FACP
Linda E. Pinsky, MD, FACP
Gary S. Ferenchick, MD, FACP
Editors

Teaching in the Hospital
Jeff Wiese, MD, FACP
Editor

Mentoring in Academic Medicine
Holly J. Humphrey, MD, MACP
Editor

Leadership Careers in Medical Education
Louis Pangaro, MD, MACP
Editor

Teaching Medicine Series

Jack Ende, MD, MACP
Series Editor

Mentoring in Academic Medicine

Holly J. Humphrey, MD, MACP
Editor

ACP Press
American College of Physicians • Philadelphia, Pennsylvania

Director, Publishing Operations: Linda Drumheller
Developmental Editor: Marla Sussman
Production Editor: Suzanne Meyers
Publishing Coordinator: Angela Gabella
Cover Design: Kate Nichols
Index: Kathleen Patterson

Printed in the United States of America
Printing/Binding by Versa Press
Composition by ACP Graphic Services

Library of Congress Cataloging-in-Publication Data

Mentoring in academic medicine / [edited by] Holly Humphrey.
    p. ; cm. -- (ACP teaching medicine series)
  Includes bibliographical references.
  ISBN 978-1-934465-45-5
  1. Mentoring in medicine. I. Humphrey, Holly. II. American College of
Physicians. III. Series: ACP teaching medicine series.
  [DNLM: 1. Mentors. 2. Teaching--methods. 3. Education, Medical--
methods. 4. Faculty, Medical. W 18 M549 2010]
  R834.M46 2010
  610.71--dc22
                          2009053111

11 12 13 14 / 10 9 8 7 6 5 4 3

Contributors

Clarence H. Braddock III, MD, MPH, FACP
Associate Dean for Medical Education
Stanford School of Medicine
Stanford, California

William T. Branch Jr., MD, MACP
Professor of Medicine
Emory University School of Medicine
Director, Division of General Internal
  Medicine
Grady Campus
Atlanta, Georgia

Jada Bussey-Jones, MD, FACP
Associate Professor of Medicine
Director, Primary Care Center
Emory University School of Medicine
Atlanta, Georgia

Capt Gerald Dodd Denton, MC, USN, MD, MPH, FACP
Associate Professor of Medicine
Vice Chair, Educational Programs
Uniformed Services University
Bethesda, Maryland

Thomas R. Hecker, PhD
Assistant Dean for Administration
University of Pennsylvania School of
  Medicine
Philadelphia, Pennsylvania

Col Paul A. Hemmer, MC, USAF, MD, MPH, FACP
Vice Chairman, Educational Programs
Uniformed Services University
Bethesda, Maryland

Stacy Higgins, MD, FACP
Assistant Professor of Medicine
Program Director, Primary Care Track
Emory University
Atlanta, Georgia

Holly J. Humphrey, MD, MACP
Professor of Medicine
Dean for Medical Education
University of Chicago Pritzker School of
  Medicine
Chicago, Illinois

Joseph C. Kolars, MD, FACP
Professor of Medicine
Senior Associate Dean for Education and
  Global Initiatives
University of Michigan Medical School
Ann Arbor, Michigan

Victoria A. Mulhern
Executive Director, Faculty Affairs and
  Professional Development
University of Pennsylvania School of
  Medicine
Philadelphia, Pennsylvania

Darcy A. Reed, MD, MPH
Associate Program Director, Internal
  Medicine Residency
Assistant Professor of Medicine
Mayo Medical School
Rochester, Minnesota

Steven F. Reichert, MD, FACP
Clinical Assistant Professor
Weill Medical College of Cornell
  University
New York, New York
Residency Program Director, Internal
  Medicine
Flushing, New York

Arthur H. Rubenstein, MD, MBBCh, MACP
Dean
University of Pennsylvania School of
  Medicine
Executive Vice President
University of Pennsylvania Health System
Philadelphia, Pennsylvania

Contributors (continued)

Kelly Smith, MPP
Communications and Residency Advising
  Manager
University of Chicago Pritzker School of
  Medicine
Chicago, Illinois

Lawrence G. Smith, MD, FACP
Dean
Hofstra University School of Medicine
Chief Medical Officer
North Shore-LIJ Health System
Great Neck, New York

Abey K. Thomas, MD
Fellow, Division of Nephrology
New York Hospital Queens
Flushing, New York

Ian L. Tong, MD
Clinical Instructor
Stanford University Hospitals
Stanford, California
Medical Director, Veterans Outreach
Palo Alto, California

Thomas R. Viggiano, MD, MEd
Professor of Medicine and Medical
  Education
Associate Dean, Faculty Affairs
Mayo Medical School
Mayo Clinic
Rochester, Minnesota

Delese Wear, PhD
Professor of Behavioral Sciences
Northeastern Ohio Universities
Rootstown, Ohio

Scott M. Wright, MD
Professor of Medicine
Johns Hopkins Bayview Medical Center
Baltimore, Maryland

Joseph Zarconi, MD, FACP
Professor of Internal Medicine
Northeastern Ohio Universities College
  of Medicine
Rootstown, Ohio

I learned at the foot of a master in U.S. medicine. I dedicate this book to him, Dr. Arthur Rubenstein, my former teacher, department chair, and most significant mentor. I further dedicate this book to the students, residents, and chief residents at The University of Chicago, who provided enthusiastic "reverse mentoring" and inspiration for a lifetime.

Acknowledgments

This book is meant to be a helpful guide to all who care about guiding the next generation. The seeds for this endeavor were planted decades ago by my mentors, to whom I owe my career. Ideally, I would call them all out by name, but that would require a book of its own.

I wish to acknowledge the professional support provided by Dana Levinson and Kelly Smith, who assisted with every aspect of the preparation of this book. They provided far more than the technical expertise and the focus on detail that every good editor relies on—they also nurtured my demeanor through their good humor and generosity of spirit. Their expertise and disposition create an atmosphere of professionalism and a good deal of enjoyment.

Contents

Visit www.acponline.org/acp_press/teaching
for additional information.

About the *Teaching Medicine* Series

This book series, *Teaching Medicine*, represents a major initiative from the American College of Physicians. It is intended for College members but also for the profession as a whole. Internists, family physicians, subspecialists, surgical colleagues, nurse practitioners, and physician assistants—indeed, anyone involved with medical education—should find this book series useful as they pursue one of the greatest privileges of the profession: the opportunity to teach and make a difference in the lives of learners and their patients. The series is composed of six books:

- *Theory and Practice of Teaching Medicine*, edited by me, considers how medical learners learn (how to be doctors), how medical teachers teach, and how they (the teachers) might learn to teach better.

- *Methods for Teaching Medicine*, edited by Kelley M. Skeff and Georgette A. Stratos, builds on this foundation but focuses on the actual methods that medical teachers use. This book explores the full range of techniques that encourage learning within groups. The authors present a conceptual framework and guiding perspectives for understanding teaching; the factors that support choices for particular teaching methods (such as lecturing vs. small group discussion); and practical advice for preceptors, attendings, lecturers, discussion leaders, workshop leaders, and, finally, course directors charged with running programs for continuing medical education.

- *Teaching in Your Office*, edited by Patrick C. Alguire, Dawn E. DeWitt, Linda E. Pinsky, and Gary S. Ferenchick, will be familiar to many teaching internists. It has been reissued as part of this series. This book remains the office-based preceptor's single most useful resource for preparing to receive medical students and residents into an ambulatory practice setting or, among those already engaged in office-based teaching, for learning how to do it even better.

- *Teaching in the Hospital* is edited by Jeff Wiese and considers the challenges and rewards of teaching in that particular setting. Hospitalists as well as more traditional internists who attend on the inpatient service will be interested in the insightful advice that this book provides. This advice focuses not only on how to conduct rounds and encourage learning among students and house officers but also on how to frame and orient the content of rounds for some of the more frequently encountered inpatient conditions.

- *Mentoring in Academic Medicine,* edited by Holly J. Humphrey, considers professional development across the continuum of medical education, from issues pertaining to students to residents to faculty themselves, as well as issues pertaining to professional development of special populations. Here is where the important contributions of mentors and role models are explored in detail.

- *Leadership Careers in Medical Education* concludes this series. Edited by Louis Pangaro, this book is written for members of the medical faculty who are pursuing—or who are considering—careers as clerkship directors, residency program directors, or educational leaders of departments or medical schools, careers that require not only leadership skill but also a deep understanding of the organization and administration of internal medicine's educational enterprise. This book explores the theory and practice of educational leadership, including curricular design and evaluation; and offers insightful profiles of many of internal medicine's most prominent leaders.

Jack Ende, MD, MACP
Philadelphia, 2010

Mentoring and Fostering Professionalism in Medical Education: An Introduction and a View From the Trenches

Life is no brief candle to me; it is a sort of splendid torch which I've got a hold of for the moment and I want to make it burn as brightly as possible before handing it on to future generations.

—George Bernard Shaw

When I was asked to edit this book on mentoring and professional development, I leapt at the opportunity, which is quite unlike my usual response to invitations for new responsibilities. Generally, I carefully study my commitments, determine how a new opportunity fits with both my calendar and my family obligations, weigh the pros and cons of the proposal, and finally determine whether I have sufficient intrinsic energy for the project.

This invitation was different. In many ways, I owe my entire career to mentoring. As the beneficiary of the wisdom, guidance, and generosity of my mentors, I knew that my answer could be nothing other than affirmative. It is also the case that the new medical school curriculum at the University of Chicago, implemented in summer 2009, is built around scholarship and discovery, with mentoring as a fundamental component for the experiential learning of our students.

Why am I so passionate about this topic? Having reached the rank of a senior faculty member, I have had more than a few decades to consider and evaluate the choices I made over the course of my career. When looking back, I am struck by how many times I stood at a crossroads and made a decision that would determine the next set of choices and opportunities. Several key decisions stand out: 1) choosing a path as a clinician-educator; 2) determining whether to focus on pulmonary medicine, critical care, or a combination of both; 3) deciding when and how to fit children into our two-physician family; and 4) coming close, on at least a few occasions, to leaving academic medicine completely.

Those instances when I considered leaving were precipitated by the simultaneous needs of children, aging parents, and a growing list of work-related responsibilities. What made the difference? First and foremost was a supportive husband who not only shared the responsibilities of home and family but also provided compassionate leadership and good humor, making each day fun-filled. His support was followed by unwavering encouragement and flexibility from my mentors. They nourished nascent dreams into reality far beyond what I was able to visualize or imagine. One thing my mentors had in common is that they were all men. Another is that they were men with wives who have professional careers of their own.

Before I had any real mentors, I had a large number of role models—more senior residents and faculty. These expert clinicians modeled compassion, integrity, and optimism in the face of challenge and difficulty. In time, some of those role models became mentors. While I cannot underestimate the impact that my experiences with traditional mentors (dyad or one-on-one relationships) had on my personal and professional development, peer mentors also heavily influenced my career. The years spent as a resident and fellow were intense learning experiences of the power of peer mentoring, learning skills and knowledge from superior colleagues, and gaining perspective and perseverance drawn from the strength of colleagues. After I became internal medicine residency program director, my interactions with the first several chief residents who served with me continued to feel like peer mentoring relationships because our ages and years of experience in medicine were similar. With time, however, my relationships with the chief residents changed, and I began to experience the value and benefit of reverse mentoring.

This concept originated in the business sector and involves younger members of the organization, with substantially less seniority, teaching more senior managers how to use technology and computing applications (1). My students helped me set up my first podcast and oriented me to Facebook and Twitter. The real benefit from reverse mentoring went beyond technology tutorials to developing a relationship based on meaningful work with a shared goal. Over many years, in the weekly 2-hour meetings with my chief residents, I not only learned some great practical tips for creating PowerPoint presentations but, more important, I stayed in touch with how the interns were managing stress and which residents were struggling with broken relationships or financial issues. The chief residents kept me in touch with our house staff in ways that I could not have accomplished on my own. They kept my heart in the trenches and my head out of the clouds. It is also the case that my career was supported and propelled forward by mentoring networks, largely through the Association of Program Directors in Internal Medicine, the American College of Physicians, and, more recently, the American Board of Internal Medicine and the Association of American Medical Colleges. These organizations inspired new ideas and perspectives, and, in my early years as a program director, they helped me develop a growing career in academic medicine. Networks are increasingly recognized as important vehicles for mentoring and professional development among colearners who share knowledge in an environment of mutual learning and trust (2).

How do we think about mentoring and the impact on professionalism? Only many years after my most intense mentoring experiences do I begin to see the subtext of what I was learning from my mentors all along. I was learning medicine not only as a discipline but also as a profession by absorbing the history of professionalism and the virtues, attitudes, and behaviors of a professional. Supporting and fostering a culture of professionalism among physicians, ensuring that the values of the profession are transmitted from one generation to the next, and encouraging professionalism in the behaviors and daily interactions of physicians are topics of intense focus among academic medical leaders and medical educators. There is a widespread perception that the professionalism of physicians has faltered in recent years, whether from the generational changes among those entering the profession or the pernicious influence of corporate culture and capitalism. At a minimum, we can say that the concept of "professionalism" is changing, as inevitably as the generations of those in the profession change. Nevertheless, there are core beliefs and central tenets related to what professionalism as a physician means, and no other activity has more potential to support their preservation or to shape how professional values in medicine evolve than mentorship. Intense personal bonds between mentor and mentee can shape not just individuals but also institutional culture and medicine in general. Therefore, what it means to be a mentor must be explored in depth, and this book is intended to play a role in this important process.

Just as the concept of "professionalism" means many things to many people, so too does the idea of "mentorship." These ideas vary among students, residents, and faculty, depending on where they are in their education and career, what they seek from the mentoring relationship, what their professional goals are, and what mentoring experiences have been available for them. It is useful, therefore, to look at best practices and program initiatives for mentorship and mentoring across the continuum of professional development—from student to resident to faculty member. It is also useful to examine how these best practices and program initiatives might consider individual qualities, be they personal attributes (such as sex or race/ethnicity) or professional cohorts (for example, foreign medical school graduate, clinician educator).

This book explores mentorship both theoretically and practically. It reviews current scholarship in the field, explores various definitions of mentorship, and provides practical suggestions. The book is divided into three sections: I) Professional Development Through Mentoring and Role-Modeling, II) Mentoring Across the Continuum, and III) Mentoring Special Populations.

The first section of book begins with a chapter by Lawrence G. Smith, who sets up a framework for the book by discussing the challenges of educating the professional physician and sustaining a culture of professionalism in academic medicine. His chapter explores specific needs and concerns at various stages of professional development and identifies the impact and significance of mentoring and role-modeling as valuable tools for educating for professionalism. The following chapter, which I wrote, provides an overview of the fundamentals of mentoring, including theory and practice, and describes the impact of mentoring, particularly in such nuanced and complicated areas as career choice, personal satisfaction, and professionalism. The next chapter, written by Delese Wear and Joseph Zarconi, considers how mentoring might be used to foster a questioning and inquiring perspective among medical professionals and to encourage students to become independent thinkers and fierce patient advocates. This chapter has a perspective not frequently heard in the discussion of mentorship or professionalism and challenges us to reconsider our assumptions, to evolve fresh directions and approaches for our interaction with new generations entering medical school, and to reflect on what professionalism in medicine might mean or look like as the century progresses. This section ends with a chapter from Darcy A. Reed and Scott M. Wright, who discuss the impact of role models in promoting professionalism and humanism in medicine. Reed and Wright reinforce Wear and Zarconi's message by reminding us of the importance of heroes and the value of aspiring toward heroism.

The second section describes mentoring across the continuum of medical education. Gerald Dodd Denton and Paul A. Hemmer start us off with a discussion of mentoring medical students, focusing on practical elements that faculty members, clerkship directors, and departmental leaders should consider to foster professionalism in medical students and to develop faculty in their role as mentors for medical students. Residency is a period of professional development in which preparation and guidance for careers are paramount, but the requirements and expectations of residency mean that mentorship is too often sacrificed for more pressing or urgent matters. Joseph C. Kolars reminds us of the value of mentorship during this stage and provides principles, techniques, and best practices for structuring the mentoring relationship between residents and faculty for a mutually productive and rewarding interaction. Several chapters are devoted to mentoring of faculty. Thomas R. Viggiano gives a sweeping overview of current research and best practices on mentoring faculty for academic careers, and Stacy Higgins, William T. Branch Jr., and Jada Bussey-Jones explore how traditional mentoring of faculty might be supported and enhanced through formal peer mentoring programs, which have specific value and resonance for clinician educators. Because the professional development of clinician-educator faculty in academic medicine has often been overlooked, and because mentors are frequently in short supply, exploring other options for such faculty to consider in order to ensure they receive the mentorship that will support their advancement—personal and professional—is crucial. This section ends with a chapter by Thomas R. Hecker, Victoria A. Mulhern, and Arthur H. Rubenstein on the successful mentoring of faculty for research careers, encompassing strategy not only for the mentoring relationship itself but also for how to foster an institutional environment where mentoring is valued, recognized, and rewarded.

The third section focuses on specific populations that have special mentoring needs and challenges. While the percentage of women and men choosing medicine is roughly equal, women continue to be underrepresented among senior faculty and academic leaders, are disproportionately represented among various disciplines of medicine, and are more likely than men to leave academic medicine. Kelly Smith and I provide a chapter on special issues and considerations for mentoring women.

The ongoing challenge of recruiting and retaining students, residents, and faculty who are underrepresented in medicine persists and underscores the need to provide effective mentorship to minorities. Clarence H. Braddock III and Ian L. Tong share insights, challenges, and strategies for mentoring underrepresented minority students, residents, and faculty. This section ends with Steven F. Reichert and Abey K. Thomas's valuable exploration of mentoring a particularly vulnerable group of residents: foreign medical school graduates. This cohort represents a significant percentage of all residents training in the United States, and this chapter provides strategies and best practices for supporting their ongoing medical education and future careers in the United States health care system.

I began this introduction by discussing my passionate belief in the importance of mentoring. The book concludes with my own lessons learned from the mentor who shaped my professional development—and indeed, the professional lives of many others.

Holly J. Humphrey, MD, MACP
Chicago, Illinois, 2010

REFERENCES

1. **Murphy J, Adamst A.** Exploring the benefits of user education: a review of three case studies. Health Information and Libraries Journal. 2005;22(Suppl 1):45-58.
2. **Kram KE, Higgins MC.** A new approach to mentoring. Wall Street Journal. 22 September 2008:R10-R11.

Section I

Professional Development Through Mentoring and Role-Modeling

1

Educating the Professional Physician

Lawrence G. Smith, MD, FACP

> But how shall we educate men of goodness, to a sense of one another, to a love of truth? And more urgently, how shall we do this in a bad time?
> —*Daniel Berrigan*

Medical educators have long focused on the development of the professional physician as one of the ultimate products of their education system. Achieving this goal has been accomplished by using mentoring and role-modeling, as well as classic teaching methods. Those methods include lecture, laboratory, and traditional clerkships to teach a core curriculum of basic science, followed by specialty-oriented rotations primarily on inpatient hospital services. In today's health care environment, the old model of medical education is no longer working; it fails to address the younger generation's culture and learning styles, and the inpatient service is no longer sufficient on its own for robust clinical education.

In the past, the key teachers of professionalism have been the master clinicians, specialists, and scientists who populated the faculties of our medical schools. These master teachers have been replaced by teaching hospitalists. Much of the day-to-day teaching has always been left to trainees only a few steps further advanced than the students, who may know the mechanics of care but are not the role models of mature professionalism. There has been a strong tradition of generosity on the part of the physician community to volunteer their time, energy, and role-modeling to train the next generation of physicians. This has been challenged by time pressures on clinicians, managed care

KEY POINTS

- In today's health care environment, there is a need for a new model of medical education that reflects the modern practice of medicine, addresses the younger generation's culture and learning styles, and also serves the needs of our patients.
- Acquisition of the professional traits and behaviors of a doctor is a personal transformation that occurs in stages and must be guided by mentors and role models.
- Physician burnout is pervasive in the healing professions and poses a true threat to medical professionalism; medical educators must strive to create a professionally supportive work culture in which individuals know to ask for help early to prevent the slide toward professional dysfunction.
- A growing body of literature suggests that certain personal attributes may predict physician resilience; further research is required to determine how medical educators can foster resilience and therefore minimize burnout among physicians.
- Medical educators must come to better understand the new generation of physicians to develop the best way to facilitate professionalism in the workplace.
- New medical school admission screening methods may help predict which individuals will excel in the noncognitive areas of medicine, such as professionalism.
- Professionalism is difficult to assess, but research suggests that good measures of professionalism will incorporate peer feedback and will recognize individualized developmental needs.
- Mentorship is a key component in the young physician's professional development.

demands for productivity, and professional isolation. All of these stressors have made effective mentoring more difficult to achieve.

During the medical education process there is a hope of gradual professionalization of the students until they are welcomed as full-fledged members of the medical profession. This chapter will enumerate and discuss challenges and threats to professional education, with specific emphasis on the struggle to instill professional values and attitudes in young physicians that are consistent with the modern practice of medicine.

❖ Challenges and Threats to Professional Education

Many challenges face medical educators in this new millennium because of the extreme changes that have occurred in our health care system (Box 1-1). Ever-increasing data show that the health care work force is inadequate and, more specifically, inadequately supplied with physicians trained in the United States. There appears to be overspecialization of physician graduates and an inappropriate geographic distribution of physicians, leading to a mismatch of the skill set of the graduates to population needs. There is a sense that recent graduates have less well-honed clinical skills, less dedication to medicine, and a poor work ethic. Furthermore, the emerging physician workforce is burdened with extraordinary educational debt that may well influence their choice of career and where and how they practice. The traditional models of teaching do not address the learning styles of the new generation, specifically in the use of technology. Most traditional models have only begun to explore the extraordinary opportunities that now exist to enhance learning through the use of educational technology. Traditional models have failed to put the learner at the right site of care in an ever-changing model of care that has shifted to ambulatory delivery, chronic disease management, and highly technologic interventions. All of this takes place in a shifting environment

Box 1-1. Challenges to Medical Educators

- ► Changing patient demographics
- ► Generational student issues
- ► Pressured hospital teaching service
- ► Chronic illness
- ► Physician workforce mismatch to care needs
- ► Wasteful models of care
- ► Consumerism
- ► Managed care
- ► Conflict of interest
- ► Student debt
- ► Technologic/data-driven care

where an aging population with serious chronic disease now challenges the entire system; data transparency threatens physician autonomy; and the "Oslerian" hospital service is now a technologically driven, computer controlled, impersonal, time-pressured, "high-through-put" patient factory (1–5). With the explosion of highly specialized physicians, patients have many doctors, but no one is in charge (6). The new limits on resident work hours have produced schedules that emphasize shift work over personal patient ownership. All this cries out for change.

The four pillars of medical education—science, humanism, health of the public, and professionalism—are all critical foundations for the practice of medicine, yet clearly need to be retrofit into a modern model of care. Scientific knowledge has become so expansive that future physicians cannot be expected to learn the minute details of every area of biomedical science. However, key concepts of basic, translational, and clinical research and their application to clinical practice through evidence-based medicine will continue to be essential aspects of any successful medical school curriculum. Medical schools have failed to teach scientific concepts that are durable and translate into sophisticated clinical thinking. Moving molecular science to the bedside has proven to be far more difficult than physiologic science. Yet an absolute commitment to a current, scientifically sophisticated knowledge base and expert technical and clinical skills is part of the compact of the profession with society.

The knowledge base of medical practice is moving so rapidly that the old model of knowing everything is clearly untenable. Medical educators are being pushed to recognize that adults learn best through active learning, where they take ownership of their own process of learning and focus on problem-solving, reasoning, and self-directed learning (see *Theory and Practice of Teaching Medicine*, another book in the *Teaching Medicine* series [7]). Technology is changing how teaching and learning take place. Educators must teach patient-centered care while being student-centered in the organizational design of the curriculum. Teaching and measuring communication skills are essential to produce effective, as opposed to simply knowledgeable, physicians. Educators must learn better ways to both define and teach modern scientific concepts that can be used to conceptualize the patient at the bedside, not simply to pass the Step 1 U.S. Medical Licensing Examination. And last but not least, young medical students must be encouraged to embrace the personal transformation from layperson to a physician capable of practicing the art of medicine: humanism, empathy, communication skills, and all the other attributes that build a trusting relationship between doctor and patient (8, 9). Although these skills often appear to be innate, research suggests that they may be teachable and certainly can be evaluated through a variety of assessment tools. It is often these skills that separate the "knowledgeable" from the "effective" physician.

Looking ahead, population health will undoubtedly become a key "basic" science of medical school curricula. Future physicians will no longer be trained only to engage a single patient one encounter at a time. Physicians of the future will be responsible for assessing and improving the health of the population in which they live, and these essential skills must be taught early in medical education and reinforced throughout training and practice (10–13). This will include active advocacy for social justice, universal access to care, elimination of health disparities, and shared responsibility for the health of the public.

Professionalism is more important than ever. This is an era when physicians can do more, patients can benefit from both preventive and therapeutic care, and the science explaining medical disease is advancing at an incredible pace. Physicians, patients, and society are dissatisfied with the status quo. Medical educators must focus on the development of professionalism that is relevant to the modern practice of medicine, is acceptable to a new generation of physicians, and serves the needs of patients. It is not acceptable to blame the younger generation of physicians for being who they are. If the profession cannot inclusively define itself for all dedicated physicians, it will fail.

In this chapter, professionalism will be discussed from its traditional roots and modern definitions. Educational interventions focusing on role-modeling, mentoring, and improving the learning environment, presented more fully in subsequent chapters of this book, will be discussed here as key features of teaching professionalism. Lastly, techniques for asssessing professionalism will be considered, for it is only through use of accurate milestones and metrics that teaching methods improve and the personal transformation to a professional physician is fostered.

❖ Defining Professionalism

There has been a steady and ever-increasing interest in medical professionalism in the medical literature and throughout all of medical education (Figure 1-1). Many learned people have attempted to define medical professionalism in terms of philosophical, moral, and ethical principles by looking at the historic roots of the western traditions that have defined "the good physician" (14–18). Professionalism is often discussed in terms of sets of virtues and behaviors that define "the good physician" (19, 20). There have been extraordinary attempts to find behaviors that can be observed

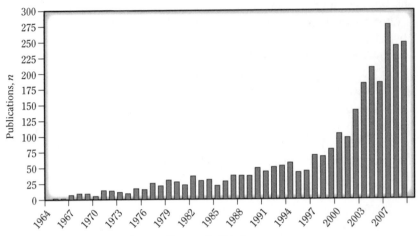

Figure 1-1 Articles on professionalism on PubMed.

and measured accurately with reproducible metrics (21). Professionalism has also been defined as a contract between the profession of medicine and society (22). This contract implies duties of both parties to the relationship, and the bond tying these parties together is trust. Others have looked at professionalism through the lens of social responsibility and even activism and advocacy (23). In the broad discussion of professionalism, there has also been significant but minimal discussion of the personal transformation from lay person to physician that distinguishes someone who *is* a physician from someone whose occupation is physician (24, 25).

There has been much pressure to define medical professionalism in educationally relevant terms to facilitate the improvement of training and evaluation. The Accreditation Council for Graduate Medical Education (ACGME) (26–29) has singled out professionalism as a core competency, and the Liaison Committee on Medical Education (30) has recently emphasized that the learning environment must be conducive to development of professionalism. The recent Milestones Project of the American Board of Internal Medicine has further emphasized the need for clear benchmarks and metrics in professional development. The public has expressed disappointment in the level of professionalism of physicians as a whole and increased interest in how medical educators plan to address this problem. The "Physician Charter on Medical Professionalism" (31), now embraced worldwide, is a document that has spurred both broad dialogue and intense focus on these issues. Even the Joint Commission has encouraged hospitals to establish zero tolerance policies for physicians whose behavior is unprofessional (32).

These external pressures come during a period when there are also many threats to appropriate physician professionalism, such as generational differences, consumerism, conflicts of interest, and burnout.

- Generational issues related to Generation X and Generation Y moving into the profession of medicine (33, 34) will be considered in more detail later in this chapter. The point here is that medical education leaders are facing pressure to bridge generational differences, particularly with the tidal wave of medical school expansion, both in the class size of existing schools and the creation of new medical schools (35).

- The *consumerism movement* tends to de-professionalize the doctor–patient relationship to make it more like a service provider–customer interaction (36–38). There has been a change for the worse in the trust relationship between the profession of medicine and society. Patients have become clients and physicians are providers. This upheaval has left many physicians feeling that they have lost their privileged position and that they no longer have to behave in special ways—all they need to do is simply provide an adequate service as a business transaction (39).

- Conflicts of interest appear to be everywhere in medicine, whether they are the large and obvious conflicts of interest with transfer of gifts and money or the very small conflicts of interest inherent in every decision a physician makes to bring someone back for further care, refer them for testing, or send them to another colleague (40–44). Conflict of interest undermines trust, which is the core ethic of the doctor–patient relationship. Money perverts professionalism, and many of the payment systems further encourage the de-professionalization of physicians. There have been intense interest and ever-increasing scrutiny of conflict of interest at the individual physician, school, and institutional levels. The continuing medical education industry has been a particular focus. It is clear that the public believes conflict of interest to be a breach of professionalism. Even the medical payment system sets up an internal conflict of interest because it makes volume the incentive instead of quality of care.

- Burnout caused by bureaucracy, depersonalization, loss of professional camaraderie, and physician disillusionment have threatened the traditional concept of the profession.

Because of all these threats to professionalism in medicine, the challenge of designing an environment that nurtures the transformation to a professional and encourages the acquisition of the attributes and duties of the profession is paramount.

What kind of attributes should the environment foster? The discussion of professionalism often involves the acquisition of the many virtues and behaviors that define the good physician (Box 1-2). Furthermore, these virtues are interpreted very differently in medicine than in the world outside of medicine. The ethics of medicine are distinctly different from the ethics of ordinary morality (39), for instance:

- In ordinary life, moral responsibility is negative. One must refrain from harming others. In medicine, doctors have a positive duty to act on behalf of their patients.
- In ordinary life, one is free to associate with whomever one chooses. In medicine, doctors must serve any patient with medical needs regardless of who they are.
- In ordinary life, one freely shares what is learned in the course of interactions with others. In medicine, confidentiality is presumed and strictly enforced.
- In ordinary life, sexual interactions are usually acceptable between adults. In medicine, nothing legitimizes physician sexual involvement with a patient.
- In ordinary life, it is considered rude to ask probing and overly personal questions. In medicine, taking a detailed history, including asking about very personal issues, is the norm.

Box 1-2. Attributes of the Good Physician

- ► Fidelity
- ► Excellence
- ► Honesty
- ► Integrity
- ► Altruism
- ► Compassion
- ► Justice
- ► Courage
- ► Embrace of *being* a physician

- In ordinary life, one expects family to act on behalf of their loved ones. In medicine, doctors should not be the physicians for their own family members.
- In ordinary life, telling a "white lie" and revealing a secret are minor infractions. In medicine, they are major breaches of professionalism.

Likewise, physicians have been given privileges to ask questions that others cannot, to examine the naked person, and to touch people in ways that are far more intimate than any other "business" interaction allows. With that privilege come the responsibility and accountability to maintain a doctor–patient relationship founded on ethics and trust, and rooted in the behaviors that patients believe are part of being a physician. Acquisition of the professional traits and behaviors of the doctor is a transformation that occurs slowly and must be guided by mentors.

❖ Stages of Professional Development

Professional transformation from lay person to physician occurs over time in stages that can be observed and described. The transformation requires students to have personal, emotionally charged interactions with patients, to reflect alone and with others about those interactions, and to observe and imitate experienced role models. Without the appropriate amount of time and learning environment for this to happen safely, socialization into the profession and personal transformation fail to occur. By looking at some of the seminal work on moral development and how this cognitive psychology framework has been applied to other professions, the stages of development of physicianship can be articulated (Table 1-1) (45–48).

Stage 1: Early Entry

In stage 1, young students enter medical school with personal behaviors that have been learned in their families and in school. Proof that these behaviors have served them well is their success in the hypercompetitive world of premedical education. When they arrive at medical school, their first exposure to the profession of medicine often produces shock and surprise when their usual behavior, which has been praised and rewarded all of their lives, is seen as unprofessional. Stage 1, therefore, is the starting point from which they begin the evolution of a physician. The angst created by the sudden realization that the rules have changed begins their movement forward.

Table 1-1. Stages of Professional Development

Stage 1: Early Entry	Stage 2: Reward/ Punishment	Stage 3: Team Member	Stage 4: Physician Self	Stage 5: Mentor
Reflex responses derive from previous non-professional life	It's all about *me*	Can hold multiple points of view	Integrated the profession (values, thinking) into a new self-identity	It's all about *others*
Rules of the profession not clearly understood	Figuring out the "rules of the game"	Relationships are critical; the "Profession" is a relationship	Professional behaviors become habitual	Holds a "big picture" perspective
Surprise and angst at adverse reactions to "usual behaviors"	What's on the test?	Motivation is the "medicine team does it this way"	Can break away from the rules and the team when appropriate	Teaches the "rules" of doctoring
	Motivation is the system's reward/ punishment	Satisfaction is from successful team and individual relationships	Leads the team	Guides the team
	Satisfaction comes from the external rewards		Can be flexible and self-critical	Nurtures the transforma-tion to physician
			Motivation is "I know the right thing to do"	Motivation is to see others succeed
			Satisfaction is internally derived (integrity)	Satisfaction derives from the accom-plishments of others

Stage 2: Reward/Punishment

In stage 2, students realize that they are immersed in a culture that has a completely new set of rules and behavioral expectations. Those who are intuitive quickly figure out a new set of rules and begin to comply with them in an effort to "succeed." However, the students' measures of personal success are the receipt of external rewards, grades, and praise. In this phase, students are trying very hard to be perceived as young citizens of the profession of medicine, but their motivation is entirely focused on themselves.

Stage 3: Team Member

In stage 3, the students begin to realize that the profession of medicine is a "club" that they would like to join. They want to be accepted by the team and they understand that medicine has its own way of understanding the world and approaching patients. They also understand that there is a social culture within the world of medicine in which they very much want to take part.

It is in stage 3 that the positive and negative influences of the hidden curriculum have so much power; students will do almost anything to fit in and be accepted by the team. Most clinical medical students, interns, and residents are in stage 3 of professional development. This should be obvious from the ultimate term of praise on so many evaluation forms, "good team player." In stage 3 of development, young physicians are able to gradually join the profession of medicine, take care of patients safely, teach younger team members, and establish internal rules that allow the process of care to take place. However, it is during this period that behaviors that would otherwise have seemed abhorrent, such as disrespect for patients, gallows humor, and many of the negative coping actions acquired by the young clinical teams, are readily accepted as normal. Here in stage 3 the reward is being accepted by the team and being part of the profession, but not quite yet being a professional.

Stage 4: Physician Self

In stage 4, the developing physicians begin to fully integrate and internalize the values and behaviors of a physician. Those values become habits, and physicians no longer think about how a lay person versus a physician would approach a situation; rather, they simply *are* physicians. They think that way, they behave that way, and it is the default way that they respond to everything in their lives. In this stage, physicians are able to get beyond the team culture, to lead and critique the team, and to do critical self-assessment. It is this stage of development to which all medical educators should strive to bring every physician-in-training. It is only at stage 4 of professional development that one can truly be seen as a professional.

These are the young physicians with the moral and personal development to be trusted by patients. They take on integrity as a way of being; they set high standards of excellence for themselves and live up to those standards even "when no one is watching." The personal reward in this stage is the personal satisfaction of being a good doctor.

Stage 5: Mentor

Stage 5 is a developmental stage that is not reached by all—in fact, it is perhaps reached by only a select few. The stage of mentor or senior physician is one where the professional focus and effort shift from themselves to the others under their charge. Mentor/senior physicians rejoice in the success of their mentees. These are the physicians who guide the transformation from lay person to professional, who explain and define the rules of the profession, who lead through role-modeling, and who are dedicated to personal excellence. Personal satisfaction is derived from the success of others. Although not everyone reaches this stage, those physicians who do must be thrust continuously into the learning environment. Through their leadership, mentoring, and role-modeling, professional development is catalyzed in others.

❖ Generational Issues

Generational differences play a key role in the current challenge of teaching professional development to emerging physicians. There are currently four generations in the American workforce (33). Much has been written about the conflict between these generations, both in the medical and nonmedical workforce, and about the significant issues that have arisen from this conflict (49–53). In fact, the endless number of papers in the medical literature on professionalism usually focuses on the virtues and behaviors of "the good physician" or on the measurement of the conflicts between generations, with the seemingly inevitable conclusion that the young generations are "unprofessional." Much of this so-called unprofessionalism focuses on a perceived lack of full commitment to being a doctor and a poor work ethic.

Table 1-2 describes the four generations currently in the workforce. The silent generation ("the veterans") comprises the most senior members of the physician community, and is seen as the generation that defines "American values." This generation, with its tendency toward conservative traditionalism, family values, and clear gender roles, in many ways defines the United States that emerged after World War II.

The Baby Boomer generation, huge in size and dominant at this time among the leadership of medicine, represents the generation that truly

Table 1-2. Generational Profiles

Characteristic	Veterans	Baby Boomers	Generation X	Generation Y
Years	1922–1945	1946–1964	1965–1980	1981–2000
Population	55 million	78 million	47 million	80 million
Style	Traditional	Personal satisfaction	Self-reliant	Modern, traditional
Size	Rapidly declining	Dominant	Small group	Large
Ethic	Respectful, loyal	Ambitious, political	Progressive, cynical	Loyal, conservative
Gender role	Classic gender roles	Mixing gender roles	Unclear	Gone
Work	Respect the system	Respect experience	Respect expertise	Respect achievement
	Work for security	Likes to work	Work to live	Change jobs easily
Heroes	Strong heroes	Strong heroes	No heroes	Anti-heroes
Seminal events	Great Depression, World War II	Vietnam	Weak United States	September 11th
Upbringing	Traditional family	Traditional family	Absentee parents	Protective parents
Reward	A job well done	Money, title, recognition	Freedom and time	Meaningful work

redefined the meaning of "workaholic." Emerging as children born into a world where the United States was a superpower and the world was redefining itself after the most devastating war, Baby Boomers brought their ambitious culture to the medical workforce. Women began to appear in greater numbers as physicians with the loss of traditional gender roles. Traditional family values began to be modified significantly. The Baby Boomer generation, with its politically savvy attitude toward life, created the plethora of Wall Street investment bankers, corporate lawyers, and high-income physicians who focus on money, title, and recognition. It is this generation that expresses the most dissatisfaction with the younger generation and yet itself has significant cynicism and loss of enthusiasm for the continued practice of medicine. They are seen as "burnt out" by the younger generations.

Generation X trainees born after 1980 and their more junior counterparts, Generation Y, are now medicine's residents and students today. These are generations whose principle mantra is balance in life. They reject workaholism and many other values of the Baby Boomers. This conflict has created a significant rift in the culture of medicine because of these core differences in values.

Unlike the very large Baby Boomer generation, Generation X is small, only 47 million. They grew up in a family structure that was in transition and often found themselves latch-key children. Their culture was characterized by pragmatism and cynicism, informality, and the ultimate irritating question, "Is this going to be on the test?" Traditional gender roles have become unclear, and Generation X individuals are highly skeptical of institutions and authority. Their behavior in the workplace is, "Give me the goal; don't tell me how to do it. I am leaving when I am done." People in this generation do not believe in "paying your dues" and do not instinctively respond well to hierarchy and chain of command. Some of these characteristics can potentially cause problems in the medical workplace. Generation X individuals look for freedom and time and will trade income, specialty choice, and prestige for them (54–56).

Generation Y, the current medical school generation, grew up in the protective environment of the safe, new nuclear family. Moving back toward more traditional values, this generation still does not want to pay its dues and is totally wired to a digital world. These individuals are looking for meaning in their work. Generation Y is also the generation that has stayed in their parents' homes longer than any prior generation and actively resists growing up. Both Generations X and Y have presented significant problems for university educators and no doubt present similar problems to medical educators (57–59).

The event that dramatically announced the arrival of Generation X was the work hour restrictions that began in New York State after the Libby Zion case (60) with the New York State 405 Regulations (61); see also *Leadership Careers in Medical Education*, another book in the *Teaching Medicine* series (62). Work hour restrictions have since become national ACGME requirements that were recently reviewed by the Institute of Medicine (63). There is enormous public pressure to reduce work hours as a means of improving patient safety. Although work hour restrictions in their current and future form are the effort of regulators, younger generations have been "blamed" by the older generation. Baby Boomers cannot get past the loss of the old culture of total workaholism in the pursuit of medicine; they see these younger doctors as slackers (64, 65). There are also many other differences between these two generations. Generations X and Y have been raised in a time when learning increasingly takes place on computer screens instead of books, where everything comes in short sound bites, where everyone multitasks continuously, and technology is hard-wired in their brain. These are the generations that grew up without clear heroes and as such have had trouble finding appropriate role models in their own professional and personal development.

However, there is little evidence that Generations X and Y are any more or less professional than any previous generation of physicians. The extreme focus on work hours as a surrogate for all "professionalism" distracts the discussion from the real issues. Although younger physicians may trade preferred specialty choice and income for time and life balance, there is no evidence that when younger physicians practice medicine, they lack the vigor, intellectual commitment, and dedication to their patients that older physicians have. The role of medical educators should be to encourage the development of the essential attributes of "the good physician," as opposed to constantly focusing on a reticence to an unlimited work commitment. Young physicians must be prepared for the future medical environment that will be the context of their lives so that they can be professionals and be professionally satisfied in their practice. Ultimately, the challenge to physician leadership is that, regardless of what generation physicians represent, they flexibly and respectfully define excellence and professionalism in terms that are completely acceptable to all generations and focused on the patient. Physician leaders need to be the people who build bridges, not barriers, within the profession of medicine. Too much effort has gone into the endless mourning of the loss of unlimited work hours. Physician leaders and educators need to get past this, move forward, and begin to regain control of the evolution of the profession. Medicine must never compromise on what is essential and can never allow entry into the profession of those who do not embrace the personal transformation to being a doctor.

In approaching this younger generation, educators must understand the differences in their learning styles, their different expectations of teachers, role models, and mentors, their approach to work, and their appropriate demand for balance in life (Box 1-3). If educators understand the context and the culture of who these young people are, the best way to challenge them to be the finest physicians they can be becomes much more straightforward.

❖ Nature Versus Nurture

One of the ongoing debates in medical education is whether professionalism is an innate set of personal characteristics and attributes or whether it can be learned during medical school (66–71). Under the former hypothesis, students either have it or do not have it. The inevitable conclusion of this belief is that much more energy and focus should be spent on choosing

---

Box 1-3. Factors Influencing Teaching Strategies for Generations X and Y

- ▶ Entitled mindset
- ▶ Technological identity
- ▶ Immersion in virtual worlds
- ▶ Self-direction
- ▶ Emphasis on action over knowledge
- ▶ Constant connection to technology
- ▶ Multitasking
- ▶ Zero tolerance for delays or wasting time
- ▶ Dislike of hierarchy
- ▶ Insistence that learning must be real

---

students with the right "stuff" to enter medical school, rather than trying to change them. Substantial data suggest that much of personal development in terms of values, behaviors, and virtues is in fact established before one arrives in medical school and that the impact of medical education may be minimal to possibly negative in the development of these types of virtuous behaviors (72–78). In fact, there is reason to believe that cynicism and self-entitled behavior actually increase as a result of medical education. The ordeal of training and the pernicious power of the hidden curriculum may transform students in the wrong direction.

The alternative argument is that the right curriculum and the right role-modeling will encourage students to behave in ways that will actually transform them into "the good physician" (see the "Memorable Moments" section in *Theory and Practice of Teaching Medicine* [7]). There is likewise some less than convincing evidence that this can take place. However, it has been shown that virtuous, professional physicians may have better relationships with patients (79–81).

As this unprecedented era of expansion of both medical school class size and medical schools themselves begins, it is possible that to graduate highly professional physicians, a completely new method of student admissions may be in order. Some experiments using different interviewing and admission techniques have already taken place but have failed to show significant progress in predicting which students excel in the noncognitive areas of medicine. Among these more innovative admissions criteria are leadership roles, life and work experience, multitasking ability, and problem-solving skills (82–86). There is a clear challenge to medical educators to broaden research to discover the best admission process and to challenge the value of traditional criteria that have historically defined the best applicants: grades, MCAT scores, research accomplishments, and prestige of the undergraduate college. The hope is that in the next era of medical school acceptance processes, medical educators will be much more creative in the way in which they accept students, and much more compulsive in doing the educational research that connects success or failure in medical school to the different screening methods (see chapter 6 in *Leadership Careers in Medical Education* [62]).

It will undoubtedly be a combination of picking students with the right attributes and nurturing their personal development to physician that will be the ultimate solution to the challenge of training the next generation of physicians to the highest standards of professionalism. No one should accept as inevitable the faculty lament at graduation, "How can we be graduating that person as a physician?"

❖ Assessing Professionalism

Professionalism is difficult to define and even more difficult to assess. Medical educators should believe that the value of assessing professionalism is worth the extraordinary effort. Patients, the public in general, and the profession itself are crying out for professionalism to be assessed and improved (87, 88).

The difficulty in assessing professionalism starts with defining both a profession and professionalism. In thinking of the classic definition, one working model is that a profession consists of a group of people joined by a common body of knowledge that has been defined and then mastered through common education; by a commitment to self-assessment, professional accountability, and self-regulation; and finally by a degree of altruism that asks the members of a profession to put the well-being of others ahead of themselves. These attributes of a profession help us better formulate how an assessment plan would be defined.

In terms of medical professionalism, the program of assessment must consider many virtues, duties, and transformational characteristics of professionalism. First and foremost is the personal transformation that occurs in stages over time. This transition can occur only through real interaction between learners and the profession and patients, and with adequate time for learners to reflect on these important formative events. There is also an element of socialization into the profession that requires both personal and group reflection and the opportunity to try on professional behaviors and language until they become one's own (89). Milestones need to be articulated in easily understood terms for these stages of development. Second to the personal transformation are personal characteristics, such as the virtues of the good physician, the duties and obligations of a caregiver, the legal and ethical rules that overlie the practice of medicine, the societal expectations, and the observable behaviors that stem from these virtues, duties, and rules (90–93).

Observation itself is often problematic in every aspect of medical education. There is substantial evidence that students pass through almost their entire period of medical education with little direct observation or supervision by senior educators. Observation takes time. Careful, reliable observation requires training of the observers, certainty that the events under observation are contextually real and that the characteristics and measures have a taxonomy that is understandable, and a reliability and validity that allow evaluation to be trusted. Observation can only be intermittent. There is always uncertainty as to how representative any episodic sampling may be. How does observation separate a given behavior or action from the underlying attitude or real motivation? When should observation be categorized by global assessments? Should assessments be deconstructed into specific attributes and building blocks of what is the overall professional physician (94, 95)? What is the role of early predictors of long-term behavioral problems (96–98)? Should there be greater attention to critical incidents and use of these to trigger significant interventions? Is there a risk to overreacting?

Who should the observers be? Should they include senior physicians, junior faculty, interns and residents, peers? There is substantial evidence that peer assessment brings new and important information to the assessment of professionalism and should probably be the norm rather than the exception as medical education moves forward (99–102). Peer assessment often takes place in settings where no one is "performing for the teacher." Students often describe positive and negative behaviors about their peers that are totally missed by faculty evaluators. In fact, the method for nominations to the Gold Humanism Honor Society uses peer assessment and often results in the identification of different students than the standard school assessment techniques would have identified.

As emphasized in Ludmerer's important book on medical education (103), time is the commodity that is in greatest demand; without time, observation, assessment, and reflection do not occur. Without reflection and formative assessment, professional growth and personal development is thwarted.

There are excellent reviews of methods of approaching institutional planning for assessment of professionalism (104), but unless there is institutional buy-in to the appropriate definition, characteristics, fit with local culture, and predictive value of individual behaviors, the assessment of professionalism is likely to fall far short of its intended goal (see chapter 8 in *Leadership Careers in Medical Education* [62]). Methods currently in use, including standardized patients, surveys, peer assessment, critical incident reports, and portfolios, represent a menu of tools that only in their composite are likely to yield actionable information. Good measures will encourage true identification of the achievement of professional milestones and the individualized needs of each physician in development. They may also indicate when professionalism is faltering.

❖ Role of Mentoring and Professional Development

Medical educators often discuss the subject of appropriate mentoring (105) in relation to the career development of the physician. There are debates as to whether one can assign a mentor or whether students and young trainees need to select mentors themselves, how critical the personal match is, and ultimately what the roles of the mentor and mentee should be (106–113). There are also efforts to measure the necessity and impact of mentorship on career development (114, 115).

This discussion must begin with a working definition of mentoring. Mentoring occurs when an experienced, trusted, professional colleague offers personal expertise and advice to facilitate a less experienced person's professional growth and success. The mentor often helps the mentee establish a broader network of contacts and connections within the field and shares experience-based wisdom about the profession. On the basis of that broad definition of mentoring, it is clear that many people encountered during the life of a professional do some aspects of mentoring but may not fit the technical definition of mentor (Box 1-4) (116, 117).

The many "teachers" that each student encounters play important roles in professional development by helping to create explanatory models for the many complex skills and the knowledge needed to become a physician. Great teachers inspire and challenge the students to learn and change. As stated so eloquently by William Butler Yeats, "Education is not the filling of a pail, but the lighting of a fire."

Role models are absolutely essential to the development of the physician professional (see chapter 4 of this book). Literally all physicians who are encountered by young students are role models, whether they intend to be or not. From this absolute reality emerges the extraordinary power of

---

Box 1-4. Mentoring Roles

- ▶ Teacher
- ▶ Role model
- ▶ Coach
- ▶ Advisor
- ▶ Agent
- ▶ Good boss
- ▶ Consummate professional
- ▶ Hero

---

the hidden curriculum. It is by trying to be like members of the profession that one ultimately becomes the professional. This emphasizes the extraordinary obligation of every physician in a learning setting to be "the good physician." The job of the educational leaders is to keep the best role models visible and keep bad role models away from learners.

Similar to the teacher and role model, the coach is someone who observes and gives advice to foster the development of the skills needed to master a given task (see chapter 1 in *Teaching in the Hospital*, another book in the *Teaching Medicine* series [118]). Advisors help students understand themselves and the options open to them when facing times of decision. Agents are senior people who advocate for and put students in the right place at the right time so that they have maximum opportunity to succeed. The agent may also be wise and able to push students to the edge of their comfort zone to foster personal growth.

The boss for whom the young physician works has enormous powers to imprint on that person how things should be done. It is especially important that the youngest members of our profession work for the good bosses. A good boss sets an atmosphere conducive to professional success and satisfaction and transmits values and skills that are life-long lessons; in other words, the boss creates a work environment that is positive and rewarding. A bad boss early in a person's development is very detrimental and often encourages a self-protective rather than a risk-taking mindset.

The mentor is the person described previously, who has reached that very high level of professional development that makes him or her capable of establishing a special, durable relationship with a mentee. That relationship may progress into that of a colleague or even that of a trusted life-long friend. The greatest mentors are often recognized by many students over multiple generations.

Finally, young people need heroes. Without heroes, people often settle for who they are instead of aspiring to who they can become. One of the laments of those studying Generations X and Y is that, as a generation, they lack heroes. Heroes are people of courage who put aside their own self-interest to do the right thing. They are people who step forward when times are tough, when situations are in crisis, and when those lesser individuals shrink from the challenge. The identification of heroes, the rejoicing in their accomplishments, and the commitment to keep them ever visible in our learning environments are among the great challenges to medical education. Heroes form the ultimate image of who each person must strive to become.

❖ Physician Burnout

One of the true threats to the profession of medicine is physician burnout. It is pervasive in the healing professions and most significantly a threat to professionalism. Burnout crushes physicians' ongoing enthusiasm to embrace the highest standards of the profession.

Physician burnout is defined by three principal components: emotional exhaustion, depersonalization, and diminished feelings of personal accomplishment. Burnout, in its many forms and degrees, represents a major unresolved problem of the medical profession. Both burnout and depression related to work stress are highest among those who render care to others. Thus, burnout has been called the silent anguish of the healers, a true erosion of the soul of physicianship (119–123).

Certain personal characteristics (124–128) can make a physician more susceptible to burnout (Table 1-3). Many of them are characteristics are associated with being professional and altruistic members of the profession. Burnout tends to happen to the very best physicians who have the highest empathy for patients. Many researchers have suggested that burnout is predestined in certain physicians. Likewise, research has shown that there are also environmental factors that predispose physicians to burnout (see Table 1-3). It is intuitive that the experience of overwork, loss of control, isolation, and lose of balance in life can lead to loss of zeal for one's work. Further, there are medical school and residency program dynamics that contribute to the onset of burnout. They are related to long work hours, dissatisfaction with the learning–service balance, loss of a sense of growth and personal development, and the endless and often futile nature of an impersonal care model. Because of these medical education factors, burnout is often a "disease of our young." These educational program issues should be a wake-up call to medical educators because burnout occurs as early as the third year of medical school, internship, and early in practice.

Table 1-3. Characteristics Associated With Physician Burnout

Personal Traits Leading to Burnout	Environmental Issues Leading to Burnout	Relationship Between Medical Errors and Burnout
Medicine is a calling	Overwork	Errors cause burnout
Compulsive, impulsive	Lack of control	Burnout increases errors
Unmarried, childless	Isolation	Anxiety about future
Negative personality	Loss of community/team	errors
Female,	Role ambiguity	Poor sleep
underrepresented	or conflict	Becoming too cautious
minority	Early in training	Self-perception of giving
Living away from	Dissatisfied with	poor care
family	faculty/learning	Depression
Stressed personal	Futile care	Early retirement
relationships	Lack of time for	Isolation
Younger	personal reflection	
	Bureaucratic work	
	Lack of patient gratitude	

Medical errors and the personal reactions they cause (129–135) are significant contributors to burnout (see Table 1-3). Young physicians receive little training in how to deal with their personal reactions to medical errors. Physicians do not seek out support from their colleagues, and therefore medical errors often push people into a downward spiral of isolated anxiety from which it is difficult to emerge. Even the recent initiative for universal disclosure of medical errors to patients and their families requires cautious guidance and education of the physicians making those disclosures. Well-intentioned disclosure can result in significant negative reactions from patients and family and thus contribute to the physician's downward spiral toward burnout.

The entire medical profession needs to be on the lookout for colleagues in trouble. The signs and symptoms of burnout (Table 1-4) must be quickly identified (136). Seeking help needs to be culturally acceptable and readily available. Physicians must have a strong social network that allows them to talk through and reflect on issues related to their personal vulnerability and "empathy fatigue" of being a caregiver. As physicians slide into burnout, the risk for severe depression, substance abuse, anger, loss of personal relationships, and, ultimately, suicide, rise. Clinical performance may deteriorate, including a loss of patient trust, poor patient adherence, increased medical errors in care, and a clear sense by the patient that the physician has lost empathy and does not like being a doctor (see Table 1-5).

Table 1-4. Signs and Symptoms of Burnout

Chronic fatigue

Anger at those making demands

Self-criticism for putting up with the demands

Cynicism, negativity, and irritability

Sense of being besieged

Exploding easily at minor issues

Weight loss or gain

Sleeplessness and depression

Suspiciousness

Feelings of helplessness

Increased degree of risk-taking

Depression and mental exhaustion

Change in professional goals

Psychological withdrawal from work

Growing concern for self instead of others

Negative attitude toward life in general

To this point no interventions have been proven to successfully reverse burnout in physicians (137–140). Yet if one looks at the personal and environmental characteristics that lead to burnout, it seems obvious that leadership must act. Medical educators or senior physicians in leadership must take charge of the learning and the work environment to create a climate that allows physicians to continue to remain professional, empathetic, altruistic, and professionally satisfied. There must be time to socialize, to reflect, and to pause during the pressures of the day's work. There must be a positive culture that allows people to ask for help early in the slide toward professional dysfunction. There needs to be a trust between physicians that allows these issues to be discussed openly without fear.

Table 1-5. Effects of Burnout on Physician and Patient

Effects on Physician	Effects on Patient
Depression, suicide	Loss of patient trust
Substance abuse	Poor patient adherence
Anger	Errors
Damaged personal relationships	Loss of empathy

❖ Physician Resilience

While burnout lies at one end of the spectrum, the positive attribute of physician resilience is at the opposite end. There is a growing but small body of literature on this subject (141–143).

In one conceptual model, physician resilience is related to an adequate "coping reserve" that may be drained and replenished by external demands, but is shaped and structured by internal factors (144). This model helps explain why resilience varies among different people and also within an individual, depending on the presence of external stressors. This model may well help create strategies to foster resilience.

In some of the research papers, certain common themes emerge in predicting the physician who will be resilient versus the one likely to suffer with burnout. Among the key positive factors are 1) attitude, perception, and approach to life; 2) relationships; 3) balance and prioritization; 4) functional work environment; and 5) spirituality (Table 1-6) (141, 143).

It is imperative that dialogue in the health care field changes from the negative term "burnout" to the positive term "resilience." Medical educators and leaders must identify new ways to foster all factors that allow physicians to absorb external stresses, use their internal coping resources, and remain positive about being a doctor.

Table 1-6. Physician Resilience: Positive Factors

Themes	Examples
Attitudes, perceptions, and approach to life	Positive outlook
	Valuing of physician role
	Self-esteem
	In charge of one's destiny
Relationships	Family, colleagues, friends, community
Balance and prioritization	Professional limit-setting
	Self-care
	Activities for oneself
	Time for others
Functional work environment	Satisfying, controlled, effective staff; good partners; efficient environment
Spirituality	Religion, prayer, community

❖ Conclusion

Many challenges face medical education in the near future. The challenges of teaching modern science, understanding changing physician roles in society, fostering patient-centered care in the midst of an avalanche of new technology, and dealing with the ever-changing generational perspectives of our young demand creativity, daring, and dedication by those directing the educational enterprise.

However, in no area of medical education are these challenges greater than the challenge of nurturing professional development in young physicians. This challenge is monumental, the task unavoidable, and the rewards enormous.

> The practice of medicine is an art, not a trade; a calling, not a business; a calling in which your heart will be exercised equally with your head.
>
> —*Sir William Osler*

Acknowledgment: Many thanks to Carole M. Ingrassia for her meticulous help in the preparation of this chapter.

REFERENCES

1. **Association of American Medical Colleges.** AAMC Statement on the Physician Workforce. June 2006. Accessed at www.aamc.org/workforce/workforceposition.pdf.
2. **Kirch DG.** A word from the president: "The primary care 'crisis.'" AAMC Reporter. October 2008. Accessed at www.aamc.org/newsroom/reporter/oct08/word.htm.
3. **Salsberg E, Grover A.** Physician workforce shortages: implications and issues for academic health centers and policymakers. Acad Med. 2006;81:782-7.
4. **Dill M, Salsberg E.** Center for Workforce Studies. The complexities of physician supply and demand: projections through 2025. Association of American Medical Colleges. November 2008. Accessed at www.aamc.org/workforce/annualmeeting08/salsberg20081.pdf.
5. **Center for Workforce Studies.** Recent studies and reports on physician shortages in the US. Association of American Medical Colleges. October 2008. Accessed at www.aamc.org/workforce/recentworkforcestudies.pdf.
6. **Fred HL.** These are the days: the internship revisited [Editorial]. Tex Heart Inst J. 2007; 34:3-5.
7. **Ende J, ed.** Theory and Practice of Teaching Medicine. Philadelphia: ACP Pr; 2010.
8. **Reinertsen JL.** Zen and the art of physician autonomy maintenance. Ann Intern Med. 2003;138:992-5.
9. **Pont EA.** The culture of physician autonomy; 1900 to the present. Camb Q Healthc Ethics. 2000;9:98-113; discussion 113-9.
10. **Koo D, Thacker SB.** The education of physicians: a CDC perspective. Acad Med. 2008; 83:399-407.
11. **Finkelstein JA, McMahon GT, Peters A, Cadigan R, Biddinger P, Simon SR.** Teaching population health as a basic science at Harvard Medical School. Acad Med. 2008;83: 332-7.

12. **Ornt DB, Aron DC, King NB, Clementz LM, Frank S, Wolpaw T, et al.** Population medicine in a curricular revision at Case Western Reserve. Acad Med. 2008;83:327-31.

13. **Maeshiro R.** Responding to the challenge: population health education for physicians [Editorial]. Acad Med. 2008;83:319-20.

14. **Woodruff JN, Angelos P, Valaitis S.** Medical professionalism: one size fits all? Perspect Biol Med. 2008;51:525-34.

15. **Holsinger JW Jr, Beaton B.** Physician professionalism for a new century. Clin Anat. 2006;19:473-9.

16. Is medicine still a profession? [Editorial]. CMAJ. 2006;174:743, 745.

17. **Dhai A.** Understanding professionalism in health care in the twenty first century. SADJ. 2008;63:174, 176-7.

18. **Wagner P, Hendrich J, Moseley G, Hudson V.** Defining medical professionalism: a qualitative study. Med Educ. 2007;41:288-94.

19. **Pellegrino E.** Character formation and the making of good physicians. In: Kenny N, Shelton W, eds. Lost Virtue: Professional Character Development in Medical Education. Advances in Bioethics. Vol 10. Oxford, United Kingdom: Elsevier; 2006:1-15.

20. **Kenny N.** Searching for doctor good: virtues for the twenty-first century. In: Kenny N, Shelton W, eds. Lost Virtue: Professional character development in medical education. Advances in Bioethics. Vol 10. Oxford, United Kingdom: Elsevier; 2006:1211-33.

21. **Stern D.** A framework for measuring professionalism. In: Stern D, ed. Measuring Medical Professionalism. New York: Oxford Univ Pr; 2006:3-13.

22. **Reiser SJ.** The moral order of the medical school. In: Wear D, Bickel J, eds. Educating for Professionalism: Creating a Culture of Humanism in Medical Education. Iowa City: Univ Iowa Pr; 2000:3-10.

23. **Coulehan J, Williams PC.** Professional ethics and social activism: where have we been? where are we going? In: Wear D, Bickel J, eds. Educating for Professionalism: Creating a Culture of Humanism in Medical Education. Iowa City: Univ of Iowa Pr; 2000:49-69.

24. **Branch WT Jr.** Supporting the moral development of medical students. J Gen Intern Med. 2000;15:503-8.

25. **Pellegrino ED.** Professionalism, profession and the virtues of the good physician. Mt Sinai J Med. 2002;69:378-84.

26. **Klein EJ, Jackson JC, Kratz L, Marcuse EK, McPhillips HA, Shugerman RP, et al.** Teaching professionalism to residents. Acad Med. 2003;78:26-34.

27. **Markakis KM, Beckman HB, Suchman AL, Frankel RM.** The path to professionalism: cultivating humanistic values and attitudes in residency training. Acad Med. 2000; 75:141-50.

28. Common program requirement, general competencies. Chicago: Accreditation Council for Graduate Medical Education; 1 July 2007.

29. **Accreditation Council for Graduate Medical Education.** Outcome Project. Accessed at www.acgme.org/outcome.

30. **Liaison Committee on Medical Education.** Accreditation Standards. Medical students section: the learning environment (MS-31). June 2008. Accessed at www.lcme.org.

31. **Medical professionalism in the new millennium: a physician charter.** Project of the ABIM Foundation, ACP–ASIM Foundation, and European Federation of Internal MedicineAnn Intern Med. 2002;136:243-6.

32. **Rosenstein AH, O'Daniel M.** A survey of the impact of disruptive behaviors and communication defects on patient safety. Jt Comm J Qual Patient Saf. 2008;34:464-71.

33. **Smith LG.** Medical professionalism and the generation gap. Am J Med. 2005;118:439-42.

34. **Wass V.** Doctors in society: medical professionalism in a changing world. Clin Med. 2006;6:109-13.
35. **Cohen JJ.** Chairman's summary of the conference. In: Hager M, ed. Revisiting the medical school educational mission at a time of expansion. Charleston, SC. Josiah Macy, Jr., Foundation; 2008.
36. **Elliott C.** Disillusioned doctors. In: Kenny N, Shelton W, eds. Lost Virtue: Professional Character Development in Medical Education. Advances in Bioethics. Vol 10. Oxford, United Kingdom: Elsevier; 2006:87-97.
37. **Hickson GB, Federspiel CF, Pichert JW, Miller CS, Gauld-Jaeger J, Bost P.** Patient complaints and malpractice risk. JAMA. 2002;287:2951-7.
38. **Coulehan J.** Viewpoint: today's professionalism: engaging the mind but not the heart. Acad Med. 2005;80:892-8.
39. **Rhodes R, Smith LG.** Molding professional character. In: Kenny N, Shelton W, eds. Lost Virtue: Professional Character Development in Medical Education. Advances in Bioethics. Vol 10. Oxford, United Kingdom: Elsevier; 2006:99-114.
40. **Korn D, Ehringhaus S.** The scientific basis of influence and reciprocity: a symposium. Washington, DC: Association of American Medical Colleges; 12 June 2007.
41. **Brennan TA, Rothman DJ, Blank L, Blumenthal D, Chimonas SC, Cohen JJ, et al.** Health industry practices that create conflicts of interest: a policy proposal for academic medical centers. JAMA. 2006;295:429-33.
42. **Rothman DJ, Chimonas S.** New developments in managing physician-industry relationships. JAMA. 2008;300:1067-9.
43. **Relman AS.** Industry support of medical education. JAMA. 2008;300:1071-3.
44. **Ehringhaus SH, Weissman JS, Sears JL, Goold SD, Feibelmann S, Campbell EG.** Responses of medical schools to institutional conflicts of interest. JAMA. 2008;299:665-71.
45. **Keegan R.** The Evolving Self. Boston: Harvard Univ Pr; 1982.
46. **Kohlberg L.** Moral stages and moralization: the cognitive developmental approach. In: Lickona T, ed. Moral Development and Behavior: Theory, Research and Social Issues. New York: Holt, Rinehart and Winston; 1976:31-53.
47. **Pascarella ET, Terenzini PT.** How College Affects Students: Findings and Insights From Twenty Years of Research. San Francisco: Jossey-Bass; 1991:335-67.
48. **Forsythe GB, Snook S, Lewis P, Bartone P.** Making sense of officership: developing a professional identity for 21st century army officers. In: Snider D, Watkins G, eds. The Future of the Army Profession. New York: McGraw-Hill; 2002:357-78.
49. **Lancaster LC, Stillman D.** When Generations Collide. New York: HarperCollins; 2002.
50. **Zemke R, Raines C, Filipczak B.** Generations at Work. New York: American Management Assoc; 2000.
51. **Leahy AL.** Managing the generation gap in healthcare [Editorial]. Surgeon. 2008;6:4-5.
52. **Walker JT, Martin T, White J, Elliott R, Norwood A, Mangum C, et al.** Generational (age) differences in nursing students' preferences for teaching methods. J Nurs Educ. 2006; 45:371-4.
53. **Safer M.** The Millennials Are Coming. CBS News. 11 November 2007. Accessed at www.cbsnews.com/stories/2007/11/08/60minutes/main3475200.shtml.
54. **Henningsen JA.** Why the numbers are dropping in general surgery: the answer no one wants to hear—lifestyle! Arch Surg. 2002;137:255-6.
55. **Dorsey ER, Jarjoura D, Rutecki GW.** Influence of controllable lifestyle on recent trends in specialty choice by US medical students. JAMA. 2003;290:1173-8.
56. **Croasdale M.** Balance becomes key to specialty pick. 2003. Accessed at www.ama-assn.org/amednews/2003/09/22/prsc0922.htm.

57. **Snell JC.** Teaching Gen X &Y: an essay part 1: establishing one's self in the classroom—brief article. College Student Journal. September 2000.
58. **Snell JC.** Teaching Gen X &Y: an essay part 2: teaching strategies. College Student Journal. December 2000.
59. **Oblinger D.** Boomers, Gen-Xers & Millennials: Understanding the New Students. Educause Review. 2003;38:37-47.
60. **Brensilver JM, Smith L, Lyttle CS.** Impact of the Libby Zion case on graduate medical education in internal medicine. Mt Sinai J Med. 1998;65:296-300.
61. **New York Codes, Rules and Regulations.** 10 NYCRR Part 405. §405.4.i-ii.
62. **Pangaro L, ed.** Leadership Careers in Medical Education. Philadelphia: ACP Pr; 2010.
63. **Institute of Medicine.** Resident Duty Hours: Enhancing Sleep, Supervision, and Safety. December 2008. Accessed at www.iom.edu/Reports/2008/Resident-Duty-Hours-Enhancing-Sleep-Supervision-and-Safety.aspx.
64. **Adams D.** Generation gripe: young doctors less dedicated, hardworking? American Medical News. 2 February 2004. Accessed at www.ama-assn.org/amednews/2004/02/02/prl20202.htm.
65. **Merritt, Hawkins and Associates.** Summary of Physicians. Accessed at www.merritthawkins.com/pdf/2004_phpysician50_survey.pdf.
66. **Bebeau MJ.** Evidence-based character development. In: Kenny N, Shelton W, eds. Lost Virtue: Professional Character Development in Medical Education. Advances in Bioethics. Vol 10. Oxford, United Kingdom: Elsevier; 2006:4:47-86.
67. **Mann KV.** Learning and teaching in professional character development. In: Kenny N, Shelton W, eds. Lost Virtue: Professional Character Development in Medical Education. Advances in Bioethics. Vol 10. Oxford, United Kingdom: Elsevier; 2006:145-83.
68. **Bebeau MJ, Lewis PL.** Manual for assessing and promoting identity formation. Center for the Study of Ethical Development. University of Minnesota; 2004.
69. **Branch WT Jr.** Small-group teaching emphasizing reflection can positively influence medical students' values [Letter]. Acad Med. 2001;76:1171-2; author reply 1172-3.
70. **Branch WT Jr.** Supporting the moral development of medical students. J Gen Intern Med. 2000;15:503-8.
71. **Stephenson A, Higgs R, Sugarman J.** Teaching professional development in medical schools. Lancet. 2001;357:867-70.
72. **Coulehan J, Williams PC.** Vanquishing virtue: the impact of medical education. Acad Med. 2001;76:598-605.
73. **Epstein RM, Hundert EM.** Defining and assessing professional competence. JAMA. 2002;287:226-35.
74. **Feudtner C, Christakis DA, Christakis NA.** Do clinical clerks suffer ethical erosion? Students' perceptions of their ethical environment and personal development. Acad Med. 1994;69:670-9.
75. **Hafferty FW, Franks R.** The hidden curriculum, ethics teaching, and the structure of medical education. Acad Med. 1994;69:861-71.
76. **Hundert EM, Hafferty F, Christakis D.** Characteristics of the informal curriculum and trainees' ethical choices. Acad Med. 1996;71:624-42.
77. **Kenny NP, Mann KV, MacLeod H.** Role modeling in physicians' professional formation: reconsidering an essential but untapped educational strategy. Acad Med. 2003;78:1203-10.
78. **Wear D, Castellani B.** The development of professionalism: curriculum matters. Acad Med. 2000;75:602-11.
79. **Adamson TE, Bunch WH, Baldwin DC Jr, Oppenberg A.** The virtuous orthopaedist has fewer malpractice suits. Clin Orthop Relat Res. 2000:104-9.

80. **Becker MH, Maiman LA.** Strategies for enhancing patient compliance. J Community Health. 1980;6:113-35.

81. **Levinson W, Roter DL, Mullooly JP, Dull VT, Frankel RM.** Physician-patient communication. The relationship with malpractice claims among primary care physicians and surgeons. JAMA. 1997;277:553-9.

82. **Wagoner NE.** Admission to medical school: selecting applicants with the potential for professionalism. In: Stern D, ed. Measuring Medical Professionalism. New York: Oxford Univ Pr; 2006:235-63.

83. **Kelman E, Canger S.** Validity of interview for admissions evaluation. Journal of Veterinary Medical Education. 1994;21:2

84. **Kulatunga-Moruzi C, Norman GR.** Validity of admissions measures in predicting performance outcomes: the contribution of cognitive and non-cognitive dimensions. Teach Learn Med. 2002;14:34-42.

85. **Kulatunga-Moruzi C, Norman GR.** Validity of admissions measures in predicting performance outcomes: a comparison of those who were and were not accepted at McMaster. Teach Learn Med. 2002;14:43-8.

86. **Stern DT, Frohna AZ, Gruppen LD.** The prediction of professional behaviour. Med Educ. 2005;39:75-82.

87. **Stern D.** A framework for measuring professionalism. In: Stern D, ed. Measuring Medical Professionalism. New York: Oxford Univ Pr; 2006:3-13.

88. **Stern DT, Frohna AZ, Gruppen LD.** The prediction of professional behaviour. Med Educ. 2005;39:75-82.

89. **Merton RK, Reader GG, Kendal PL, eds.** The Student Physician. Introductory Studies in the Sociology of Medical Education. Cambridge, MA: Harvard Univ Pr; 1957.

90. **Arnold L, Stern DT.** What is medical professionalism? In: Stern D, ed. Measuring Medical Professionalism. New York: Oxford Univ Pr; 2006:15-37.

91. **Kao A.** Ethics, law and professionalism: what physicians need to know. In: Stern D, ed. Measuring Medical Professionalism. New York: Oxford Univ Pr; 2006:39-52.

92. **Hafferty F.** Measuring professionalism: a commentary. In: Stern D, ed. Measuring Medical Professionalism. New York: Oxford Univ Pr: 2006:281-306.

93. **Mangione S, Kane GC, Caruso JW, Gonnella JS, Nasca TJ, Hojat M.** Assessment of empathy in different years of internal medicine training. Med Teach. 2002;24:370-3.

94. **Veloski J, Hojat M.** Measuring specific elements of professionalism: empathy, teamwork and lifelong learning. In: Stern D, ed. Measuring Medical Professionalism. New York: Oxford Univ Pr; 2006:117-45.

95. **Arnold EL, Blank LL, Race KE, Cipparrone N.** Can professionalism be measured? The development of a scale for use in the medical environment. Acad Med. 1998;73:1119-21.

96. **Papadakis M, Loeser H.** Using critical incident reports and longitudinal observations to assess professionalism. In: Stern D, ed. Measuring Medical Professionalism. New York: Oxford Univ Pr; 2006:159-73.

97. **Papadakis MA, Hodgson CS, Teherani A, Kohatsu ND.** Unprofessional behavior in medical school is associated with subsequent disciplinary action by a state medical board. Acad Med. 2004;79:244-9.

98. **Ginsburg S, Kachan N, Lingard L.** Before the white coat: perceptions of professional lapses in the pre-clerkship. Med Educ. 2005;39:12-9.

99. **Klamen D, Williams R.** Using standardized clinical encounters to assess physician communication. In: Stern D, ed. Measuring Medical Professionalism. New York: Oxford Univ Pr; 2006:53-74.

100. **Norcini J.** Faculty observations of student professional behavior. In: Stern D, ed. Measuring Medical Professionalism. New York: Oxford Univ Pr; 2006:147-57.

101. **Arnold L, Stern D.** Content and context of peer assessment. In: Stern D, ed. Measuring Medical Professionalism. New York: Oxford Univ Pr; 2006:175-94.

102. **McCormack WT, Lazarus C, Stern D, Small PA Jr.** Peer nomination: a tool for identifying medical student exemplars in clinical competence and caring, evaluated at three medical schools. Acad Med. 2007;82:1033-9.

103. **Ludmerer KM.** Time to Heal. New York: Oxford Univ Pr; 1999.

104. **Martinez R.** Professional role in health care institutions: toward an ethics of authenticity. In: Wear D, Bickel J, eds. Educating for Professionalism: Creating a Culture of Humanism in Medical Education. Iowa City: Univ of Iowa Pr; 2000:35-48

105. **Grady-Weliky TA, Kettyle CN, Hundert EM.** The mentor-mentee relationship in medical education: a new analysis. In: Wear D, Bickel J, eds. Educating for Professionalism: Creating a Culture of Humanism in Medical Education. Iowa City: Univ of Iowa Pr; 2000:105-19.

106. **Farrell SE, Digioia NM, Broderick KB, Coates WC.** Mentoring for clinician-educators. Acad Emerg Med. 2004;11:1346-50.

107. **Palepu A, Friedman RH, Barnett RC, Carr PL, Ash AS, Szalacha L, et al.** Junior faculty members' mentoring relationships and their professional development in U.S. medical schools. Acad Med. 1998;73:318-23.

108. **Jackson VA, Palepu A, Szalacha L, Caswell C, Carr PL, Inui T.** "Having the right chemistry": a qualitative study of mentoring in academic medicine. Acad Med. 2003; 78:328-34.

109. **Sambunjak D, Straus SE, Marusic A.** Mentoring in academic medicine: a systematic review. JAMA. 2006;296:1103-15.

110. **Baugh SG, Sullivan, SE.** Mentoring and career development. Guest Editorial. Career Development International. 2005;10:425-8.

111. **Rose GL, Rukstalis MR, Schuckit MA.** Informal mentoring between faculty and medical students. Acad Med. 2005;80:344-8.

112. **Straus SE, Chatur F, Taylor M.** Issues in the mentor-mentee relationship in academic medicine: a qualitative study. Acad Med. 2009;84:135-9.

113. **Zerzan JT, Hess R, Schur E, Phillips RS, Rigotti N.** Making the most of mentors: a guide for mentees. Acad Med. 2009;84:140-4.

114. **Pololi LH, Knight SM, Dennis K, Frankel RM.** Helping medical school faculty realize their dreams: an innovative, collaborative mentoring program. Acad Med. 2002;77: 377-84.

115. **Berk RA, Berg J, Mortimer R, Walton-Moss B, Yeo TP.** Measuring the effectiveness of faculty mentoring relationships. Acad Med. 2005;80:66-71.

116. **Steiner JF, Curtis P, Lanphear BP, Vu KO, Main DS.** Assessing the role of influential mentors in the research development of primary care fellows. Acad Med. 2004;79: 865-72.

117. **Keyser DJ, Lakoski JM, Lara-Cinisomo S, Schultz DJ, Williams VL, Zellers DF, et al.** Advancing institutional efforts to support research mentorship: a conceptual framework and self-assessment tool. Acad Med. 2008;83:217-25.

118. **Wiese J, ed.** Teaching in the Hospital. Philadelphia: ACP Pr; 2010.

119. **Meadors P, Lamson A.** Compassion fatigue and secondary traumatization: provider self care on intensive care units for children. J Pediatr Health Care. 2008;22:24-34.

120. **Gundersen L.** Physician burnout. Ann Intern Med. 2001;135:145-8.

121. **Maslach C, Jackson SE.** Burnout in organizational settings. Applied Social Psychology Annual. 1984;5:133-53.
122. **Chopra SS, Sotile WM, Sotile MO.** STUDENTJAMA. Physician burnout. JAMA. 2004; 291:633.
123. **DeValk M, Oostrom C.** Burnout in the medical profession. Occupational Health at Work. 2007;3:1-5.
124. **Muscatello MR, Bruno A, Carroccio C, Cedro C, La Torre D, Di Rosa AE, et al.** Association between burnout and anger in oncology versus ophthalmology health care professionals. Psychol Rep. 2006;99:641-50.
125. **Dyrbye LN, Thomas MR, Huschka MM, Lawson KL, Novotny PJ, Sloan JA, et al.** A multicenter study of burnout, depression, and quality of life in minority and non-minority US medical students. Mayo Clin Proc. 2006;81:1435-42.
126. **McManus IC, Keeling A, Paice E.** Stress, burnout and doctors' attitudes to work are determined by personality and learning style: a twelve year longitudinal study of UK medical graduates. BMC Med. 2004;2:29.
127. **Meltzer LS, Huckabay LM.** Critical care nurses' perceptions of futile care and its effect on burnout. Am J Crit Care. 2004;13:202-8.
128. **Spickard A Jr, Gabbe SG, Christensen JF.** Mid-career burnout in generalist and specialist physicians. JAMA. 2002;288:1447-50.
129. **Fahrenkopf AM, Sectish TC, Barger LK, Sharek PJ, Lewin D, Chiang VW, et al.** Rates of medication errors among depressed and burnt out residents: prospective cohort study. BMJ. 2008;336:488-91.
130. **Waterman AD, Garbutt J, Hazel E, Dunagan WC, Levinson W, Fraser VJ, et al.** The emotional impact of medical errors on practicing physicians in the United States and Canada. Jt Comm J Qual Patient Saf. 2007;33:467-76.
131. **Shanafelt TD, Bradley KA, Wipf JE, Back AL.** Burnout and self-reported patient care in an internal medicine residency program. Ann Intern Med. 2002;136:358-67.
132. **West CP, Huschka MM, Novotny PJ, Sloan JA, Kolars JC, Habermann TM, et al.** Association of perceived medical errors with resident distress and empathy: a prospective longitudinal study. JAMA. 2006;296:1071-8.
133. **Consumer Affairs.** Physician burnout linked to medical errors. 2005. Accessed at www.consumeraffairs.com/news04/2006/09/doctors_medical_errors.html.
134. **Engel KG, Rosenthal M, Sutcliffe KM.** Residents' responses to medical error: coping, learning, and change. Acad Med. 2006;81:86-93.
135. **Fischer MA, Mazor KM, Baril J, Alper E, DeMarco D, Pugnaire M.** Learning from mistakes. Factors that influence how students and residents learn from medical errors. J Gen Intern Med. 2006;21:419-23.
136. **Castelo-Branco C, Figueras F, Eixarch E, Quereda F, Cancelo MJ, González S, et al.** Stress symptoms and burnout in obstetric and gynaecology residents. BJOG. 2007; 114:94-8.
137. **Linzer M, Visser MR, Oort FJ, Smets EM, McMurray JE, de Haes HC; Society of General Internal Medicine (SGIM) Career Satisfaction Study Group (CSSG).** Predicting and preventing physician burnout: results from the United States and the Netherlands. Am J Med. 2001;111:170-5.
138. **McCray LW, Cronholm PF, Bogner HR, Gallo JJ, Neill RA.** Resident physician burnout: is there hope? Fam Med. 2008;40:626-32.
139. **Zellmer DD.** Teaching to prevent burnout in the helping professions. Analytic Teaching. 2005;vol 24: no. 1.

140. **CMA Policy.** Physician health and well-being. Ottawa, Ontario, Canada: Canadian Medical Assoc; 1998.

141. **Weiner EL, Swain GR, Wolf B, Gottlieb M.** A qualitative study of physicians' own wellness-promotion practices. West J Med. 2001;174:19-23.

142. **Huby G, Gerry M, McKinstry B, Porter M, Shaw J, Wrate R.** Morale among general practitioners: qualitative study exploring relations between partnership arrangements, personal style, and workload. BMJ. 2002;325:140.

143. **Jensen PM, Trollope-Kumar K, Waters H, Everson J.** Building physician resilience. Can Fam Physician. 2008;54:722-9.

144. **Dunn LB, Iglewicz A, Moutier C.** A conceptual model of medical student well-being: promoting resilience and preventing burnout. Acad Psychiatry. 2008;32:44-53.

2

Fundamentals of Mentoring and Professional Development

Holly J. Humphrey, MD, MACP

> Mentors are guides. They lead us along the journey of our lives. We trust them because they have been there before. They embody our hopes, cast light on the way ahead, interpret arcane signs, warn us of lurking dangers and point out unexpected delights along the way (1).
>
> —*Laurent Daloz*

Visit an exhibition by a new artist, attend a performance of a world-class orchestra or opera company, and read the background description of the artist, featured soloist, or conductor. Along with a recounting of previous operatic roles or a listing of recordings or prior exhibitions, one invariably finds the name of the teacher with whom the artist studied. In the context of music and art, "whom one studies with" carries enormous significance—not simply as an instructor of art or music but as a master of a particular technique or style or approach. These nuances of practice are potentially replicated, enlarged, and interpreted through the voice, eyes, ears, or hands of the protégé.

In science, the laboratory carries similar importance. What is the reputation of the senior scientist? Is the laboratory one with a reputation of high-quality, high-impact science or one more committed to publishing quantity, regardless of the significance and integrity of the work? Whose laboratory one trains in lays the fundamental groundwork for a scientist's career—not only in learning the approach to research and to tackling questions that arise and failures that ensue, but in such broad and diverse areas as the organization of the laboratory, how to interact and collaborate with the larger network of scientists in the field, and how to consider and engage with other questions provoked by their work.

KEY POINTS

- Mentoring is a critical component of any profession and transcends all disciplines. Mentoring encourages protégés to reflect on how their work contributes to their profession and to the larger society.
- Mentoring literature is built on the scholarship of developmental psychologists Erik Erikson and Daniel Levinson, educator Laurent Daloz, and educational psychologists Jeanne Nakamura and David Shernoff.
- Professional values and practices are transmitted across generations through the teacher–student and mentor–protégé relationships.
- Ideal mentors provide a supportive environment that challenges and inspires the protégé.
- Ideal protégés will have realistic expectations of the mentor and are receptive to constructive criticism.
- Common models of mentoring include the traditional dyad model, in which an experienced older teacher provides guidance to a novice; layered mentoring, in which protégés are assigned to mentoring groups at each level of training; and peer mentoring, in which a group of individuals with similar interests mentor one another.
- Mentoring is the vehicle through which professional values are imprinted and transmitted from one generation to the next.

In clinical medicine, the senior physicians whom students learn from and residents train with hold equally significant implications. Learning medicine under the tutelage of a master clinician has enormous import to the habits of mind, clinical reflexes, diagnostic acumen, or procedural techniques that more junior colleagues learn and ultimately perfect. Sometimes these daily interactions with clinician-teachers move into longer-lasting, more enduring relationships. In addition to teaching and learning the knowledge and skills of clinical medicine, and considering the practical and very real issues of career development, one begins to see and appreciate the importance of self-reflection and the bigger questions relating to the contribution of one's work to the profession and to society. When this happens, a mentoring relationship is born. In this relationship, not only is the career of the individual protégé enhanced and developed, but the field is advanced and the elements of the profession are rediscovered, with the primacy of service to the patient as the highest priority. Taken together, the betterment of the profession and ultimately of society is possible.

Both the concept of mentoring and the concept of professional development are slippery. They are difficult to define, measure, and evaluate. While this conundrum reflects reality, it should not deter an exploration of these concepts so vital to the future of physicians, their patients, and the tenets of professionalism. A willingness to wrestle with these concepts will, in the best circumstance, lead to new insights and applications.

This chapter explores traditional as well as current concepts underlying mentoring theory and practices. The chapter considers the characteristics and behaviors of ideal mentors and of ideal protégés. In addressing models of mentoring, one realizes that mentoring is not a one-way process and that current social network theory may someday help explain the myriad influences on the development of a professional. The chapter ends with an invitation to consider the profound implications for imprinting and ultimately for transforming individuals, the institutions employing them, and the profession itself. Together, individuals and institutions influence the evolution of a profession. To the extent that this evolution respects the core values of the profession, then the evolutionary adaptation will continue to benefit the larger society. When those fundamental values are compromised, this evolution may occur to the detriment of patients, the profession, the physicians themselves, and society as a whole.

❖ Mentoring Theory

The idea of mentoring is an ancient one, deriving from Homer's epic poem *The Odyssey*. The goddess of wisdom, Athena, takes the form of Mentor, an old and trusted friend of Odysseus to whom Odysseus has entrusted the care of his son, Telemachus (2). Mentor provides guidance, protection, and education, sharing wisdom and nurturing during a transitional period for Telemachus. In so doing, he demonstrates many of the basic qualities and roles that continue to be associated with mentors in modern life: coach, teacher, guardian, protector, and kindly parent.

Elements of mentoring transcend all disciplines, professions, and contexts and have equal relevance in classrooms, boardrooms, laboratories, and clinical settings. It is no wonder, then, that numerous texts and theorists drawn from such fields as business, social psychology, education, and medicine have attempted to define what mentoring is and why it matters. The social psychologist Mihaly Csikszentmihalyi said, "Mentoring—it is how young men learned to be hunters and young women weavers; how farmers, builders, and healers learned their craft. Mentoring is still an essential link in the chain of maintaining the pattern of culture, yet one that is still not that well understood" (3).

Today's mentoring literature ranges from the goal-oriented, "how to succeed" business literature (4) to the programs focused on training a new generation of scientists sponsored by the Howard Hughes Medical Institute (5). Mentoring has long been considered an intrinsic aspect of academic medicine, at every stage of medical education and in the development of faculty. Mentoring is associated—perhaps not rigorously, but frequently—with key outcomes in academic medicine (6, 7). It is difficult to quantify the impact that mentoring has (7) or even to quantify all the components of mentoring. In many ways, mentoring as a concept is nebulous to mentors and protégés (8). Further, the impact of mentoring is most often reported on outcomes that themselves are highly nuanced and ambiguous, such as career choice, personal satisfaction, and professionalism, in addition to more easily quantifiable outcomes of career success (9). Mentoring is highly dynamic and fluid, as well as symbiotic, making it difficult to determine which key elements lead to desired outcomes.

Although this chapter cannot comprehensively review the classic contributions to mentoring literature, there are several scholars—Erik Erikson, Daniel Levinson, Laurent Daloz, and, most recently, Jeanne Nakamura and David Shernoff—whose work is strongly relevant and has been referenced broadly throughout the literature.

Erik Erikson

> A person does best at this time to put aside thoughts of death and balance its certainty with the only happiness that is lasting: to increase, by whatever is yours to give, the goodwill and higher order in your sector of the world (10).
> —*Erik Erikson, 1974*

Erikson is one of the first developmental psychologists to assert that development continues throughout adulthood. In describing the eight developmental stages of the life cycle, he identified the middle stage of adult life as the period when creative and meaningful work gains in value. The significant task of those at this stage is to perpetuate culture by transmitting values. Such a role is clearly related to parenting but also has profound relevance for mentoring. Erikson writes that the struggle of this developmental stage is to achieve generativity, the concern for establishing and guiding the next generation (11). Erikson's work highlights the value and meaning of mentoring from the perspective of the mentor, rather than the protégé.

Daniel Levinson

As a man passes 40, his task is to assume responsibility for new generations of adults ... He must find new ways to combine authority and mutuality— accepting his own responsibility and offering leadership, yet also taking them seriously as adults, inviting their participation and fostering their growth toward greater independence and authority (12).

—Daniel Levinson, 1978

Similar to Erikson, Levinson's work considers the developmental stages of life. It is during midlife that an individual's relationship to work and career gains in relevance. Levinson writes eloquently and powerfully about the impact of mentoring, not on mentors but on the protégé. A mentor, by embodying what can be accomplished for younger individuals, provides the path forward. Levinson describes a mentor as an individual who is characteristically a half-generation older than the protégé (separating the mentor from the parent), whose role includes teaching, guiding, and socializing into a profession (13). Levinson was also one of the first to specifically discuss gender discrepancies in mentoring, both in terms of the availability of mentors and their differential impact on protégés.

Laurent Daloz

The question for us as teachers is not whether but how we influence our students. It is a question about a relationship: Where are our students going and who are we for them in their journey? (1, 13)

—Laurent Daloz, 1999

One of the key concepts set forth by Daloz is the importance of a mentor during periods of transition. Because transitions are periods of rapid growth and directional change, mentors are needed to provide support, challenge, and vision. Figure 2-1 shows the interaction between support and challenge. *Support* is essential and consists of listening for genuine understanding and mirroring so that protégés can see their self-reflection in order to enhance understanding. Support also consists of providing structure, setting positive expectations, serving as an advocate, and ultimately making the interactions special. The *challenge* is created by identifying tasks, heating up dichotomies, constructing hypotheses, and setting high standards. Finally, *vision* occurs through modeling, keeping traditions, offering a map, and once again providing a mirror.

Figure 2-1 illustrates Daloz's idea that mentors must achieve a balance in their mentoring by affirming the validity of the protégé's experience and providing challenge, which will ultimately enhance that protégé's sense of agency in the world. But providing support and challenge in balanced

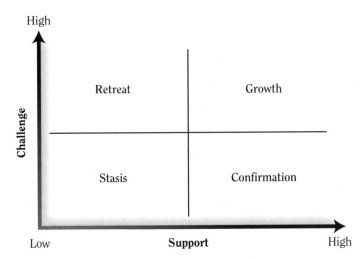

Figure 2-1 Effects of support and challenge on development. When the challenge faced by the protégé and the support provided by mentors are both high, the greatest amount of growth and development will be achieved. Reproduced with permission from Daloz L. Mentor: Guiding the Journey of Adult Learners. 2nd ed. New York: Jossey-Bass; 1999.

measure are not sufficient; mentors must also help their protégés— through modeling, guidance, and reflection—obtain a vision of where they want to go (14). Mentors also serve as keepers of tradition—or "keepers of meaning" (15). In this way, mentors pass on traditions to future generations.

Jeanne Nakamura and David Shernoff

> The relationship (between novice and experienced practitioner) has the potential to play a role not only in the development and future success of the individual student, but also the perpetuation and transformation of the domain of professional knowledge and practice, and the evolution of the social field, or professional community, to which mentor and student belong. In short, it affects both professionals and the profession (16).
> —*Jeanne Nakamura and David Shernoff, 2009*

The work of Nakamura and Shernoff examines how the practices of a profession are passed from one generation to the next. By studying mentors who serve as both outstanding moral exemplars and highly accomplished scientists, they examine the dynamics of the teacher–student relationship and ultimately uncover the transmission of values and practices across generations of scientists. Nakamura and Shernoff explore the social transmission of professional lineages and in so doing have developed insights about the practices of mentors and their potential impact on a field over subsequent generations. Table 2-1 illustrates an example of the impact of a mentoring lineage by providing examples of well-known mentors and their protégés in physics and painting, as well as characters from a well-known film.

Just as genes are the unit of transmission of biological material from one generation to the next, the "meme" is the unit of cultural transmission of cherished practices and values across generations. As the cultural analogues to genes, memes serve as a basis for explaining the spread of ideas, values, and beliefs from one generation to the next. Memes evolve by natural selection, similar to biological evolution. They spread through the attitudes and behaviors that they generate in their hosts.

By using qualitative research methods, Nakamura and Shernoff identified the memes that were most strongly transmitted across three lineages of mentors and protégés involved in scientific research. Those memes were displaying honesty and integrity in research, treating people fairly, providing intellectual freedom and guidance, and creating a laboratory structure that was facilitative. Table 2-2 shows the number of scientists who inherited each meme from their mentor throughout the mentoring generations that followed.

Table 2-1. Examples of Mentoring Lineages*

Physics Mentors	Protégés
Lord Rayleigh	J.J. Thomson
J.J. Thomson	Ernest Rutherford
Ernest Rutherford	Niels Bohr
Niels Bohr	Linus Pauling, Werner Heisenberg, Aage Bohr
Painting Mentors	**Protégés**
Jean-Baptiste-Camille Corot	Camille Pissaro
Camille Pissarro	Paul Gauguin, Paul Cézanne
Star Wars Mentors	Protégés
Yoda	Obi-Wan Kenobi
Obi-Wan Kenobi	Luke Skywalker

*The long-lasting impact of a single mentor across multiple generations is seen in many different fields.

Table 2-2. Good-Work Memes: Lineage Members Who Inherited Each Meme

Meme	Gall Lineage ($n = 13$)	Motulsky Lineage ($n = 11$)	Lewontin Lineage ($n = 12$)	Chi-square
Honesty, integrity, and ethics in research	8	7	7	0.07
Treating people equally, fairly	5	4	7	1.42
Providing intellectual freedom and guidance	6	5	4	0.52
Creating a facilitative lab structure	8	2	8	6.48*

Unless otherwise noted, values in table are numbers of members. Reproduced with permission from Nakamura J, Shernoff DJ. Good Mentoring: Fostering Excellent Practice in Higher Education. San Francisco: J Wiley; 2009.

*$P < 0.05$

Characteristics and Behaviors of Ideal Mentors

The scholarly literature—both classic and contemporary—and the insights underlying much of the mentoring theories provide a broad overview of how to approach mentoring. They also provide a framework for considering how these concepts might be applied in a practical context. In other words, they help answer the question, What are the characteristics and behaviors to which mentors should aspire?

Many authors have sought to identify the key elements of mentoring and then translate them into practical suggestions and advice. One recent book on mentoring identified six primary themes: 1) what excellent mentors do (matters of skills); 2) the traits of excellent mentors (matters of style and personality); 3) arranging the mentor–protégé relationships (matters of beginning); 4) knowing oneself as a mentor (matters of integrity); 5) when things go wrong (matters of restoration); and 6) welcoming change and saying goodbye (matters of closure) (3).

The more recent work by Nakamura and Shernoff demonstrates the critical role of supportive relationships. These relationships provide a context for positive advising experiences—in fact, support dwarfs all other attributes studied. The authors found six distinct components of supportiveness (Box 2-1) (16).

Although mentoring is a key determinant of academic success (17), medical educators rarely receive training in the mentoring process (18). Literature from the academic research and business world—where

Box 2-1. Six Components of Supportive Relationships

1. Consistent availability and involvement
2. Balance between freedom and guidance
3. Atmosphere of and resources fostering supportiveness
4. Frequent, specific positive feedback
5. Students treated as respected collaborators
6. Mentors demonstrating an individual interest in the protégé

mentoring is a prevalent and strongly valued aspect of the professional culture—offers numerous lists, tables, and strategies for mentors (19–22). Table 2-3 provides specific suggestions from two senior scientists who also were highly effective mentors.

Clearly, key skills involve communication (with an emphasis on listening), an ability to help the protégé with specific tasks and problems, and serving as a source of inspiration and confidence for the protégé—the positive and supportive aspect that Nakamura and Shernoff have described. Perhaps most important is the quality of trust in the relationship. Protégés should have no doubt that their mentors are acting selflessly and on their behalf, even when they are giving negative feedback or critiquing the pro-

Table 2-3. Tips From Two Highly Successful Principal Investigators

Screen potential students carefully

Require intellectual playtime

Use student's talents

Provide fast feedback

Let early success drive students

Get a mega-whiteboard to track projects

Help students network

Be vicious with manuscript reviews

Mentor a person, not just a scientist

Train scientists to be storytellers

Push mentees out of the nest

Reproduced with permission from Evans J. Mentoring magic: how to be an effective mentor. Tips from two highly successful principal investigators. The Scientist. 2008;22:70.

tégés' work. Such investment on the behalf of mentors shows that they value both the person and his or her goals (23).

A recent conference on mentoring identified several valuable characteristics of effective mentors in academic medicine (18), including:

- Being knowledgeable
- Being responsive and available
- Showing interest in the mentoring relationship
- Understanding the protégé's capabilities and potential
- Motivating protégés to challenge themselves
- Acting as advocates for protégés

Finally, there is something much harder to quantify—that element of "right fit" or chemistry to develop an effective and satisfying mentoring relationship (24).

Research on the impact of mentoring in medicine demonstrates that mentoring leads to greater career satisfaction, sense of psychosocial support, and success (25, 26). Several specific qualities of mentoring are related to a protégé's satisfaction with the mentoring relationship, including communication (keeping in touch and not abusing power), skills and academic guidance (advice on career goals and research and communication skills), and professional development (providing counsel on decisions and helping to building networks) (18). Given the importance of mentoring for the development of younger trainees in medicine, formal programs—both to increase mentoring and to improve faculty skills in mentoring—are clearly warranted.

❖ Characteristics and Behaviors of Ideal Protégés

Several articles provide helpful guidance on how protégés might maximize the opportunity to learn from a mentor (8, 27). Mentors are inspired by seeing a passionate protégé who is not afraid to facilitate the relationship. Mentoring is enhanced when the protégé has realistic expectations of the mentor, including the time the mentor has available for the protégé. This extends beyond face-to-face meeting time to encompass time to write letters, make phone calls, and help promote the protégé. All of these activities are part of a mentor's repertoire, but the protégé must be careful to not make too many demands. Protégés also have the most to gain when they can accept criticism and hear critiques not as a personal failing but as a way to learn and improve their work. The protégé who can accept a mentor's imperfections will be best able to learn from the mentor's areas of strength. In fact, Perlmutter (27) states that the ideal advisor is a composite of various imperfect humans.

Zerzan and colleagues (8) outlined several characteristics of ideal mentees—namely that they aspire to self-assessment, are receptive, take initiative and responsibility, and demonstrate honesty and appreciation. These authors advocate that the mentee take ownership of and direct the relationship by managing the work of the relationship via planning, setting meeting agendas, asking questions, listening, completing assigned tasks, and requesting feedback. Furthermore, mentees ideally are aware of their own knowledge and skill gaps and identify their goals in 3-month, 1-year, and 5-year increments.

❖ Mentoring Models

Mentoring appears in many forms and formats. The traditional mentoring relationship is a dyad—an older, more experienced individual who serves as a guide and teacher for a novice in a field. Because of the range of activities that a mentor might need to serve—from career planning to research guidance to editing a manuscript to setting up a professional network—multiple mentors often fulfill this variety of needs. Further, it may be that protégés benefit from exposure to multiple mentors, which allows them to gain a broader variety of opinions, experiences, and expertise than they otherwise might (8). Co-mentoring is one approach, perhaps most often seen among those who are pursuing research careers (28). Co-mentors are peers who partner to serve all the mentoring needs of their protégé. Protégés have reported that this arrangement provided greater depth and breadth for them, and mentors consider it is a less demanding, time-consuming experience (24).

Mentoring relationships can evolve organically, on the basis of shared interests or personal "fit," or by assignment through a formal mentoring relationship sponsored by the program, department, or institution. In addition to the choice and the assignment model, there is a third alternative called layered mentoring. This is used primarily at the resident level, when protégés are assigned to mentoring groups drawn from every level of training. In the layered mentoring model, faculty members are assigned a mentoring group and, in addition to overseeing the regular meetings of this group, help to facilitate traditional, dyad mentoring relationships for the group members (29).

This model is closely related to peer mentoring (which is discussed at greater length in chapter 8 of this book). Peer mentoring refers to a group of individuals with similar backgrounds engaged in similar work—often at different stages of the continuum of professional development—who meet regularly to mentor each other (30). Peer mentoring groups are sometimes led by faculty mentors, and there is evidence that having such guidance makes the peer mentoring experience more robust (31). In addition, one of the key limitations associated with traditional dyad mentoring is the failure to move beyond a highly hierarchical relationship to one that is more mutually supportive and fluid (32). Layered mentoring or peer mentoring may be more empowering for participants. Today, the impact of social networks on behavior, including health behaviors, speaks to the powerful influence of peers and these informal social networks (33).

There are numerous barriers to finding a mentor and to having a positive mentoring experience. Some reports conclude that certain groups—women, underrepresented minorities, clinician-educator faculty, for example—are less likely to have mentors or to be satisfied with the mentoring relationship (21, 22). Because of this, it is important to consider all models of mentoring so that trainees at all levels can find the mentoring and support they need. Finally, institutions can do a great deal to develop, reward, and support mentors, and in this way enhance an institutional culture of mentoring (Table 2-4) (18). While being mentored offers protégés many benefits, including personal and professional development, there are also

Table 2-4. Tips to Promote Effective Mentors: Three Domains

Mentors	Mentors or Protégés	Institutions
Know yourself	Know yourself	Develop mentors
Work with students who are a good match	Seek a good fit with mentor	Heighten awareness of gender and cultural issues
Address individual differences	Seek a good fit in a learning/working environment	Provide education on professional boundaries
Think out loud	Play an active role in the learning process	Reward mentors (academic recognition, protected time)
Create a community that complements and amplifies the direct transmission of knowledge, values, and practices	Seek out multiple influences	Support mentors (peer support, referral panels, mentors for mentors)

Adapted with permission from Ramani S, Gruppen L, Krajic Kachur E. Twelve tips for developing effective mentors. Med Teacher. 2006; 28:404-408, and from Nakamura J, Shernoff DJ. Good Mentoring: Fostering Excellent Practice in Higher Education. San Francisco: J Wiley; 2009.

key advantages for the institution, such as increased trust and morale, improved retention, and enhanced organizational commitment (10). Finally, it's important to realize that those who are mentored are most likely to mentor others, thereby sustaining a valuable tradition (28).

❖ Leaving a Legacy of Values

Example is not the main thing in influencing others, it is the only thing (34).
—*Albert Schweitzer*

Mentoring is a key avenue through which one may leave a living legacy and simultaneously help shape the future of a field (16). The science historian Thomas Kuhn points out that paradigms change most readily when a discipline attracts highly motivated practitioners who look forward to solving puzzles and making discoveries (35). Medicine offers many intrinsic rewards, including helping patients and making novel contributions to knowledge. Those who work closely with medical students continue to report that the young people entering the field possess virtues of altruism and dispositions that are service-oriented (36). Mentors can teach students how to apply those intrinsic values in the context of clinical medicine. Nakamura and Shernoff point out that even universal norms in a profession may not be obvious to the neophyte (16). To feel compassion is one thing; to apply it during discussions of end-of-life considerations with a patient is quite another. At the bedside and in the office, students and residents see myriad examples—both good and bad. A mentor provides daily examples and in so doing helps students and residents translate their core values into a professional context with another human being.

Sometimes the core values and responsibilities of a profession are shortchanged. When this happens, the result is "compromised work" (37). In their book *Good Mentoring*, Nakamura and Shernoff (16) point out the following about "compromised work":

> if work that shortchanges a profession's core responsibilities ... prevails within a field or even within the institution where training takes place, novices may absorb the prevailing norms and practices without ever having occasion to question the alignment of these norms and practices with their own extraprofessional commitments. Susceptible to the available social cures, they may tacitly learn from the wider field until or unless they encounter a respected model who questions and diverges from the common practice.

Many forces can undermine the values and virtues on which the profession of medicine is based. Gardner and colleagues point out that "the relationship between practitioners and the public they serve is always in a delicate balance with the professionals interested in securing more rights and the public interested in seeking more services. Over time this tension can result in a fruitful synergy or degenerate into conflict" (38). Learning to manage the complex, high-technology, profit-driven terrain characterizing today's health care environment requires mentors who embody the highest ethical standards and virtues of a professional to guide and show the way. In Nakamura and Shernoff's study, modeling was especially important for the transmission of skills and knowledge (16). The authors opined that seeing good work modeled consistently is probably an important influence when forces undermining good work prevail. They go on to say that "exhortations to do the right thing are simply not compelling if the individual does not walk the talk." Most authors agree that it is both modeling and conversation about the issues—the nuance, the complexity—that is most ideal in transmitting the values and practices of a profession. Thus, mentoring in the clinical setting can either contribute to what has become known as "the hidden curriculum" or be a powerful antidote to the unspoken messages, actions, and behaviors that undermine the profession (39).

Over time, especially with the long apprenticeships that once characterized medical education and training, students and residents were imprinted with the application of values to the clinical practice of medicine. Is this possible today? Different teaching attending physicians may be assigned each week in the inpatient setting, or even daily in the outpatient setting. The chance to interact for extended periods with any one attending may no longer exist. This has led some to propose elaborate advising systems, written guides to career success, and virtual or online mentoring programs. While there may be valuable information gained from these methods, they cannot replace the interpersonal, regular exchanges that occur in the classic model of mentoring for guidance and support. To do otherwise would be analogous to raising children in a virtual way by e-mail, text messaging, or Skype sessions. These modalities may facilitate information exchange, but they surely do not provide nurturing—the nuanced interactions involving compassionate limit-setting or re-direction needed for healthy growth and development. They cannot replace the importance of presence and modeling. Likewise, the same guidance once provided by the senior clinician during an entire month-long rotation or longer may require departments and institutions to reconsider how their clinical education programs are structured.

In the face of a rapidly changing society and the competing demands on the medical profession, mentoring is critical to medical education and ultimately to patients and society. Despite its nebulous nature, mentoring in medicine serves not only the protégé and the mentor but ultimately patients, the profession, and society. Mentoring in clinical medicine is about not just transmitting knowledge and skills but also tending to the core values of the profession.

Einstein said it best:

> It is not enough to teach a man a specialty.... It is essential that the student acquire an understanding of and a lively feeling for values.... It is this personal contact with those who teach—not through textbooks. It is this that primarily constitutes and preserves our culture (40).
>
> —*Albert Einstein, 1952*

Acknowledgments: Special thanks to Dana Levinson for extensive assistance and guidance with the preparation of the manuscript and to Kelly Smith for editorial expertise in bringing the manuscript to completion.

REFERENCES

1. **Daloz L.** Effective Teaching and Mentoring: Realizing the Transformational Power of Adult Learning Experiences. San Francisco: Jossey-Bass; 1986.
2. **Homer.** Fagles R, translator. The Odyssey. New York: Viking Penguin; 1996.
3. **Johnson WB, Ridley CR.** Elements of Mentoring. Revised ed. New York: St. Martin's Pr; 2008.
4. **Csikszentmihalyi M.** Forward. In: Nakamura N, Shernoff DJ. Good Mentoring. Fostering Excellent Practice in Higher Education. San Francisco: J Wiley; 2009.
5. **Ensher EA, Murphy SE.** Power mentoring: how successful mentors and protégés get the most out of their relationships. San Francisco: Jossey-Bass; 2005.
6. **The Wisconsin Project for Scientific Teaching.** Accessed at http://scientificteaching.wisc.edu.
7. **Sambunjak D, Straus SE, Marusic A.** Mentoring in academic medicine: a systematic review. JAMA. 2006;296:1103-15.
8. **Zerzan JT, Hess R, Schur E, Phillips RS, Rigotti N.** Making the most of mentors: a guide for mentees. Acad Med. 2009;84:140-4.
9. **Rogers J, Monteiro FM, Nora A.** Toward measuring the domains of mentoring. Fam Med. 2008;40:259-63.
10. **Zachary LJ.** Creating a Mentoring Culture: The Organization's Guide. San Francisco: Jossey-Bass; 2005.
11. **Erikson EH.** Dimensions of a New Identity. New York: Norton; 1974.
12. **Erikson EH.** Identity and the Life Cycle. New York: Norton; 1959.
13. **Levinson D, Darrow C, Klein E, Levinson M.** The Seasons of a Man's Life. New York: Knopf; 1978.
14. **Daloz L.** Mentor: Guiding the Journey of Adult Learners. 2nd ed. New York: Jossey-Bass; 1999.
15. **Vaillant GE.** Mental health. Am J Psychiatry. 2003;160:1373-84.
16. **Nakamura J, Shernoff DJ.** Good Mentoring: Fostering Excellent Practice in Higher Education. San Francisco: J Wiley & Sons; 2009.

17. **Sackett DL.** On the determinants of academic success as a clinician-scientist. Clin Invest Med. 2001;24:94-100.
18. **Ramani S, Gruppen L, Kachur EK.** Twelve tips for developing effective mentors. Med Teach. 2006;28:404-8.
19. **Evans J.** Mentoring magic: how to be an effective mentor. Tips from two highly successful principal investigators. The Scientist. 2008;22:70.
20. **Delong TJ, Gabarro JJ, Lees RJ.** Why mentoring matters in a hypercompetitive world. Harvard Business Review. 2008; January:115-21.
21. **Bland C, Taylor A, Shollenberger S.** Mentoring systems: benefits and challenges of diverse mentoring partnerships. AAMC Faculty Vitae. September 2006. Accessed at www.aamc.org/members/facultydev/facultyvitae/fall06/feature.htm.
22. **Rose GL, Rukstalis MR, Schuckit MA.** Informal mentoring between faculty and medical students. Acad Med. 2005;80:344-8.
23. **Adams JU.** How to be a good mentor. The Scientist. 2004;18:56.
24. **Jackson VA, Palepu A, Szalacha L, Caswell C, Carr PL, Inui T.** "Having the right chemistry": a qualitative study of mentoring in academic medicine. Acad Med. 2003;78:328-34.
25. **Ramanan RA, Phillips RS, Davis RB, Silen W, Reede JY.** Mentoring in medicine: keys to satisfaction. Am J Med. 2002;112:336-41.
26. **Wasserstein AG, Quistberg DA, Shea JA.** Mentoring at the University of Pennsylvania: results of a faculty survey. J Gen Intern Med. 2007;22:210-4.
27. **Perlmutter DD.** Are you a good protégé? Chronicle of Higher Education. 18 April 2008. Accessed at http://chronicle.com/article/Are-You-a-Good/45755.
28. **Luckhaupt SE, Chin MH, Mangione CM, Phillips RS, Bell D, Leonard AC, et al.** Mentorship in academic general internal medicine. Results of a survey of mentors. J Gen Intern Med. 2005;20:1014-8.
29. **Humphrey HH, Levinson DL, Smith K.** Mentoring women and minorities throughout residency and beyond. In: Henderson MC, ed. APDIM Toolkit. 9th ed. Washington, DC: Association of Program Directors in Internal Medicine; 2007.
30. **Bussey-Jones J, Bernstein L, Higgins S, et al.** Repaving the road to academic success: an alternative approach to mentoring. Society for General Internal Medicine. 2006. Accessed at www.sgim.org/userfiles/file/AMHandouts/AM04/Workshops/WA11.pdf.
31. **Pololi LH, Knight SM, Dennis K, Frankel RM.** Helping medical school faculty realize their dreams: an innovative, collaborative mentoring program. Acad Med. 2002;77:377-84.
32. **Pololi L, Knight S.** Mentoring faculty in academic medicine. A new paradigm? J Gen Intern Med. 2005;20:866-70.
33. **Thompson C.** Are your friends making you fat? The New York Times Magazine. 10 September 2009:MM28.
34. **Schweitzer A, Anderson E, eds.** Thoughts for Our Times. New York: Peter Pauper Press; 1975.
35. **Kuhn T.** The Structure of Scientific Revolutions. Chicago: Univ of Chicago Pr; 1970.
36. **Reddy ST, Farnan JM, Yoon JD, Leo T, Upadhyay GA, Humphrey HJ, et al.** Third-year medical students' participation in and perceptions of unprofessional behaviors. Acad Med. 2007;82:S35-9.
37. **Gardner H.** Irresponsible work. In: Gardner H, ed. Responsibility at Work. San Francisco: Jossey-Bass; 2007.
38. **Gardner H, Csikszentmihalyi M, Damon W.** Good Work. When Excellence and Ethics Meet. New York: Basic Books; 2001:17.
39. **Hafferty FW.** Beyond curriculum reform: confronting medicine's hidden curriculum. Acad Med. 1998;73:403-7.
40. **Einstein A.** Education for independent thought. New York Times. 5 October 1952.

3

Challenging the Profession: Mentoring for Fearlessness

Delese Wear, PhD

Joseph Zarconi, MD, FACP

> A defining characteristic of good teaching is a tendency to push on the existing order of things (1).
>
> —*Mike Rose, Possible Lives*

As the current medical literature bears out, mentorship has multiple meanings. We would argue that because of the multiplicity of meaning, traditional conceptualizations of one-on-one mentorship do not work well as a model for the transmission of lessons of professionalism at the undergraduate level.

The same can be said about professionalism. As the term grew in popularity during the past 10 or 15 years—indeed, medical educators have argued for its presence in every curriculum document, manuscript, conference paper, and specialty board position statement—its meaning became more slippery and varied. In some locales, it became synonymous with ethical behavior, in others with etiquette and good manners surrounding punctuality and dress. Professionalism mandates crept across the medical education landscape like kudzu, as Coulehan likes to describe it (2). This has led to what some called "overuse of the word 'professionalism' itself," with students often viewing it as "a collection of excessive directives, lectures, rules, and moral pronouncements that they found repetitive and patronizing" (3), and well-meaning educators confusing "professionalism conversations with conversations about rules of common decency, civil behavior, and the *Golden* Rule" (4).

That said, medical educators have vast teaching opportunities to help their students and residents develop as caring, thoughtful, and

KEY POINTS
- Mentors need to "nudge" students toward critical self-knowing and promote broader understanding of their own beliefs and values, where they come from, and how they are evolving throughout their professional development.
- Exposing students to the broadest array of alternative landscapes and narratives develops their abilities to see through many lenses.
- Mentors should expose the forces that influence the students' professional development, the health and care of patients, and the culture of medicine, and help students to develop approaches to challenge these forces if appropriate.
- It is important to break down the silence of students and honor their voices in ways that can meaningfully shape how medicine is, or can be.
- Several strategies based on innovative curricula and faculty development hold promise for encouraging professional growth and development of future physicians.

respectful physicians who work on behalf of the patients and communities they serve. Thinking about these opportunities requires crafting a different language and a different set of assumptions about mentoring and professionalism than the ones currently used. To think about these opportunities requires what Parker Palmer (5) calls "the courage to teach," for it is *teachers* who "possess the power to create conditions that can help students learn a great deal—or keep them from learning much at all. Teaching is the intentional act of creating those conditions, and good teaching requires that we understand the inner sources of both the intent and the act."

This chapter explores how ideas of "courage" and fearlessness might be applied in the mentoring relationship; the "inner sources" of teachers' intentions and actions; and the conditions created by teachers who are at any moment also mentors, role models, or advisors. The literature on both mentoring and professionalism is examined, and the relationship between these concepts is explored; the intention is to clarify both mentoring and professionalism in a manner that will be helpful for medical teachers. This discussion is not meant to disparage traditional forms of mentoring aimed at career development or academic advancement. Rather, a case is made for broader and more comprehensive mentoring objectives that complement traditional objectives and for approaches to mentoring that promote the humanistic and professional ideals of the medical profession.

❖ Mentoring Medical Students: Current Conceptions

A current MEDLINE search of the terms *mentor* or *mentoring* with *medical student* yields over 70 entries. One of those articles, Buddeberg-Fischer and Herta's "Formal Mentoring Programmes for Medical Students and Doctors—A Review of the Medline Literature" (6), provides an excellent overview of the goals and structures of such programs. Most programs position mentoring with some aspect of career development or specialty selection, such as shadowing experiences with surgeons or family physicians or descriptive curriculum interventions to raise interest in community medicine or geriatrics. Some are an introduction to medical student life; others focus on women and other underrepresented groups, such as mentoring efforts targeting women interested in surgery. Most suggest a traditional one-on-one mentoring structure, which is a voluntary experience outside the required curriculum; others involve group mentoring, which is often attached to curricular experiences.

Seven articles specifically mention professional development (distinct from the career or specialty issues cited above) as a goal of the mentoring relationship. Two of them describe the same program (7, 8): the LOCUS (Leadership Opportunities with Communities, the Medically Underserved, and Special Populations) program at the University of Wisconsin, a program that involves service to underserved and special populations. Another article describes a portfolio project to promote professionalism (9), and still another focuses on professionalism in emergency medicine (10). Two others address curricular issues relevant to mentoring professionalism: one a comparison of the merits of reflective writing and one-on-one sessions with mentors (11), the other the development of the "college" system within medical schools as a site for groups of students to address professionalism issues with mentors (12). Finally, one article describes informal mentoring between faculty and medical students that addresses "implicit knowledge about the 'hidden curriculum' of professionalism" (13).

Interestingly, none of these referenced programs resemble the classic one-on-one definition of mentoring that usually involves a personal relationship between a more experienced and, most often, older person with someone less experienced and younger. In that construct, the former acts as a guide or sponsor, offering knowledge, support, inside information, advice, challenges, and sometimes opportunities for collaboration.

Whether in dyads or small groups, as in the "college" system, or in multiple-mentoring models (6), certain assumptions about what mentoring should accomplish are relatively constant. Many of these assumptions concern instructive and socializing functions, such as "shaping," "forming," or "accelerating" a "career trajectory" (14, 15). Some descriptions seem clearly corporate-based, focusing on career "development," "satisfaction," "path," or "productivity" (14); others cite functions such as helping students prepare a vitae or improve their interview techniques (15). And while some— particularly those focusing on mentoring and professionalism—mention values and ethical perspectives as embedded in the mentoring relationship, almost all assume that those terms speak for themselves. Taherian and Shekarchian, for example, speak of "developing values and an ethical perspective" along with helping trainees learn "the unwritten rules of the game" (15). However, they never critically dissect what those values and ethical perspectives are; how they overlap and sometimes contradict each other (depending on how, where, and by whom the terms are being used); and, most important, whose interests are served when mentors urge and model particular values and ethical perspectives. Anyone who has spent time in medical education would recognize that myriad values circulate throughout the environment, that ethical inquiry looks different depending on one's position, and that different clinical specialties enact divergent conceptions of "humanism" and other abstractions traditionally uttered in the discourses on professionalism.

An illustrative case in point is a recent article offering "twelve tips for developing effective mentors," in which the authors state that "a mentor is someone who is a counselor and a teacher and instructs, admonishes and assists a junior trainee or colleague in attaining success" (14). While this article presents valuable ideas on mentoring aimed at career success, its perspective on mentoring is narrowly focused on mentee success. As a result, it is "mentee focused" rather than directed toward better patient care.

In a decade-old editorial, John Bligh asks how a mentor differs from someone responsible for the educational development of a doctor-in-training, that is, a teacher (16). The author believes that although teaching differs from the usual conceptions of mentoring, at the medical school level the focus should be on mentoring embedded in a richer conception of teaching. This model stands for far more than transmission of knowledge, and more than training in clinical skills and reasoning. In addition to those essentials, mentors-cum-teachers should forthrightly and unapologetically nurture the skills *and* values associated with critical reflection on self, profession, and society, which are at the very heart of the professionalism that should be addressed throughout medical school. The students' ability and desire to reflect on the people they are becoming and how their actions affect their patients, peers, profession, family, and society—these are at least as important to the ongoing development of their humanity as are the traits and behaviors that have become associated with professionalism. Such reflection requires that students move into the worlds their patients inhabit, outside of ambulatory settings, hospital beds, and clinics; these are the worlds formed by the messy, seemingly insurmountable cultural and structural issues that contribute so much to patients' health, well-being, and illnesses. Students should begin to question some of the very conceptions of "physician," "patient," "health," and "illness" that are firmly entrenched in both the professional and popular culture, and come to understand that objectivity, evidence, and outcomes, as important as they may be, may not explain what patients are experiencing (17). Mentoring should be grounded in what Parker Palmer calls a "profound understanding of how we're all called to stand in the ... gap between what is and what could and should be" (18).

❖ Encouraging Reflection and Critical Assessment

The remainder of this chapter proposes a theoretical conception of mentoring grounded in the belief that medical educators have the responsibility to nudge their students toward critical assessment of themselves, their clinical surroundings, the structure of medical education, and the cultural conditions that lead patients to seek care (or not to). These reflective skills form the heart of professional development and the core of mentors' responsibilities to students. The chapter concludes with some practical strategies that mentors can use to encourage fearlessness in their students, and thereby strengthen the professional and moral culture of medicine.

Values

The preceding use of the word "nudge" above is not flippant. Students arrive at the doorsteps of medical education with preformed values, typically arising from their religious beliefs, families, class-based orientations, and other life experiences. The mentor's job is to foster critical self-refection on these beliefs. For example, medical students often hold particularly uncritical beliefs in a meritocratic world. Stimulating more critical reflection on such beliefs may deepen the students' understanding and perhaps their empathy and tolerance. Thus, the role of mentors and teachers is *not* to inculcate or instill but to offer students landscapes of learning previously unseen that may influence the meanings they later bring to their work. These landscapes—always partial, always laced with human values unique to each individual—include those that may not be explicit or even visible inside the walls of hospitals, clinics, and examination rooms. In such alternative landscapes, students might consider that well-educated, economically and socially privileged persons (such as themselves) may have skewed or incomplete explanations for patients and communities in all their varieties.

Theories of mentoring from domains outside medicine offer medical educators such visions. Legal scholar Lani Guinier provides some of the most eloquent and useful descriptions of what mentoring should and should not be. She argues that a mentor is *not*—or *should not* be—the experienced faculty member in the lineage of Homer's Mentor, one who often counsels and "keeps students in line ... a pacifier of the status quo" (19). In fact, she continues,

> an effective teacher is less a role model than a mentor, an educator who empowers through feedback, guidance, and sharing rather than one who commands through example, visibility.... Mentors see learning as an active process that builds on students' emotional engagement and emphasizes the mutuality of their role in the educational conversation ... [while using] teaching techniques that foster security and respect for multiple viewpoints (19).

Demystifying the traditional image of faculty members as detached problem-solvers, Guinier "takes information from the margin to transform the educational dialogue for all [her] students," (19) even as she puzzles out loud with them over knotty cultural issues to which she has no clear answers.

In medical education, such puzzling must be central to mentoring as a counter to the cultural expectations for certainty placed on physicians. Post (20) describes her method of teaching as posing questions "that cannot be answered in one hour, in one classroom, or sometimes in an entire ... career. Questions like these remain in the classroom in a kind of intellectual suspended animation long after they have been asked." These teaching behaviors are often absent in clinical teaching, where the importance of knowing the right answers is so vital because of what is at stake. Yet this laudable striving for correctness and exactitude in the clinical domain can actually truncate medical students' emerging professional identities when faculty avoid the messy arena of values, both their own and others'. The emphasis on certainty is misapplied when physicians assume that they "know" how patients think, what patients believe, and how patients will act on medical advice. In truth, these things are not very well known at all, and students need to be reminded of this throughout their medical education.

But more needs to be said about the environment in which all this is played out, and the consequences both mentors and their students face if they "fearlessly" examine the culture of medicine, the cultures their patients inhabit, and the intersection where they meet. There are consequences when students consider how "education/science/work/life are not value-free" (21) and then choose to speak openly about such values. Here Foucault's thinking on "fearless speech" (22) holds bright promise for the mentoring relationship.

Fearless Speech, Moral Courage

Anyone close to medical education, and indeed anyone who has experienced it, knows that silence is practiced with some frequency during medical training. This silence is invoked, for example, when a student witnesses a clinical faculty member demeaning a nurse or other health care professional, a patient being ridiculed behind his back, or a faculty member aggressively questioning a student in such a way that it becomes less about learning and more about humiliation. Students quickly learn the unwritten codes of keeping their mouths shut in fear of the consequences, such as receiving poor evaluations and gaining the reputation of troublemaker. Students often tuck these experiences away as examples of negative role-modeling with the belief that they will never act this way. Most do not, yet these scenarios persist with each new generation as students perceive the consequences of speaking out.

Foucault uses the word *parrhesia*, which is usually translated into English as "free speech," to form the basis of his argument that we must tell the truth even when it is likely to be met with resistance. While there is a pejorative sense of the word (similar to uncensored babbling), its more common meaning is simply to tell the truth because it is one's obligation, even if there is a risk in the telling. In their persuasive article, "Foucault's 'Fearless Speech' and the Transformation and Mentoring of Medical Students," Papadimos and Murray (23) contend that mentors pass on *parrhesiastic* values to medical students, giving them the ability to challenge the status quo and thus transform medical education and medical practice—and back them up when they are met with resistance. To quote their work:

> Medical students must become able citizens who not only possess the critical skills necessary to understand how power/knowledge operates, but they must develop the capacity to expose and to challenge this power, when required—to speak out fearlessly on behalf of their patients, their profession, themselves, and society in general. ... In sum, medical students must learn to practice parrhesia, they must speak fearlessly. This does not exactly mean that they will speak without fear; rather, it means that they will learn to have

the courage to speak under fearful circumstances—to address and to critique those institutions or individuals who control more power, knowledge, and technology. ... It means 'speaking truth to power,' as Foucault has said. Such an attitude, behavior, or value cannot exactly be 'taught' as a skill or as a piece of positive knowledge. It calls for an apprenticeship by mentors who will foster such an ethos in their students, who demonstrate parrhesia themselves, and who actively encourage new discourses in their teaching, their research, and beyond (23).

Mentors encourage medical students to practice parrhesia when they encourage students to think about how their own values and beliefs directly influence patient care and how both medical education and practice involve political and moral choices (20). This conception of mentoring is vastly different from the cultural work of traditional mentoring, which is based on the premise that to sustain strength and solidarity within cultural groups over time, strategies that allow such groups to reproduce themselves must be practiced. They need these strategies because "each new generation, each new birth must be taught, convinced, even coerced into accepting the norms for behavior within that society" (24). In fact, Powell (24) argues that traditional mentoring may actually discourage mentees from examining assumptions within academic environments that need to be challenged or even changed.

Parker Palmer provides an alternative. He identified structures and practices found in educational cultures that are divisive and hurtful to students, and suggests how these are sustained by faculty silence. Such silence, he maintains, is rooted in fear of confronting issues that might be unpopular with colleagues, administrators, or even students themselves. He writes of scenarios anyone who has taught will recognize, particularly in medical education, when students are "afraid of failing, of not understanding, of being drawn into issues they would rather avoid, of having their ignorance exposed or their prejudices challenged, of looking foolish in front of their peers" (5). But the fear "multiplies geometrically" when students' fears are mixed with their faculty's reluctance to confront such issues.

Palmer suggests that these fears are also fed by the dominant mode of knowing in most educational settings, particularly true in medical education. This mode of knowing is influenced by how we make knowledge, which thus dictates how we answer the questions, "How do we know what we know?" and "How do we know our knowledge is true?" Biomedicine's extreme emphasis on objectivity and distance—an essential stance in the creation of *some* knowledge—influences every corner of medical education. At times it makes students fearful of their subjective, utterly human, and inevitably flawed selves. A fearless mentor would challenge medical students to recognize the values, opinions, and biases that infuse the whole of medical practice, along with their own and those of everyone who teaches them.

Mentoring parrhesia, indeed mentoring fearlessness, while often exceedingly difficult, offers hope for students to develop *fortitude*, one of the virtues that Pellegrino and Thomasma argue are essential to medical practice. Pellegrino and Thomasma differentiate fortitude from physical courage, characterizing it as a form of "moral courage, for example, the willingness of the individual to suffer personal harm for the sake of the moral good" (25). And while traditional forms of medical education, particularly in clinical settings, rightly focus much of the student's attention on what to *do*, and how to do it, this form of mentoring shifts the student's consciousness on how to *be* in medical work. Clearly, physical courage is required in stepping in to manage a victim of multiple trauma or to resect an inflamed appendix. But moral courage is required in serving the good of the patient and profession, as when a student stands to resist derogatory humor being directed at a patient. A focus on moral courage reminds students that they may resist enculturation in the practices and behaviors that characterize some negative aspects of medicine's culture—arrogance, lack of empathy, and disdain for patients. Further, when students respond to mentoring that encourages fearlessness, and reject such practices (even in "fearful circumstances"), they often find that they are not alone, and that others on the team respond to the positive moral turns that can result. As students develop greater comfort in enacting moral courage to defend how they wish to be as physicians, they also develop their potential to mentor others on the health care team. In turn, they can influence the cultures of medicine and medical education in positive and meaningful ways. They develop consciousness and influence not only on how they can be as physicians but on how medicine can be.

❖ Mentoring and Professionalism: Some Immodest Proposals

As stated here and elsewhere (26–29), the professionalism "movement" began as a list of virtues that medical educators seized upon and promoted with the belief that the meaning of the terms and worth of the movement were apparent to all educators, students, and accrediting and governing bodies. Indeed, the concept is probably less viable for the current generation of medical students, even though the impulse that fueled its widespread attention remains critical to the education of young physicians. That impulse—to find ways to describe the values, attitudes, and behaviors important to caring, socially responsive physicianhood and then talk to students, residents, and attending physicians about how to take up these challenges in their lives—remains one of the most important tasks of medical education and beyond. This challenge involves urging students to reflect on their emerging professional selves, to consider how institutional structures are influencing who they are becoming, and to compare who they are becoming to what brought them to medicine in the first place. At the same time, faculty members should look in the mirror and model to students through their talk and actions that they are co-wanderers with their students, sharing their vulnerability. Parker Palmer offers several "immodest proposals" for the education of professionals that may help them "keep their hearts alive in settings where people too often lose heart … [and] stand up to and sometimes against the institutions from which their paychecks, and perhaps their identities, come" (5). The following describes three of these proposals, which go to the heart of mentoring.

First—and possibly one of the most difficult tasks for medical educators and mentors—"we must help our students debunk the myth that institutions possess autonomous, even ultimate, power over our lives" (5). This is where cultivating a fearlessness in students comes into play as faculty, too, name and confront the practices within and outside medical education that diminish one's humanity and that of others. This fearlessness is enacted when faculty model skills of critical inquiry, which may lead students to examine and question the nature of medical knowledge; the social, economic, and hierarchical organization of medical institutions; and the relationships between medical institutions and all groups in society. Such pursuits would emphasize to students how medical education shapes their professional identities both negatively and positively.

This first challenge may be one of the most difficult medical educators face as they teach students who seem to learn at every opening that they should never challenge authority, particularly in clinical settings. It is one thing to argue the validity of a test item but quite another to question, however respectfully and appropriately, a clinical faculty member's actions or attitudes toward a patient. *This is just not done.* This thinking, however, gives students a "cheap ethical out," but to be fair, the medical environment instructs students that "powers" will harm them if crossed (5). In addition, students come to believe that even if they do speak out, little will change; this belief is often reinforced by examples they witness. The urgings and encouragement arising from fearless mentoring would suggest that "if we are even partly responsible for creating institutional dynamics, we possess some degree of power to alter them. The education of a new professional would help students understand and take responsibility for the myriad ways we co-create and re-create institutional pathologies" (5).

Second—and similarly—the education of young professionals guided by fearlessness would invalidate the assumption that one's emotions should be suppressed to become an excellent physician. Educators would help students understand that it is the mark of a professional to honor one's own emotions as well as the emotions of patients, families, and other caregivers. Palmer argues that students should be helped to

> honor and attend to their feelings, especially painful ones like anxiety, anger, guilt, grief, and burnout. Students would learn to explore feelings about themselves, the work they do, the people with whom they work, the institutional settings in which they work, and the world in which they live. They would learn that painful feelings are not signs of personal weakness, sources of shame, or irrelevant to the complex challenges of knowing, working, and living (5).

In fact, the kind of mentoring proposed here identifies "emotion as a source of knowledge and a catalyst for understanding, rather than a distraction from one's academic development" (30). It helps students to consider how to integrate their emotional, intellectual, and physical lives in ways that make sense to each of them (even as faculty acknowledge their ongoing challenges in this arena).

A third proposal for the education of physicians focuses squarely on fearlessness. Medical students should be encouraged to explore how power relative to patients, students, faculty, formal and informal social networks, and accrediting bodies operates in medical education, training hospitals, systems of health care delivery, the communities they serve, and the culture at large. Such fearlessness necessitates involvement beyond the current formulaic undergraduate curriculum, moving students beyond the physician–patient framework to broader considerations of the health concerns of the poor, inadequate nutrition, unsafe work and living conditions, abuse, and addictions. Students should be asked to consider the influence of such issues as the following:

- Financial rewards on patient care
- How government agencies regulate and sponsor how and what knowledge is made and who benefits most from certain kinds of knowledge
- Who gets to make public policy and who doesn't
- The interests of the pharmaceutical industry, the insurance industry, government lobbies, and business.

This is the wide-angle lens described earlier. Mentors should help students use this lens to assess their roles and responsibilities as physicians in an education system that often fails to address such issues, much less question them. Such mentors help students refine and refocus their radar as they read the medical environment for meanings, particularly those that help them develop a concept of professionalism that is not limited to good etiquette (31).

Medical educators teach values explicitly and implicitly every day to students and residents who sit in their classrooms; who watch them on rounds, at the bedside, and with their peers and coworkers; who talk with them informally in hallway conversations; and who know something of their lives outside medicine. Nobel laureate Toni Morrison writes that such influence on students, often unacknowledged, is seen through what students are asked to read, how discussions and debates are guided, how students are "nudged" to explore particular issues, all of which are "inscribed" on one's teaching. "Like it or not," she writes,

> we are paradigms of our own values, advertisements of our own ethics.... Now the question of how to teach values becomes less fraught. How do we treat each other? The members of our own profession? How do we respond to professional and political cunning, to raw and ruthless ambition, to the plight of those outside our walls? What are we personally willing to sacrifice, give up for the "public good"? What gestures of reparation are we personally willing to make? What risky, unfashionable research are we willing to undertake? (32)

These are questions critical to the teacher and mentor in any setting, in any academic domain. They are also the mark of the teacher and mentor who is not embarrassed to use words such as "kindness" and "compassion"; who is not afraid to speak openly with students about her successes and failures, her struggles for meaning and balance; who is willing to confront institutional directives surrounding professionalism that are "formulaic ... menus of phrases, courses, and temporary forms of behavior that a student can taste without swallowing" (32). This is the mentoring for fearlessness we propose here for medical students.

❖ Strategies for Mentoring for Fearlessness

The goals of effective mentoring, and particularly, mentoring for fearlessness, have been elaborated in this chapter to include at least the following:

- To "nudge" students toward critical self-knowing, promoting broader understanding of their own beliefs and values, where they come from, and how they are evolving throughout their professional development

- To expose students to the broadest array of alternative land-scapes and narratives, which in turn develops their abilities to see through many lenses
- To demystify faculty so that students not only learn how to solve problems and arrive at answers, but also witness the manner in which all faculty also struggle with quandary and uncertainty
- To expose the forces of power that influence the students' pro-fessional development, the health and care of patients, and the culture of medicine, and help students develop approaches to challenge such forces when appropriate
- To break down the silence of students and honor their voices in ways that can meaningfully shape how medicine is, or can be.

This chapter has discussed approaches to achieving these goals. Yet, to achieve them requires deliberate and systematic commitment to fostering mentors and mentorship that can challenge traditional structures and cultures in medicine and medical education. One such strategy emerging among medical schools is the dedication of valued time throughout the curriculum for students to develop their reflective skills, to process their experiences in medical school, and to expand their understanding of self and of the world of medicine. Often called *Doctoring* courses, these programs expose students to relevant topics or issues on which they are invited to reflect, both in writing and in small-group discussions. Topics reflect where students are in the curriculum and what they are experiencing in their socialization. They can include exposure to imaginative as well as medical literature, film, poetry, and other media as a way of exposing them to "alter-native landscapes and narratives."

A second strategy relies on students' writing narratives in the clinical environment as a means for "changing the conversations" (33). These narratives are used to discuss and explore implications for the students' professional development and are used in faculty development work. Such strategies are meant to create safe-space conversations that may disrupt what has been called the "hidden" or "informal" curriculum, and to create disturbance in the organizational culture of medicine. Similar techniques could be used on inpatient clinical teaching services if faculty mentors set aside a portion of each day's rounding activities for reflective conversations with residents and students about what took place that day on rounds. When the team has laughed or joked about a morbidly obese patient on the service, for example, the team can openly discuss why they resort to the use of derogatory humor, whether it feels right to do so, and whether they should pursue alternative ways to mange one's responses to such patients.

Such regular focusing on "what just happened here" in the clinical setting may promote individual and group reflection and break down the usual silences of team members who hesitate to challenge the more traditional culture and systems of care.

All of these strategies, of course, depend on vigorous faculty development. Attending faculty members, as well as residents in their role as teachers, must have their own consciousness raised about how students develop their professional identities, and how the clinical educational culture affects the students' and faculty's development. Faculty must be able to reflect and lead discussions on the forces of power in medicine and medical education; to encourage reflective writing and discussion; and to create learning environments where all participants, medical students included, are given voice and encouraged to use it constructively. Similarly, faculty incentives and rewards systems must be recalibrated to reward and celebrate achievements in this sort of mentoring.

The opportunities in medical education are many, and the privilege of mentoring medical students in preparation for a life of service in medicine is an honored one. Clearly, many well-meaning educators across many institutions have developed successful ways to nudge students toward lives in medicine enriched by conscious professional commitment and satisfaction. Challenges remain, however, and some are increasingly exacerbated by increasing (and rightful) emphasis on science and technology in medical education, the dramatic acuity of illness particularly in hospital settings, and a stressed health care workforce. Yet the obligation shared by medical educators everywhere is that of training future physicians who are capable of rich understanding of self as well as of patients, able to see through myriad lenses and comprehend many landscapes, capable of managing quandary and uncertainty, conscious of power relationships and how they influence the culture of medicine, confident to advocate at all times for their patients and for their subsequent trainees, and, when appropriate, "to push on the existing order of things." Mentoring for fearlessness offers some hope that the efforts of the medical education community can facilitate the achievement of such ends.

REFERENCES

1. **Rose M.** Possible Lives: The Promise of Public Education. New York: Penguin; 1996.
2. **Coulehan J.** You say self-interest, I say altruism. In: Wear D, Aultman J, eds. Professionalism in Medicine: Critical Perspectives. New York: Springer; 2006:104.

3. **Goldstein EA, Maestas RR, Fryer-Edwards K, Wenrich MD, Oelschlager AM, Baernstein A, et al.** Professionalism in medical education: an institutional challenge. Acad Med. 2006;81:871-6.
4. **Engel JD, Zarconi J, Pethtel LL, Missimi, SA.** Narrative in Health Care: Health Patients, Practitioners, Profession, and Community. Oxford: Radcliffe; 2008:128.
5. **Palmer P.** The Courage to Teach: Exploring the Inner Landscape of a Teacher's Life. San Francisco: Jossey-Bass; 1998.
6. **Buddeberg-Fischer B, Herta KD.** Formal mentoring programmes for medical students and doctors—a review of the Medline literature. Med Teach. 2006;28:248-57.
7. **Carufel-Wert DA, Younkin S, Foertsch J, Eisenberg T, Haq CL, Crouse BJ, et al.** LOCUS: immunizing medical students against the loss of professional values. Fam Med. 2007;39:320-5.
8. **Haq C, Grosch M, Carufel-Wert D.** Leadership Opportunities with Communities, the Medically Underserved, and Special Populations (LOCUS). Acad Med. 2002;77:740.
9. **Kalet AL, Sanger J, Chase J, Keller A, Schwartz MD, Fishman ML, et al.** Promoting professionalism through an online professional development portfolio: successes, joys, and frustrations. Acad Med. 2007;82:1065-72.
10. **Van Groenou AA, Bakes KM.** Art, Chaos, Ethics, and Science (ACES): a doctoring curriculum for emergency medicine. Ann Emerg Med. 2006;48:532-7.
11. **Baernstein A, Fryer-Edwards K.** Promoting reflection on professionalism: a comparison trial of educational interventions for medical students. Acad Med. 2003;78:742-7.
12. **Murr AH, Miller C, Papadakis M.** Mentorship through advisory colleges. Acad Med. 2002;77:1172-3.
13. **Rose GL, Rukstalis MR, Schuckit MA.** Informal mentoring between faculty and medical students. Acad Med. 2005;80:344-8.
14. **Ramani S, Gruppen L, Kachur EK.** Twelve tips for developing effective mentors. Med Teach. 2006;28:404-8.
15. **Taherian K, Shekarchian M.** Mentoring for doctors. Do its benefits outweigh its disadvantages? Med Teach. 2008;30:e95-9.
16. **Bligh J.** Mentoring: an invisible support network [Editorial]. Med Educ. 1999;33:2-3.
17. **Miller FA, Mellon WD, Waitzkin H.** Experiencing community medicine during residency: the La Mesa housecleaning cooperative. In: Wear D, Bickel J, eds. Educating for Professionalism: Creating a Climate of Humanism in Medical Education. Iowa City, IA: Univ of Iowa Pr; 2000:134-49.
18. **Palmer P.** Politics of the brokenhearted. Accessed at www.commonweal.org/new-school/pdf_files/Politics%20of%20the%20Brokenhearted.pdf.
19. **Guinier L.** Of gentlemen and role models. In: Wing AK, ed. Critical Race Feminism. New York: NYU Pr; 2003:106-13.
20. **Post DW.** The politics of pedagogy: confessions of a black woman law professor. In: Wing AK, ed. Critical Race Feminism. New York: NYU Pr; 2003:131-9.
21. **Benishek LA, Bieschke KJ, Park J, Slattery SM.** A multicultural feminist model of mentoring. J Multicult Counsel Devel. 2004;32:428-42.
22. **Foucault M.** Fearless Speech. Los Angeles: Semiotext(e); 2001.
23. **Papadimos TJ, Murray SJ.** Foucault's "fearless speech" and the transformation and mentoring of medical students. Philos Ethics Humanit Med. 2008;3:12.
24. **Powell BJ.** Mentoring: one of the master's tools. Initiatives. 1999;19-31.
25. **Pellegrino ED, Thomasma DC.** The Virtues in Medical Practice. New York: Oxford Univ Pr; 1993:109.

26. **Wear D, Zarconi J.** Can compassion be taught? Let's ask our students. J Gen Intern Med. 2008;23:948-53.

27. **Wear D, Kuczewski MG.** The professionalism movement: can we pause? Am J Bioeth. 2004;4:1-10.

28. **Wear D, Nixon LL.** Literary inquiry and professional development in medicine: against abstractions. Perspect Biol Med. 2002;45:104-24.

29. **Wear D, Castellani B.** The development of professionalism: curriculum matters. Acad Med. 2000;75:602-11.

30. **McGuire FM, Reger J.** Feminist co-mentoring: a model for academic professional development. NWSA J. 2003;15:54-72.

31. **Kahn MW.** Etiquette-based medicine. N Engl J Med. 2008;358:1988-9.

32. **Morrison T.** How can values be taught in the university? In: Denard CC, ed. What Moves at the Margin: Selected Nonfiction. Jackson: Univ Pr of Mississippi; 2008:191-7.

33. **Inui T, Cottingham AH, Frankel RM, Litzelman DK, Mossbarger DL, Suchman AL, et al.** Educating for professionalism at Indiana University School of Medicine: feet on the ground and fresh eyes. In: Wear D, Aultman JM, ed. Professionalism in Medicine: Critical Perspectives. New York: Springer; 2006:165-84.

4

Role Models in Medicine

Darcy A. Reed, MD, MPH
Scott M. Wright, MD

> Role model: a person considered as a standard of excellence in a partic-
> ular behavioral or social role for another person to emulate (1).

Role models are ubiquitous. Everywhere you go, there is someone doing something noteworthy from which you can learn. Role models are different from teachers, who aim to impart knowledge or skill to learners through lessons and instructions. Role models are also distinct from mentors, who actively and purposively attempt to support the advancement and success of mentees. Mentors and mentees have formal relationships with mutually agreed-upon goals and expectations, whereas role models might not even know that another individual looks up to them as an inspiring exemplar.

There is no need to personally know, meet, see, or touch an individual for him to serve as an inspiring role model. Role models can be appreciated over great distances and despite the passage of long periods of time. For example, the work ethic, courage, and leadership skills of heroes of the past or those living far away (such as Abraham Lincoln, Martin Luther King, Gandhi, or Nelson Mandela) may serve as bright beacons to strive toward.

This chapter reviews and discusses the sociologic basis for role-modeling and the underpinnings illustrating why observation is an effective method for learning complex matters. Examples of role models in contemporary life will also be explored. What is known about role models in medicine will be described, with emphasis on the importance of role models in teaching and promoting professionalism

---

KEY POINTS

- Role models are distinct from mentors, who have formal relationships with mentees that consist of mutually agreed-upon goals and expectations. Role models might not even know that they are considered inspiring exemplars.
- Role-modeling is an integral component of medical education because process of learning in medicine is often conceptualized as an apprenticeship. Role-modeling conveys the skills, attitudes, values, and ethics of the profession.
- Role models shape the professionalism of learners and affect the learning environment.
- Medical trainees selectively pick and choose among the behaviors of various models. There are three specific patterns of modeling: 1) classic modeling, 2) active rejection, and 3) inactive orientation.
- Role-modeling in medicine is characterized by modifiable behaviors that can be learned and practiced.
- Role models may enhance their effectiveness by being intentional about their modeling through "role-modeling consciousness," which refers to purposeful, continuous self-reflection on one's own behaviors in real time.

---

and humanism in medicine. The chapter ends with suggestions for how physicians can serve as more effective role models for medical learners.

❖ Psychologic and Sociologic Basis for Role Models

I hear and I forget. I see and I remember (2).

—*Confucius, 551– 479 BC*

Early psychologists and zoologists discovered that animals and people have an innate propensity to imitate behaviors they see (3, 4). While studying the Japanese macaque, scientists laid out an offering of rice in the sand, figuring the monkeys would take a while to pick it up off the sand. However, one female grabbed big handfuls of rice and sand and took them down to the water. When she threw them in the water, the rice floated and the sand sank, and she skimmed the rice off the surface of the water. Soon all the other monkeys began to do it, too. The expression "monkey see, monkey do" characterizes observational learning, and it is simply illustrated in the children's classic *Caps for Sale: A Tale of a Peddler, Some Monkeys, and Their Monkey Business* (5).

In humans, imitative practices start very early (4). Meltzoff and Moore found a reliable tendency for newborn infants (age 12 to 21 days) to imitate specific behavior they had just seen (6). Bandura and colleagues (7) worked with school-aged children to understand the spectrum of issues that could be absorbed through observational learning; through this work they described social learning theory (7). They discovered that almost anything can be learned through observation, including personality traits, problem-solving skills, aesthetic preferences, phobias, addictions, cognitive development, moral judgments, and moral behaviors.

❖ Contemporary Role Models

Without an antecedent adjective, a role model is assumed to be positive and exemplary. Of course, there are many negative role models who set bad examples, and yet others still look up to them with reverence. In a famous Nike commercial, the former NBA player Charles Barkley had this to say: "I am not a role model. I am not paid to be a role model ... Parents should be role models. Just because I can dunk a basketball doesn't mean I should raise your kids" (8). Many took offense to this advertisement, claiming that select individuals who are handsomely rewarded for their talents and held up as stars need to acknowledge that many people, particularly youths, consider their behaviors and decorum the standard to follow.

Emulating the behaviors and adopting the perspectives of others can be taken too far; religious fanaticism and cults are notable examples of this phenomenon. Unfortunately, individuals may lose the ability to make rational decisions and will blindly follow the commands of others, even when these decisions put them in danger or even cause their own premature death. This is certainly role-modeling gone bad.

In the U.S. military, exemplary behaviors are noted and recognized with awards and ultimately promotions. The military hierarchical system of ranks encourages individuals to carefully look up to superiors in order to understand and acquire the expected norms in conduct and behavior. Similarly, many businesses acknowledge excellent effort put forth and results realized by employees, often publicizing achievement in formats such as "employees of the month."

In his acclaimed book *The Tipping Point* (9), Malcolm Gladwell notes that certain individuals are uniquely placed in positions where their influence can be powerful—both in terms of the number of people looking to them and the intensity of the impact that they have on others. Gladwell recounts multiple examples of how such individuals serve as change agents and give rise to all sorts of phenomena, including new behaviors, fads, fashions, speech patterns, and ways of being.

In sum, human behavior has long been, and continues to be, very suggestible.

❖ Role Models in Medicine

Role-Modeling as an Effective Teaching Method

Role-modeling is an integral component of medical education. Because the process of learning in medicine is often conceptualized as an apprenticeship, role-modeling is a particularly important method for conveying the skills, attitudes, values, and ethics of the profession (10–13).

While teachers may believe that they can direct and control the learning process as it pertains to role-modeling, studies suggest that imitation or integration of specific behaviors modeled by teachers is actually a selective process purposely employed by learners. In a study of learning methods used by pediatric residents in an outpatient continuity clinic, Balmer and colleagues (12) reported that residents relied on role models as an "implicit and intentional learning strategy." By observing the behaviors of their clinic preceptors, pediatric residents obtained "templates" for communication and decision-making that they adapted into their own practice (12). Structured frameworks for recording observations of preceptors' behaviors may help medical trainees to more precisely note the positive behaviors that they wish to emulate, as well as encourage faculty to explicitly model professionalism (13).

Shuval and Adler (14) prospectively followed two classes of medical students to understand the ways in which medical trainees learn from their physician teachers. The results showed that medical trainees selectively picked and chose among the behaviors of various models. Three specific patterns of modeling were noted: 1) classic modeling, wherein learners recognize what they are witnessing and attempt to adjust their behavior to become more like the model; 2) active rejection, in which learners identify attributes that they purposely want to avoid and strive to be "unlike" the model; and 3) inactive orientation, wherein the learner is not affected one way or the other by the interaction with the model (Figure 4-1) (14). As learners advance in training and experience, they begin to more thoughtfully consider the various behaviors that they are observing (14), and they can more judiciously reflect on attributes that they want to incorporate into their repertoire versus those that they wish to avoid.

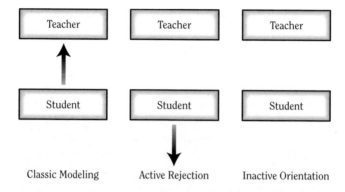

Figure 4-1 Three patterns of modeling observed by Shuval and Adler (14).

Differences Between Role Models and Mentors

Observational learning in medicine does not require that the models be aware that they are serving in this role (12). This underscores an important distinction between role models and mentors in medicine. Because much of this book is devoted to mentors and mentoring, a clear understanding of the differences between a mentor and a role model is needed. Mentoring relationships are usually longer-lasting than relationships with role models, and the scope of the interaction is often correlated with the mentees' productivity and the extent to which mentors benefit from the relationship (15). Formation of the relationship between mentors and mentees is intentional, and both the mentor and mentee actively sustain and grow the relationship to achieve shared goals (16). Finally, beyond general career guidance, mentors often help mentees with specific tasks, such as completing research projects, securing residency positions or faculty appointments, or preparing applications for academic promotion (17). Mentors are often in the same subspecialty as the mentee and possess specific skills that the mentee works to acquire through the mentoring relationship.

Conversely, data suggest that interactions between learners and their role models are typically brief (18). In fact, role models may never interact directly with an individual learner, yet through the learner's observations alone, the role model may profoundly influence the learner's professional development. Role models are chosen by the learner, with or without knowledge and involvement of the model, because by definition, a role model is someone who is *perceived* (by the learner) to embody a standard of excellence to be emulated. Thus, role-modeling lies "in the eye of the beholder"—the learner's. Role models teach primarily by example, and rather than trying to mold the learner, role models inspire learners by their conduct. Although role models may counsel and advise learners (19), role models are generally selected by learners because they possess globally desirable attributes that learners wish to acquire and sustain throughout their own careers (20–22).

Attributes of Role Models in Medicine

Limited data address the characteristics that make an individual a positive role model in medicine. A case–control study of 341 department of medicine attending physicians at four teaching hospitals (23) found that several modifiable behaviors were independently associated with being named by learners as an excellent attending physician role model (Box 4-1).

In another study among surgical faculty, behaviors that correlated with being identified as a role model by surgical residents included stimulating critical thinking among learners through use of literature, allowing for autonomy so that learners could make independent decisions, and attending didactic sessions with trainees (24). The implication of both of these studies is that role-modeling appears to be characterized by modifiable behaviors that can be learned and practiced.

In other studies, learners identified both innate attributes (such as personality and general affect) and modifiable factors (including clinical and teaching skills) as the most important characteristics of physician role models (18, 19, 21). In a qualitative study of the characteristics of physician role models, commonalities among physicians named as role models by medical students included demonstrating dedication to one's specialty and patients, love of teaching, and genuine interest in the needs and welfare of students (18).

The attributes and behaviors of negative role models have been largely overlooked in the literature, despite an acknowledgment that repeated

---

Box 4-1. Modifiable Behaviors Associated With Being Named an Excellent Attending Physician Role Model

▶ Dedicating a greater percentage of total work effort to teaching

▶ Spending more time conducting rounds and teaching while serving as an attending in the hospital

▶ Emphasizing the doctor–patient relationship in one's care and teaching

▶ Teaching the psychosocial aspects of medicine

exposures to negative examples probably adversely affects professional development (25). When physician-teachers were asked to describe barriers that prevented them from being effective role models, they identified being impatient, overly opinionated, and overextended (26). Individuals who have difficulty remembering names and faces, or those who choose not to focus on such recognitions, are thought to be less effective role models (26). Learners also identify specific behaviors, such as lacking sensitivity toward patients, failure to support students with difficulties, and disinterest in humanistic contact with students, as characteristics of negative models (27, 28).

These findings leave open the possibility that positive role-modeling behavior can be learned and that negative role-modeling can be avoided. Although the learning derived from role-modeling is not contingent upon awareness or purposeful participation by the model (12), role models may enhance their effectiveness by being intentional about their modeling. Experienced role models specifically think about their own behaviors when interacting with learners (26) and try to consistently demonstrate only positive examples for learners. This has been described as "role-modeling consciousness" (26), purposeful, continuous self-reflection on one's own behaviors that occurs in real time in the teaching setting.

Figure 4-2 depicts a framework for role-modeling in medicine that emphasizes intentional display of desirable attributes and behaviors by the model. In this framework, the physician role model uses his or her "role-modeling consciousness" to intentionally exemplify the specific characteristics and skills while simultaneously limiting barriers (26). Effective role models can consistently "shift the balance" toward positive role-modeling behaviors that may be emulated by others. Effective role-modeling, of course, also depends on active, focused observation on the part of the learner (see Figure 4-1) (13, 29, 30). Learners need to pay attention, internalize their observations, reflect on them, and mold their subsequent behavior on the basis of what was observed and learned (25).

Impact of Role Models on Professionalism

Role models shape the values, attitudes, and ethics of learners and thus have an effect on the learners' professionalism (31, 32). Experts implore that professionalism be taught (33); most U.S. medical schools have formal professionalism curricula in place (34). Unfortunately, traditional didactic instruction is probably insufficient to inculcate professional behavior (10, 35). Role-modeling, on the other hand, is identified by deans nationwide as one of the most important methods for fostering professionalism among students (36). Senior residents report that they learn more about profes-

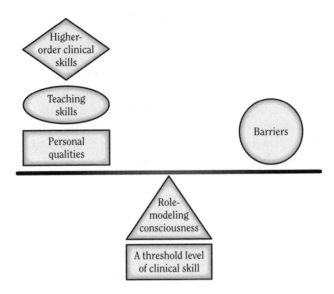

Figure 4-2 Conceptual model of role-modeling in medicine.

sionalism by observing role models than by traditional didactic or case-based instruction (11). Likewise, Feudtner and colleagues found that increasing the number of hours of ethics education in a formal curriculum did not decrease the erosion of ethical behavior among medical students (37). Through their conduct and example, role models send clear signals about the accepted values and behaviors of the profession (38, 39). Since role-modeling is probably one of the most effective ways to instill professionalism, it is crucial that faculty be mindful and intentional about the behaviors they exhibit in front of learners (40).

When asked about the core values that attending physicians most want and try to pass on to trainees, attending physicians identified caring, respect, communication, and integrity (38). These values are consistent with those identified by the American Board of Internal Medicine (32) and others (31, 41–43) as fundamental attributes of medical professionalism. Data indicate that teaching faculty acknowledge personal responsibility for the moral and professional development of their learners (38), yet many would suggest that teachers need to be far more explicit about the professional attitudes and values that learners should acquire (10, 33, 42, 44).

Role-Modeling and Career Choice
In addition to shaping the professionalism of learners, role models also influence learners' choices of career. Exposure to sufficient positive role models in a given subspecialty during medical school substantially

increased the odds that a medical student would choose that specialty for residency training (19). Likewise, observation of negative behaviors or dissatisfaction among physicians in a certain specialty may cause learners not to select that specialty (45). Students who view a given clinical preceptor as a good role model are substantially more likely to consider the preceptor's specialty for their own career (46). Residents claim to recall more numerous encounters with positive role models in their chosen field than with physicians in other specialties during medical school (20).

Issues of Gender and Ethnicity

The sex of the role models, particularly the availability of female role models in certain specialties, may influence career choice among female learners (45, 47–49). Similarly, ethnic and cultural diversity among faculty members helps today's diverse student body find attending physicians who are similar to themselves. It is believed that the more similarities between a learner and a physician-teacher, the more likely it is that the faculty member will serve as a role model for the trainee (50).

Impact of Role Models on the Learning Environment

Whenever and wherever learners gather, a learning environment exists (51). The learning environment is thought to consist of institutional culture (52), formal and hidden curricula (53), and the learning climate (54, 55). As shown in Figure 4-3, role models influence learners within all three elements of the learning environment.

Institutional culture includes official policies and procedures, reward systems, rituals, customs, and norms. Role models may influence institutional culture in their roles as leaders and teachers; however, the way in which role models respond to the culture, such as policies or actions of leadership, can create strong impressions on learners and influence how they will respond to similar stimuli and situations.

In his important work on the learning environment, Hafferty (53) described three distinct "curricula" in medical education: the formal curriculum, the informal curriculum, and the hidden curriculum. The formal curriculum is the set of learning experiences that are planned, written, and officially endorsed by the medical school or training program. The informal curriculum is the spontaneous, unplanned interaction that occurs between students and teachers outside of formal educational experiences. Physician-teachers, functioning as role models, not only direct this spontaneous education but also set the tone for the learning. The hidden curriculum is a "set of influences" associated with organizational structure and culture. These influences include the unplanned messages sent by role models and per-

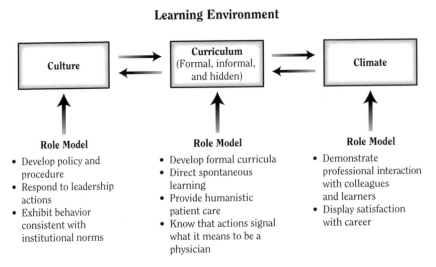

Figure 4-3 Role models can significantly influence all three components of the learning environment in medicine: culture, curriculum, and climate.

ceived by learners about what it means to be a physician, what it takes to succeed, and what constitutes "right" and "wrong" within medicine (53).

Learners' perceptions of institutional culture and curricula (formal, informal, and hidden) constitute the learning climate. Climate is distinguished from culture in that culture consists of the norms, values, and assumptions of an organization, while climate is composed of individuals' *perceptions* of these elements: what they are noticing and sensing (54). In teaching by example, role models may exert considerable sway over learners' perceptions of the appropriate way to interact with patients, colleagues, and multidisciplinary health care teams (39, 56), thereby influencing the learning climate.

Students and residents learn from both positive and negative role-modeling within the learning environment. Lingard and colleagues (57) observed communication among multidisciplinary teams in the operating room and identified a high frequency of "tension" events related to team communication. Junior residents responded to tension in the environment by mimicking the undesirable behaviors of the staff surgeon, which intensified, rather than resolved, interprofessional conflict (57). The investigators concluded that novices (junior residents) were sensitive to tension events and are predisposed to respond with less than ideal behavior (57). A second study characterized intimidation and harassment experienced by surgical trainees in the operating room. While trainees acknowledged being harassed, they rationalized that such behaviors from their teachers was "good intimidation," part of the established surgical culture, and possibly an effective learning tool (58). These disconcerting observations demonstrate that the behaviors of negative role models may be excused, accepted, and even emulated by learners, and they underscore the importance of role-modeling on the development of values and attitudes among trainees.

Peers are also powerful role models in the learning environment, especially within the hidden curriculum. The messages peers communicate about "what is really important" and "how to survive" constitute core learning experiences throughout physicians' professional development. Learners identify peers as role models and influential sources for learning about professionalism (59). Much to the dismay of teachers and education administrators, the messages communicated by peers through the hidden curriculum seem largely beyond the reach of faculty. However, faculty role models are in a position to mediate some of the unwanted messages that permeate the hidden curriculum, including those originating from peers, by 1) setting positive examples and 2) entering into meaningful relationships with learners that can counteract undesirable influences of hidden curricula and institutional culture (60).

Because role models exert considerable influence within all aspects of the learning environment, they can be bestowed the responsibility of changing it fundamentally (61, 62). Some educators suggest that students and residents are not learning the intended norms of the profession because faculty physicians are not consistently modeling the desired behaviors (44, 63). The negative messages of the hidden curriculum represent the greatest barrier to promoting humanism in medical schools (61), and explicit role-modeling of humanistic care by physician-teachers has been identified as the primary method to overcome these negative influences (61). Research on relationship-centered medical education suggests that meaningful relationships between teachers and learners can be the critical mediating factor in the hidden curriculum (60). Indeed, a "critical mass" of positive role models will be needed to combat the negative influences of the learning environment and promote the desired attitudes, values, and behaviors of the profession (56). Several educational initiatives (61–63) have addressed this challenge, including the notable Gold Humanism Honor Society (64) sponsored by the Arnold P. Gold Foundation. This initiative brings together laudable cohorts of individuals (medical students who exemplify excellence in humanism) and celebrates their accomplishments so that they may serve as role models and positively influence the values of their institutions.

In the end, responsibility for providing trainees with role models essential for their development as professionals resides with the faculty.

Box 4-2 lists just some of the exercises faculty may find useful as they step up to assume this vital role.

In the end, responsibility for providing trainees with role models essential for their development as professionals resides with the faculty. Box 4-2 lists just some of the exercises faculty may find useful as they step up to assume this vital role.

Box 4-2. Exercise for Becoming a More Effective Role Model

▶ Think about an individual whom you consider a true role model. Ask yourself:
  • What about this individual do you hope to emulate?
  • Which of his or her attributes have you already adopted?
  • How has this helped your professional development?
▶ Examine your own behaviors:
  • What undesirable behaviors should you try to avoid?
  • What behaviors should you further cultivate?
▶ Recognize that learners are watching you all the time
  • Point out behaviors you would like them to notice
  • Explain why you do what you do
  • Strive to consistently act professionally, even beyond the confines of the medical teaching environment

---

REFERENCES

1. Webster's New World Dictionary, College Edition. New York: World Publishing Company; 1959.
2. **Confucius.** World of Quotes. Accessed at www.worldofquotes.com/author/Confucius/1/index.html.
3. The Primates: Life in the Trees. Accessed at www-personal.umich.edu/~phyl/anthro/lifetrees.html.
4. **Damon W, Lerner RM.** Handbook of Child Psychology: Theoretical Models of Human Development. Hoboken, NJ: J Wiley; 2006.
5. **Slobodkina E.** Caps for Sale: A Tale of a Peddler, Some Monkeys, and Their Monkey Business. New York: HarperCollins; 1968.
6. **Meltzoff AN, Moore MK.** Imitation of facial and manual gestures by human neonates. Science. 1977;198:74-8.
7. **Clark D.** Albert Bandura. Accessed at www.skagitwatershed.org/~donclark/ hrd/history/bandura.html.

8. **Higbee A.** American topics. The New York Times. 7 June 1993. Accessed at www. nytimes.com/1993/06/07/news/07iht-topi_13.html.

9. **Gladwell M.** The Tipping Point: How Little Things Can Make a Big Difference. Boston: Little, Brown; 2000.

10. **Ludmerer KM.** Instilling professionalism in medical education [Editorial]. JAMA. 1999; 282:881-2.

11. **Brownell AK, Côté L.** Senior residents' views on the meaning of professionalism and how they learn about it. Acad Med. 2001;76:734-7.

12. **Balmer D, Serwint JR, Ruzek SB, Ludwig S, Giardino AP.** Learning behind the scenes: perceptions and observations of role-modeling in pediatric residents' continuity experience. Ambul Pediatr. 2007;7:176-81.

13. **Jones WS, Hanson JL, Longacre JL.** An intentional modeling process to teach professional behavior: students' clinical observations of preceptors. Teach Learn Med. 2004;16: 264-9.

14. **Shuval JT, Adler I.** The role of models in professional socialization. Soc Sci Med. 1980; 14A:5-14.

15. **Luckhaupt SE, Chin MH, Mangione CM, Phillips RS, Bell D, Leonard AC, et al.** Mentorship in academic general internal medicine. Results of a survey of mentors. J Gen Intern Med. 2005;20:1014-8.

16. **Zerzan JT, Hess R, Schur E, Phillips RS, Rigotti N.** Making the most of mentors: a guide for mentees. Acad Med. 2009;84:140-4.

17. **Sambunjak D, Straus SE, Marusic A.** Mentoring in academic medicine: a systematic review. JAMA. 2006;296:1103-15.

18. **Althouse LA, Stritter FT, Steiner BD.** Attitudes and approaches of influential role models in clinical education. Adv Health Sci Educ Theory Pract. 1999;4:111-22.

19. **Wright S, Wong A, Newill C.** The impact of role models on medical students. J Gen Intern Med. 1997;12:53-6.

20. **Wright S.** Examining what residents look for in their role models. Acad Med. 1996; 71:290-2.

21. **Elzubeir MA, Rizk DE.** Identifying characteristics that students, interns and residents look for in their role models. Med Educ. 2001;35:272-7.

22. **Wallace AG.** Educating tomorrow's doctors: the thing that really matters is that we care. Acad Med. 1997;72:253-8.

23. **Wright SM, Kern DE, Kolodner K, Howard DM, Brancati FL.** Attributes of excellent attending-physician role models. N Engl J Med. 1998;339:1986-93.

24. **Maker VK, Curtis KD, Donnelly MB.** Are you a surgical role model? Curr Surg. 2004;61:111-5.

25. **Kenny NP, Mann KV, MacLeod H.** Role-modeling in physicians' professional formation: reconsidering an essential but untapped educational strategy. Acad Med. 2003;78:1203-10.

26. **Wright SM, Carrese JA.** Excellence in role modelling: insight and perspectives from the pros. CMAJ. 2002;167:638-43.

27. **Maheux B, Beaudoin C, Berkson L, Côté L, Des Marchais J, Jean P.** Medical faculty as humanistic physicians and teachers: the perceptions of students at innovative and traditional medical schools. Med Educ. 2000;34:630-4.

28. **Beaudoin C, Maheux B, Côté L, Des Marchais JE, Jean P, Berkson L.** Clinical teachers as humanistic caregivers and educators: perceptions of senior clerks and second-year residents. CMAJ. 1998;159:765-9.

29. **Bandura A.** Social Foundations of Thought and Action. Englewood Cliffs, NJ: Prentice Hall; 1985.

30. **McGee SR, Irby DM.** Teaching in the outpatient clinic. Practical tips. J Gen Intern Med. 1997;12 Suppl 2:S34-40.

31. **Stern DT, Papadakis M.** The developing physician—-becoming a professional. N Engl J Med. 2006;355:1794-9.

32. **American Board of Internal Medicine.** Project Professionalism. Philadelphia: American Board of Internal Medicine; 1994.

33. **Cruess SR, Cruess RL.** Professionalism must be taught. BMJ. 1997;315:1674-7.

34. **Kao A, Lim M, Spevick J, Barzansky B.** Teaching and evaluating students' professionalism in US medical schools, 2002-2003 [Letter]. JAMA. 2003;290:1151-2.

35. **Reynolds PP.** Reaffirming professionalism through the education community. Ann Intern Med. 1994;120:609-14.

36. **Bickel J.** Promoting Medical Students' Ethical Development: A Resource Guide. Washington, DC: Assoc of American Medical Colleges; 1993.

37. **Feudtner C, Christakis DA, Christakis NA.** Do clinical clerks suffer ethical erosion? Students' perceptions of their ethical environment and personal development. Acad Med. 1994;69:670-9.

38. **Wright SM, Carrese JA.** Which values do attending physicians try to pass on to house officers? Med Educ. 2001;35:941-5.

39. **Wear D.** On white coats and professional development: the formal and the hidden curricula. Ann Intern Med. 1998;129:734-7.

40. **Epstein RM.** Mindful practice. JAMA. 1999;282:833-9.

41. **Viggiano TR, Pawlina W, Lindor KD, Olsen KD, Cortese DA.** Putting the needs of the patient first: Mayo Clinic's core value, institutional culture, and professionalism covenant. Acad Med. 2007;82:1089-93.

42. **Epstein RM, Hundert EM.** Defining and assessing professional competence. JAMA. 2002; 287:226-35.

43. **Swick HM.** Toward a normative definition of medical professionalism. Acad Med. 2000; 75:612-6.

44. **Cooke M, Irby DM, Sullivan W, Ludmerer KM.** American medical education 100 years after the Flexner report. N Engl J Med. 2006;355:1339-44.

45. **Mutha S, Takayama JI, O'Neil EH.** Insights into medical students' career choices based on third- and fourth-year students' focus-group discussions. Acad Med. 1997;72:635-40.

46. **Hunt DK, Badgett RG, Woodling AE, Pugh JA.** Medical student career choice: do physical diagnosis preceptors influence decisions? Am J Med Sci. 1995;310:19-23.

47. **McMurray JE, Schwartz MD, Genero NP, Linzer M.** The attractiveness of internal medicine: a qualitative analysis of the experiences of female and male medical students. Society of General Internal Medicine Task Force on Career Choice in Internal Medicine. Ann Intern Med. 1993;119:812-8.

48. **Neumayer L, Konishi G, L'Archeveque D, Choi R, Ferrario T, McGrath J, et al.** Female surgeons in the 1990s. Academic role models. Arch Surg. 1993;128:669-72.

49. **Saxon LA, Rao AK, Klarich KW.** Shortage of female cardiologists: exploring the issues. Mayo Clin Proc. 2008;83:1022-5.

50. **Wright SM, Carrese JA.** Serving as a physician role model for a diverse population of medical learners. Acad Med. 2003;78:623-8.

51. **Maudsley RF.** Role models and the learning environment: essential elements in effective medical education. Acad Med. 2001;76:432-4.

52. **Scott T, Mannion R, Davies H, Marshall M.** The quantitative measurement of organizational culture in health care: a review of the available instruments. Health Serv Res. 2003;38:923-45.

53. **Hafferty FW.** Beyond curriculum reform: confronting medicine's hidden curriculum. Acad Med. 1998;73:403-7.
54. **Gershon RR, Stone PW, Bakken S, Larson E.** Measurement of organizational culture and climate in healthcare. J Nurs Adm. 2004;34:33-40.
55. **American Medical Association.** Initiative to Transform Medical Education Phase 3: Program Implementation. Recommendations for Optimizing the Medical Education Learning Environment. Chicago: American Medical Assoc; 2008:5-6.
56. **Branch WT Jr.** Deconstructing the white coat [Editorial]. Ann Intern Med. 1998; 129:740-2.
57. **Lingard L, Reznick R, Espin S, Regehr G, DeVito I.** Team communications in the operating room: talk patterns, sites of tension, and implications for novices. Acad Med. 2002;77:232-7.
58. **Musselman LJ, MacRae HM, Reznick RK, Lingard LA.** 'You learn better under the gun': intimidation and harassment in surgical education. Med Educ. 2005;39:926-34.
59. **Maker VK, Donnelly MB.** Surgical resident peer evaluations-what have we learned. J Surg Educ. 2008;65:8-16.
60. **Haidet P, Stein HF.** The role of the student-teacher relationship in the formation of physicians. The hidden curriculum as process. J Gen Intern Med. 2006;21 Suppl 1:S16-20.
61. **Branch WT Jr, Kern D, Haidet P, Weissmann P, Gracey CF, Mitchell G, et al.** The patient-physician relationship. Teaching the human dimensions of care in clinical settings. JAMA. 2001;286:1067-74.
62. **Rose GL, Rukstalis MR, Schuckit MA.** Informal mentoring between faculty and medical students. Acad Med. 2005;80:344-8.
63. **Stern DT.** Practicing what we preach? An analysis of the curriculum of values in medical education. Am J Med. 1998;104:569-75.
64. **The Arnold P. Gold Foundation.** The Gold Humanism Honor Society. Accessed at http://humanism-in-medicine.org/cgi-bin/htmlos.cgi/03713.1.2191019918818156392/intros/gGhhs.html?srchString = Programs%20Medical%20Students%20%26%20Faculty%20Gold%20Humanism%20Honor%20Society.

Section II
Mentoring Across the Continuum

5

Mentoring and Fostering Professionalism in Medical Students: From the Classroom to the Clerkship

Capt Gerald Dodd Denton, MC, USN, MD, MPH, FACP
Col Paul A. Hemmer, MC, USAF, MD, MPH, FACP

Previous chapters in this book have presented the principles underlying mentorship and professionalism, allowing this chapter to focus on the more practical elements that faculty members, clerkship directors, and department leaders should consider to foster professionalism in medical students. The underlying approach and understanding of professionalism for this chapter are those of Pellegrino, already noted in chapter 3—that professionalism is fulfilling a promise of duty and a promise of expertise (1). This chapter discusses mentoring students in the preclerkship setting but primarily addresses mentoring in the clerkship, including an overview of specific challenges, a discussion of clerkship activities geared toward promoting professionalism, and identification of some key opportunities for mentoring medical students. Institutional efforts that can support mentors are also discussed.

❖ Mentoring Preclinical Students

For most medical students, beginning medical school represents their first exposure to the education, research, and patient care of the medical profession (see also chapter 1 of this book). This is the time that students should begin to adopt the physician-specific behaviors that influence professional development throughout their careers. Role

KEY POINTS

- Faculty should be involved in preclinical courses and model commitments to duty and expertise in everyday work.
- Clerkship faculty should maintain a positive outlook, budget time for teaching, and allow appropriate independence.
- The clerkship director should establish a fair, transparent grading mechanism and be available to students; letters of recommendation should be clear and balanced.
- The clerkship director should avoid conflicts of interest in actively recruiting students during the clerkship.
- Clerkship experiences for students should include activities specifically designed to address professionalism and mentorship, such as home visits, reflective writing, and portfolios.
- Departments should establish interest groups, offer research opportunities for students, and provide faculty development for house staff.
- The department chair should be visible to students in the educational program, actively encourage teaching by faculty, and be a role model.
- Medical schools should formally recognize professionalism with ceremonies and awards.

models (chapter 4), in particular, can contribute powerfully to early formation of a professional identity (2), and participation in the preclinical curriculum is an important way for individual faculty to begin to nurture professional development.

Students are eager to see how medicine comes to life in the application, integration, and understanding of basic science and clinical medicine. Teaching in a preclinical course—whether lectures, small groups, or clinical skills courses—allows faculty to model desirable behaviors and engage the students. Faculty members, whether "clinical" or "basic science," should be open and prepared to not just be role models but rather function as mentors as students approach them with questions or seek advice and guidance. Mentoring starts with faculty describing their jobs and emphasizing parts of their careers that are most satisfying, while acknowledging and discussing ways to moderate more stressful aspects. It also means being able to recognize personal limitations and therefore helping to guide the student to someone better suited to help; in other words, helping the students discover a "functional mentor" who can assist them with a specific area (3).

Clinical faculty who desire to mentor should teach in preclinical courses and participate in interest groups or other student organizations. They should bring a positive attitude and engaging approach to their participation (Table 5-1). They should also build collaboration with the basic science faculty and not dismiss or criticize the basic science curriculum. Such criticism, whether overt or subtle, hardly fosters the respect of medicine's scientific underpinning, and it represesnts a negative aspect of the "hidden curriculum" (described in chapter 4 of this book, and by Snyder [4] as "what students learn throughout the experience of attending medical school that is not necessarily part of stated educational aims"). Instead, help the students to understand how what they are learning applies to patient care, research, and education.

An individual faculty member may use several approaches in the preclinical years to positively influence students' professional development (Box 5-1). Early patient contact experiences, beyond what students receive in clinical skills courses, support development of professional values. Such experiences allow early socialization into the profession and motivate

Table 5-1. Do's and Don'ts for Faculty and Departments When Mentoring and Fostering Professionalism in Medical Students (Internal Medicine Example)

DO

Be a positive role model

Offer to write letters of recommendation

Invite students to train in internal medicine

Budget time for students

Allow appropriate independence

Recruit positive role models

Establish internal medicine interest groups

Sponsor white coat ceremonies and other formal recognitions of professional responsibilities

Offer research opportunities

DON'T

Complain about working environment

Display arrogance or greed

Fail to disclose conflicts of interest

Forget that students are always watching

Box 5-1. Encouraging Professionalism in Students in the Preclinical Years

▶ Model the commitments to duty and expertise expected of the students and be explicit about how this occurs within the daily approach to research, education, or patient care.

▶ "Think aloud" about what it means to be a professional; trainees often miss, or misinterpret, nonverbal cues, so discuss even what you believe to be obvious aspects of duty and expertise.

▶ Be honest, respectful, and reflective in discussions with students, including being mindful of how you speak about others and of an individual student's career thoughts or choice.

▶ Direct students to individuals or groups who can help demonstrate the core of professionalism, such as encouraging students to be involved in teaching courses, institutional committees, professional organizations, and community service.

▶ Offer membership in professional societies, such as the American College of Physicians; this can be an important way to mentor professional values through emphasizing service and leadership responsibilities.

students to master preclinical materials in anticipation of future patient care (5). Patient-centeredness, a component of humanism, may develop from early patient contacts in medical school, especially if home visits are included (6). Indeed, many medical schools are beginning to offer early patient contact for just these reasons. Even if these are simply "shadowing" experiences in which the student might participate only limitedly in patient care, a faculty member should understand that the student is always watching, and will learn about professional conduct as much from what is said (and not said) as what is done.

❖ Mentoring Students in the Clerkships

Faculty have even more exposure to students during the clinical years. Thus, there is greater potential for clinical and community-based faculty to mentor students. Because many students are seeking to identify their future careers at this time (7), clinical faculty are key role models and mentors in this process. In the case of internal medicine, for example, faculty might identify students with facility in this field, such as a humanistic approach to patient care, patient-centeredness, and the ability to embrace complexity while acting with simplicity (8). Discussing with students how these personality traits and approaches to care fit with a career in internal medicine may facilitate mentoring relationships. Do not underestimate the power of inviting students to "join your club." (See Table 5-2 for suggestions on mentoring during the clerkship.) The outpatient setting and inpatient settings offer different opportunities for mentors, although certainly some behaviors are effective in both settings (Box 5-2).

In the inpatient setting, there are often multiple levels of learners simultaneously, and everyone from intern, resident, attending faculty, and nonmedical faculty has the chance to serve as teacher and mentor to students. The challenges to fostering professional development are many, from the "hidden curriculum" to hospital policies that limit a student's ability to document in the medical record. Allow students to have a meaningful role in patient care, through supervised independence and hands-on experiences, which will also attract students to the specialty. For example, students are often enamored with procedures. Help them to understand the context of the procedure and that procedures are something done *with* patients, not *to* patients. Integrate students into the informed consent process, and let them see how faculty explain their reasoning to patients; listen to the patient's wants, needs, and fears; and reach agreement. If not

Table 5-2. Do's and Don'ts for Clerkship Directors When Mentoring and Fostering Professionalism in Medical Students

DO

Establish a fair process for evaluation, feedback, and grading

Be readily available for students

Use activities designed to promote professionalism (e.g., reflective writing exercises, home visits, teaching attending physicians)

Use portfolios

DON'T

Allow pharmaceutical gifts to students

Encourage pharmaceutical industry–supplied meals during conferences and call nights

Allow efforts to recruit students to your discipline interfere with the integrity of the evaluation and grading process

---

Box 5-2. Effective Mentor Behaviors

▶ Set clear expectations—for teachers and learners—in the approach to the rotation; communicating what is expected is fundamental to being fair to students.

▶ Maintain a positive outlook and avoid complaining about logistic problems that are out of students' control; by the same token, be honest about your career and life.

▶ Budget appropriate time for students in the outpatient setting to interact with patients and, if possible, choose patients carefully to promote both an enjoyable and an educational experience.

▶ Engage the student in the learning process. Faculty should not only expect students to read and learn about their patients but also be willing to learn from what the student discovers; it is empowering for students to know that they can "teach the teacher."

▶ Foster a student's transition from merely reporting about patients to interpreting, managing, and even educating (10). In other words, help foster the student's sense of ownership in patient care and learning.

---

in place, consider deploying faculty to meet with students to give them a safe environment to talk about their struggles, concerns, and difficulties (9). Fostering a student's "growing independence" (10) enables them to function at higher levels and may lead to greater interest in a given specialty.

❖ Challenges to Mentoring in the Clerkships

There are many challenges to mentoring professionalism in the clinical years. In particular, fatigue and sleep deprivation may cause students to take shortcuts and lose their focus. Recent moves to limit resident and student hours to ensure patient safety have improved quality of life for residents and students, which has reduced the fatigue that used to permeate medical education (11). On the other hand, duty hour limitation has led to work compression and discontinuity of patient care and mentoring relationships (11). These influences are direct threats to professionalism. Stress surges during periods of intense patient care can also be barriers to developing professionalism. Students often lack confidence in themselves, which leads to imitation of resident behaviors that may or may not be appropriately adaptive (12).

Beyond the hidden curriculum, faculty should be aware that students often encounter a "disavowed curriculum" in school—that the very things overtly stated to be inconsistent with the tenets of professionalism are, in fact, manifest in the educational environment (13). While society and faculty hope that positive professional behaviors are consistently taught, these unintentional curricula are very powerful and convey mostly maladaptive behaviors. For example, students may pick up on cues from residents, faculty, peers, and clerkship or residency program directors that grades, not the mastery of material, are the principal motivator for studying. Students may be encouraged (by intent or not) to learn disease processes outside of the context of the patient, leading to dehumanization. For example, students are often concerned that they "don't have enough time to read," to prepare for examinations, losing sight of the fact that textbook medicine comes to life only in the presence of patients. Students may join in "gripe sessions" about faculty or fellow students, leading to erosion of interpersonal skills. In response, mentors can model appropriate behavior, give feedback on maladaptive behaviors, and share personal reflections on the influence of the hidden curriculum with students to raise awareness of its effects (12). This must happen in the most direct way possible, a clear acknowledgment of its presence and active steps to correct the issue. Unfortunately, many faculty *think* they are correcting the deficits seen, but students may misinterpret nonverbal cues and vague statements (14, 15).

Students somehow pick up habits during the clinical years—such as listening to the heart and lungs through a patient's clothes—that were certainly not taught in physical examination courses. Even the most idealistic students may lose their focus on the patient as a person and refer to patients as disease processes, such as "the diabetic with a necrotic foot" on the ward team or "the alcoholic with cirrhosis" in the clinic. Strong mentoring relationships and aggressive faculty approaches to combat this behavior are warranted (15).

Certain characteristics of faculty encourage unprofessional behaviors among students. Chaotic, unsupervised rotations may prevent students from understanding therapeutic approaches and cause a lack of appreciation for clinical reasoning. Arrogant faculty who do not listen to the input of junior trainees marginalize students (and can end up making mistakes). Abuse of power by faculty can be a major source of student dissatisfaction, lack of interest in internal medicine, and poor professional development (12).

Conflicts of interest are troubling to medical students, even though they are not always recognized. Physicians, especially those teaching students, should avoid situations in which their self-interest is placed ahead of the patient's interests. Conflicts of interest are easily disclosed during lectures, but practices such as referring patients for testing at facilities owned or controlled by the ordering physician, accepting gifts from pharmaceutical companies, and overtreating or overcharging patients for services to enhance physician income are poor examples to provide for physicians in training and must be avoided even if not explicitly prohibited by the institution.

❖ Clerkship-Specific Activities to Promote Professionalism

By using as an example the internal medicine clerkship, certain key activities can promote student professionalism and can be easily integrated into the program as required elements. Some of the activities described below may be implemented in other courses and clerkships but are discussed in the context of the internal medicine clerkship.

Reflective writing exercises (also described in chapter 3) can be used to promote professionalism. Reflection requires students to apply their personal beliefs and values to the moral or ethical dimensions of their experience. Formal exercises requiring reflection require students to think about their experiences and to consider what they personally value. Seminal events, such as the death of a patient, a medical error, an unexpected outcome, or witnessed professional or unprofessional behavior may be designated a "critical event" for reflection. Reflective writing exercises may take the form of formal written essays, blog-writing, or presentation and discussion of ethical issues applicable to particular situations. Faculty involvement in the review and processing of critical events is essential to validate the experience and to ensure that the reflection is understood within the context of professional growth (16, 17).

Portfolios, or collections of students' original works, may enhance developing professionalism. Mentors should be assigned to review portfolios to reinforce positive aspects, validate the experiences, and show their value in the context of the student's life. Portfolios can be graded, but primarily they should be evaluated on pass-fail criteria. Portfolios can include discussions of thought-provoking events, ethical case studies, or case scenarios. Portfolios can include traditional written work, such as histories and physical examinations with analyses, artwork, literary writing, or almost anything valued by the clerkship director, department, and student. Portfolios can be developed and stored online, electronically, or in traditional written form. As enduring documents representing significant effort, portfolios may be referenced repeatedly over time, reinforcing positive professional behaviors, and clearly illustrating professional growth (18).

Home visits are a wonderful way to encourage patient-centered care and humanistic qualities in medical students, while affording students with opportunities to understand disease processes in the context of patients' lives. Students performing home visits have much more time to interact with patients while in the home and can develop more meaningful relationships with them. Most research into home visits has shown that students highly value them; many students describe these visits as one of the "most important" experiences during medical school (see also the "Memorable Moments" section of *Theory and Practice of Teaching Medicine*, another book in the *Teaching Medicine* series [19]) and that they allowed the students to grow in professional values (20–22).

Letters of recommendation and the process of residency application are an important and often overlooked venue in which to instill professional behaviors. Students often ask faculty to write letters of recommendation in support of residency applications (23, 24). These letters might be personal letters of recommendation, based on direct experience working with the student, or departmental letters of recommendation intended to summarize a student's achievement during clerkships or rotations. While letters of recommendation serve an important role in the residency application process, residency program directors often find the information to be unhelpful or not fully representative of the student's abilities (23).

Faculty, including the clerkship director, have an obligation to write letters of recommendation that are honest and fair representations of student achievement. Letters should discuss areas in which the student has done well and areas in which the student needs improvement. Recommendations should be unambiguous—the program director should not have to decode adjectives. In fact, it may be time to consider letters of recommendation as letters of evaluation, much as the traditional "dean's letter" has become the medical student performance evaluation. Such an approach to writing recommendation letters sets a tone of respect and honesty toward the student and the program director, and reflects on the professionalism of the faculty member writing the letter.

When a student asks for a letter of recommendation, faculty should meet with the student to discuss the letter. An understanding of the student's career goals and expectations of the content of the letter is necessary to write an appropriate letter. The faculty member should disclose the content of the letter, including the sources of information used in the letter. Faculty members should be direct about what they will write and how it will be balanced; essentially, there should be "informed consent" about the process. Individual faculty should disclose to students if he or she is uncomfortable writing a supportive letter.

Table 5-3 lists recommended elements of a letter of reference (23, 24). This is intended not as an all-inclusive list but rather addresses elements helpful to faculty members and clerkship directors writing such letters.

❖ Responsibilities of the Clerkship Director

Clerkship directors enjoy a unique position in the professional development of medical students because they are responsible for involving students in sustained and meaningful interactions with patients and health care team members. Clerkship directors bridge the gap from the department to the student, and link the clinical and basic sciences for students. Essentially, clerkship directors oversee each medical student's "growing independence" (10) by constructing excellent educational training programs, designing and implementing curriculum, developing faculty, and providing mentorship.

A fair and balanced process for evaluation, feedback, and grading exhibits the professionalism of the clerkship director and reflects the highest professional standards of the department. Transparency in the grading process, disclosed up-front and in writing, is one way to accomplish this. An evaluation framework that is applied uniformly across the clerkship sites and consistently over a clerkship year, paired with feedback to students based on the evaluation framework, can be reassuring and a good example of appropriate professional behavior for students to emulate. Clerkship directors should be readily available to students, with open door policies and easy access to discuss policies and procedures.

Being There, or Being Unaware

Clerkship directors should lead by example. Within the clerkship program, clerkship directors should be core teachers, and assume roles expected of all teachers, such as clinic attending, ward attending, lecturer, teaching attending, small-group leader, and so forth. Such participation is important not only in understanding the impact of the learning environment on the students and how the educational program is really working but also in allowing the clerkship director to serve as a role model to faculty and students alike. By participating in core teaching activities, the clerkship director can informally interact with teachers, understand the challenges they face, learn about areas of concern or success in the educational program, answer questions, and provide faculty development in real time.

Table 5-3. Elements to Include in Letters of Recommendation

Personal letters of recommendation

State how the faculty knows the student and the context in which the student was taught

Provide the timeframe of individual faculty/student interaction

Summarize impressions of the student's abilities and potential

Use direct quotations from the evaluation of the student

Be balanced: state what the student did well and discuss areas in need of improvement

Provide a summation: state degree of confidence that the student has the academic, personal, and professional qualities to succeed in the residency training program.

Be specific

Departmental letters of recommendation

Provide general information, common to all departmental letters, about the clerkship program(s)

- Describe the clerkship program: length, components (ambulatory and/or ward), evaluation methods (descriptive, examinations), whether grading is criterion-based or normative
- Provide a grade distribution for the student's medical school class and student's position in this distribution (if available)
- Describe unique aspects of the clerkship program that the residency needs to understand the perspective of the letter

Discuss the student's performance

- Use direct quotations from teachers' evaluations that are representative of student performance
- Be balanced and honest: any concerns about student performance should be cited and discussed
- Address areas that program directors will find informative (e.g., use the Accreditation Council for Graduate Medical Education core competencies)

Provide a summary recommendation

- Use descriptions that accurately represent the student's achievement and potential; don't speak in code or expect the residency director to decipher your language

Determine who signs the letter—clerkship director and/or department chair

Data obtained from DeZee KJ, Thomas MR, Mintz M, Durning SJ. Letters of recommendation: rating, writing, and reading by clerkship directors of internal medicine. Teach Learn Med. 2009;21:153-8; and Wright SM, Ziegelstein RC. Writing more informative letters of reference. J Gen Intern Med. 2004;19:588-93.

Clerkship directors can send a powerful message to students by taking their turn as a core teacher, as attending physician. In that role, clerkship directors have to be aware of their psychological size—their position of significant authority, particularly regarding their responsibility for student grading, may be very intimidating for the individual student working with the clerkship director. Directors should not compensate for this by changing expectations or making things easier for the student, but they can address it by helping the student grow and by evaluating and providing feedback clearly linked to the clerkship goals and expectations.

By being present in the clerkship as a teacher or attending physician, the clerkship director will have an awareness of the educational program that simply is not possible by reading critiques or meeting with teachers or students. Even more fundamentally, it allows the clerkship director to have what some have described as "face validity"—the clerkship director is seen by teacher and students, and they know the director's face (25).

Educating, Not Recruiting

Admittedly, clerkship directors are in a difficult position regarding mentoring or recruiting students into their disciplines; the primary purpose of the clerkship is to train all students in the requisite competencies, defined by the medical school and within a given discipline, regardless of the students' future career plans. However, the decline in interest in internal medicine as a career, for example, has brought the discipline to a crossroads and serves as an instructive and compelling example. Internal medicine career choice is strongly influenced by the current practice environment (in which students view internal medicine negatively) and by their educational experience on the clerkship (7). Complicating this is the decision of many students choosing internal medicine to pursue subspecialty careers (26, 27). All these forces bring pressure on the internal medicine clerkship director about whether to actively recruit students to the discipline and to primary care (particularly of the elderly), which is crucial for patient health and the effectiveness of the health care system.

Students on clinical clerkships are wary about inquiries into their career choices (28, 29). They fear retribution in the evaluation and grading process—whether intentional or not—if they discuss their true career wishes. Many students will claim to be noncommittal or even falsely state that they are interested in the discipline of the clerkship, motivated by self-preservation and a desire to keep their career options open.

Even internal medicine clerkship directors themselves are split on the issue of whether to recruit students to the field. One national survey study, however, reported that clerkship directors believe residency program directors and department chairs expect them to encourage students to enter internal medicine (30).

Despite these concerns and pressures, the clerkship director should not be seen as recruiting students for training in their discipline during the clerkship—either actual recruiting or the *perception* of recruiting. The first obligation of the clerkship director is to create an outstanding educational experience that is rigorous and fair to all students regardless of their stated career choice. Because clerkship directors give students grades, there should be no question of bias or other factors that could be construed as influencing the grading process or learning environment. A clerkship director who actively recruits students during the clerkship jeopardizes the integrity of the evaluation and grading process, which is the fundamental task in meeting the educational duty toward society: to graduate medical students who are ready for the next level of training.

During the clerkship, the clerkship director will undoubtedly encounter students who have a talent for the director's specialty or express an interest in it. The clerkship director certainly can advocate for the specialty by answering questions and by providing information and materials about careers in a manner that does not jeopardize his or her integrity. The director can extend opportunities for research and for joining professional societies to students during the clerkship.

Outside of the clerkship, clerkship directors can play an important role in mentoring students and guiding their career choice. After the clerkship, the clerkship director should be available to students to discuss career choices and options, to help students develop fourth-year clerkship schedules that will help prepare them for internship, and to play an important role in the residency application process (see earlier section on letters of recommendation). Clerkship directors should be involved in preclinical courses because this allows them to meet students early in the course of medical school and to provide a role model for how important the curriculum is to patient care.

❖ Departmental Efforts to Promote Professionalism

Clerkships and Courses

Departmental efforts are extremely important in developing mentoring relationships with students, ensuring positive professional development, and encouraging students to enter the specialty. These efforts may include structural elements within courses under the departments' control and developing extramural activities, such as interest groups and research opportunities.

Longitudinal clerkships, in which students simultaneously participate in multiple clinical clerkships over a prolonged period (often an entire academic year), are evolving. This model may promote a student's professional development by allowing the student to follow specific cohorts of patients for longer periods while working closely with a core group of faculty (31, 32). Department chairs and clerkship directors should carefully choose faculty for longitudinal experiences because of the intense exposure and profound influence such faculty may have on students. Although the benefits of longitudinal versus traditional clerkship models are still preliminary and the long-term impact of such programs on student career choice and patient relationships is unknown (33, 34), longitudinal clerkships may provide an alternative educational model that better prepares students for their "next step."

In recruiting faculty members to teach students, positive role models should always be chosen whenever possible. Those with a positive outlook who convey their interest and enthusiasm for the specialty are more likely to be appreciated by students and to develop mentoring relationships with them.

Education takes time—and time is exactly what is needed to ensure students develop enthusiasm for a specialty. Students faced with short visit times, cranky faculty, inadequate clinical space, and limited opportunity to think independently may leave the experience unsatisfied, unfulfilled, and bitter toward the specialty. Likewise, in the inpatient setting, faculty patience is a virtue because time is required for students to gather, synthesize, and communicate clinical data and their opinions. Harried, overworked faculty are not good role models, and departments should find ways to protect faculty time and reward faculty for teaching (such as through educational value units [35]). Faculty teaching can be fostered and encouraged through academies, faculty honors, and awards for teaching and by compensation for teaching.

Specialty-Specific Interest Groups and Research Opportunities

Medical student interest groups are a good way to establish a presence for that field early in the medical school calendar and put the best attributes of the specialty forward. Students may find role models or establish mentoring relationships through these interest groups. The groups should not be viewed merely as recruiting venues, as their role in increasing interest in a given specialty is unclear (36). For example, an internal medicine interest group might sponsor panel discussions on careers in internal medicine, provide workshops for skills practice in physical examination and simple procedure performance, promote humanitarian missions and free clinic experiences, and allow students to explore research opportunities. Student participation in planning and running these groups can give students leadership experiences early in medical school. Involvement of house staff, who are closer in age to students than medical school faculty, may promote interest and lead to productive mentoring relationships. Residents may have more immediate direct connections with students and can be direct and honest about the types of mentoring relationships that they have found helpful.

With regard to fostering student interest in research careers, departments should develop mechanisms to connect motivated students with clinical and bench researchers in their areas of interest. Such mechanisms need not be complicated—they could be Web-based or developed through specialty interest groups. For example, student leaders of interest groups could periodically meet with the chair or a designee or could e-mail department faculty to develop lists of faculty with research activities appropriate for medical students. These lists could be promulgated at interest group meetings or posted online. The department chair should encourage a culture of collaboration with students.

Role of the Department Chair

The department chair plays a critical role in the educational and mentoring mission (see also *Leadership Careers in Medical Education*, also part of the *Teaching Medicine* series [37]), in ways that are visible and less visible to medical students. On a personal level, medical students want to see department chairs directly involved in the educational program. In one study, students reported that they wanted chairs to be an advocate for teaching by participating in lectures; being visible in ambulatory and inpatient settings; meeting with students, often as a group, at some time during the clerkship to make clear the department's commitment to teaching; and being available to the students (38). According to another study, 82% of internal medicine department chairs were directly involved in the medicine clerkship through many of the ways listed above (39).

Department chairs should consider introducing themselves to clerkship students at the clerkship orientation. A simple welcome to the clerkship and a few minutes of comments, either in person or on video (for students who perform their clerkships across multiple sites), set the tone about the priority of the educational experience and the chair's interest in the students. Direct participation and visibility to students thereafter are also important, through participation in lectures, attendance at conferences, and engagement in student teaching rounds on occasion. Furthermore, the chairs who express their interest in the students and their teachers model important aspects of professionalism: duty and commitment.

Chairs also play a key role in supporting other educational activities in the continuum of student education. Departments oversee many preclerkship courses, including clinical skills courses; thus, the department chair has an opportunity to influence students early in their education. If the department chair helps identify course directors and selects individuals who not only are interested, available, and capable but also work well horizontally (across departmental lines) and vertically (throughout undergraduate medical education) in the curriculum, the faculty chosen will probably also be someone who can serve as a role model and mentor to students.

❖ Formal Recognition of Professional Behavior

Departments and dean's offices should formally and publicly recognize students, house staff, and faculty who show outstanding attributes of medicine. Awards ceremonies should note not only academic work but also achievement in professional values, with specific awards that may be determined by departments or peers. Measures as simple as award certificates and plaques are effective, as are higher-level, formal national recognition for deserving faculty through programs such as the Herbert S. Waxman Award for Outstanding Medical Educator through the American College of Physicians (40) and the Humanism in Medicine Awards through the Arnold P. Gold Foundation (6).

Forums to mark important passages in the growth and development of students may be provided. The White Coat Ceremony at the inception of the clinical clerkship, initiated at the University of Chicago in 1989 (41), has become common in medical schools across the United States and reminds the participants of the professional ideals of medicine. The Arnold P. Gold Foundation has developed guidelines for this important rite of passage that include students reciting an oath, such as the Oath of Hippocrates, and then donning the white coat for the first time. The ceremony usually features an address by an important physician, who might be a mentor or role model, and a celebratory reception (6).

❖ Conclusion

From their first day in medical school, students have the opportunity to consider what it means to be a physician and a medical professional. Mentorship for professionalism must be an intentional aspect of the medical school curriculum and must be integrated throughout all 4 years. This period of medical education also affords opportunities and practical strategies for faculty to develop in their roles as mentors who instill and model appropriate behaviors and values. Clerkships offer opportunities as well as challenges for mentoring students for professionalism. While faculty teachers will always have the greatest impact in mentoring students, leaders and institutions can also support and reward faculty engaged in this important part of educating medical students.

Disclaimer: The views expressed are those of the authors and do not reflect the official policy or position of the Uniformed Services University of the Health Sciences, the Department of Defense, or the U.S. Government.

REFERENCES

1. **Pellegrino E.** Humanism and the Physician: Knoxville: Univ of Tennessee Pr; 1979.
2. **Taherian K, Shekarchian M.** Mentoring for doctors. Do its benefits outweigh its disadvantages? Med Teach. 2008;30:e95-9.
3. **Thorndyke LE, Gusic ME, Milner RJ.** Find a Functional Mentor. Association Colleges of Physicians. 2009. Accessed at www.acphysci.com/aps/resources/PDFs/APS%200109_CareerWatch.pdf.
4. **Snyder B.** The Hidden Curriculum. Cambridge, MA: MIT Pr; 1973.
5. **Kamalski DM, Braak EW, Cate OT, Borleffs JC.** Early clerkships. Med Teach. 2007; 29:915-20.
6. **The Arnold P. Gold Foundation.** A Public Foundation Fostering Humanism in Medicine. Accessed at http://humanism-in-medicine.org
7. **Hauer KE, Durning SJ, Kernan WN, Fagan MJ, Mintz M, O'Sullivan PS, et al.** Factors associated with medical students' career choices regarding internal medicine. JAMA. 2008;300:1154-64.
8. **Alliance for Academic Internal Medicine.** Primer to the Internal Medicine Clerkship. A Guide Produced by the Clerkship Directors in Internal Medicine. Clerkship Directors in Internal Medicine. Accessed at www.im.org/Publications/PhysiciansInTraining/Documents/Primer2ndEd.pdf.
9. **Griffith CH 3rd, Wilson JF, Haist SA, Albritton TA, Bognar BA, Cohen SJ, et al.** Internal medicine clerkship characteristics associated with enhanced student examination performance. Acad Med. 2009;84:895-901.
10. Introduction to the Clerkship in Internal Medicine of the F. Edward Hebert School of Medicine. Accessed at www.usuhs.mil/med/clerkshiphandbook2009.pdf.
11. **Myers JS, Bellini LM, Morris JB, Graham D, Katz J, Potts JR, et al.** Internal medicine and general surgery residents' attitudes about the ACGME duty hours regulations: a multicenter study. Acad Med. 2006;81:1052-8.
12. **American Board of Internal Medicine.** ABIM Project Professionalism. 2001. Accessed at https://www.abim.org/pdf/publications/professionalism.pdf. Published 2001.
13. **Ginsburg S, Regehr G, Lingard L.** The disavowed curriculum: understanding student's reasoning in professionally challenging situations. J Gen Intern Med. 2003;18:1015-22.
14. **Ginsburg S, Lingard L, Regehr G, Underwood K.** Know when to rock the boat: how faculty rationalize students' behaviors. J Gen Intern Med. 2008;23:942-7.

15. **Burack JH, Irby DM, Carline JD, Root RK, Larson EB.** Teaching compassion and respect. Attending physicians' responses to problematic behaviors. J Gen Intern Med. 1999;14:49-55.

16. **Fischer MA, Harrell HE, Haley HL, Cifu AS, Alper E, Johnson KM, et al.** Between two worlds: a multi-institutional qualitative analysis of students' reflections on joining the medical profession. J Gen Intern Med. 2008;23:958-63.

17. **Dyrbye LN, Harris I, Rohren CH.** Early clinical experiences from students' perspectives: a qualitative study of narratives. Acad Med. 2007;82:979-88.

18. **Buckley S, Coleman J, Davison I, Khan KS, Zamora J, Malick S, et al.** The educational effects of portfolios on undergraduate student learning: a Best Evidence Medical Education (BEME) systematic review. BEME Guide No. 11. Med Teach. 2009;31:282-98.

19. **Ende J, ed.** Theory and Practice of Teaching Medicine. Philadelphia: ACP Pr; 2010.

20. **Medina-Walpole A, Heppard B, Clark NS, Markakis K, Tripler S, Quill T.** Mi Casa o Su Casa? Assessing function and values in the home. J Am Geriatr Soc. 2005;53:336-42.

21. **Denton GD, Rodriguez R, Hemmer PA, Harder J, Short P, Hanson JL.** A prospective controlled trial of the influence of a geriatrics home visit program on medical student knowledge, skills, and attitudes towards care of the elderly. J Gen Intern Med. 2009;24: 599-605.

22. **Yuen JK, Breckman R, Adelman RD, Capello CF, LoFaso V, Reid MC.** Reflections of medical students on visiting chronically ill older patients in the home. J Am Geriatr Soc. 2006;54:1778-83.

23. **DeZee KJ, Thomas MR, Mintz M, Durning SJ.** Letters of recommendation: rating, writing, and reading by clerkship directors of internal medicine. Teach Learn Med. 2009;21:153-8.

24. **Wright SM, Ziegelstein RC.** Writing more informative letters of reference. J Gen Intern Med. 2004;19:588-93.

25. **Grum C.** Annual Review of Medical Education. Clerkship Directors in Internal Medicine Annual Meeting. Nashville, TN: Clerkship Directors in Internal Medicine; 2004.

26. **West CP, Popkave C, Schultz HJ, Weinberger SE, Kolars JC.** Changes in career decisions of internal medicine residents during training. Ann Intern Med. 2006;145:774-9.

27. **Sox HC.** Career changes in medicine: Part II [Editorial]. Ann Intern Med. 2006;145: 782-3.

28. **Woolley DC, Moser SE, Davis NL, Bonaminio GA, Paolo AM.** Treatment of medical students during clerkships based on their stated career interests. Teach Learn Med. 2003;15:156-62.

29. **Woolley DC, Paolo AM, Bonaminio GA, Moser SE.** Student treatment on clerkships based on their specialty interests. Teach Learn Med. 2006;18:237-43.

30. **Hauer KE, Fagan MJ, Kernan W, Mintz M, Durning SJ.** Internal medicine clerkship directors' perceptions about student interest in internal medicine careers. J Gen Intern Med. 2008;23:1101-4.

31. **Hirsh DA, Ogur B, Thibault GE, Cox M.** "Continuity" as an organizing principle for clinical education reform. N Engl J Med. 2007;356:858-66.

32. **Ogur B, Hirsh D, Krupat E, Bor D.** The Harvard Medical School-Cambridge integrated clerkship: an innovative model of clinical education. Acad Med. 2007;82:397-404.

33. **Ogur B, Hirsh D.** Learning through longitudinal patient care—narratives from the Harvard Medical School-Cambridge Integrated Clerkship. Acad Med. 2009;84:844-50.

34. **Norris TE, Schaad DC, DeWitt D, Ogur B, Hunt DD; Consortium of Longitudinal Integrated Clerkships.** Longitudinal integrated clerkships for medical students: an innovation adopted by medical schools in Australia, Canada, South Africa, and the United States. Acad Med. 2009;84:902-7.

35. **Stites S, Vansaghi L, Pingleton S, Cox G, Paolo A.** Aligning compensation with education: design and implementation of the Educational Value Unit (EVU) system in an academic internal medicine department. Acad Med. 2005;80:1100-6.

36. **Hauer KE, Alper EJ, Clayton CP, Hershman WY, Whelan AJ, Woolliscroft JO.** Educational responses to declining student interest in internal medicine careers. Am J Med. 2005;118:1164-70.

37. **Pangaro L, ed.** Leadership Careers in Medical Education. Philadelphia: ACP Pr; 2010.

38. **McIlwain-Dunivan GC, Phelan ST, Rayburn WF.** What medical students value most during their clinical clerkships from department chairs. Am J Obstet Gynecol. 2003; 189:659-61.

39. **Hemmer PA, Alper EJ, Wong RY.** Participation of internal medicine department chairs in the internal medicine clerkship—results of a national survey. Acad Med. 2005; 80:479-83.

40. American College of Physicians Awards and Masterships. Accessed at www.acponline.org/about_acp/awards_masterships. Accessed May 26, 2009.

41. **Green K.** 20th Anniversary of the White Coat Ceremony. 16 March 2009. Accessed at www.articlesbase.com/clothing-articles/20th-anniversary-of-the-white-coat-ceremony-819135.html.

6

Principles, Techniques, and Practical Suggestions for Mentoring Residents

Joseph C. Kolars, MD, FACP

Many of the principles of mentorship presented in other chapters of this book will apply to residents and postgraduate trainees. Residents may have experienced the value of mentorship during their previous education and understand the value of further mentorship. However, their individual needs for personal growth are becoming more divergent at a time when the demands of residency are often all-consuming. As such, mentorship can end up as a luxury sacrificed in light of the requirements and expectations of training. For many, residency is the final stage of their training before embarking on a career. It is the preparation and approach to a career that often provide the impetus for mentorship.

This chapter is divided into four sections. The first examines the definition and purpose of mentorship in the lives of residents. The second focuses on preparing residents for mentoring relationships. The third explores resident approaches to selecting a mentor and managing the relationship. Finally, the fourth speaks to faculty recruitment and development. Suggestions and pointers for managing the mentoring relationship from the faculty perspective are also provided. Some of this chapter appears to be directed more at residents than faculty; however, the primary focus is on program directors and those responsible for establishing mentorship programs, to help them coach residents on maximizing the benefits of mentorship and to coach faculty on the best strategies as mentors.

KEY POINTS
- Residents, as well as faculty, often need to be educated about the value and essential ingredients of mentorship.
- Mentorship implies the professional development of an individual rather than just the acquisition of a skill or completion of a task.
- Faculty are instrumental at modeling self-reflection for residents. Self-reflection allows the development of insight, which enables residents to identify their own needs and growth opportunities.
- When serving as mentors, faculty should structure the relationship to serve the needs of the resident. Faculty development programs can be very helpful in this regard.
- Mentorship is important for residents entering academic careers, as well as those pursuing clinical positions. Their mentorship needs are likely to reflect issues pertaining to these career paths.

❖ Definition and Purpose of Mentorship: The Value Proposition for Residents

By the time learners have entered postgraduate training as residents, they have typically been successful consumers of advice. Success has been predicated on their ability to navigate educational systems and find answers to their own questions. They also have had a variety of more senior members of the field who have helped shape their development. Some of these faculty were more appropriately called "educational supervisors," who oversaw performance; "advisors," who were often charged with providing direction on technical solutions (such as scheduling and which programs to apply to); "research preceptors," who helped oversee a project; and "teachers," who may have turned them on (or turned them off) to a discipline. Residents have often begun to identify role models whose careers, or parts of a career, they would like to emulate. Residents will often assume that one or more of the roles outlined above encompasses the concept of mentoring. They may not understand a more inclusive view of mentorship, and they might find the expectation of cultivating another "parent figure" in their life to be of limited value.

"What Do You Mean by Mentorship?"

Mentorship differs from these other roles in that it focuses on the personal growth and development of the resident. One commonly cited definition of mentor is someone of advanced rank or experience who guides, teaches, and develops a novice (1). Residents can typically grasp the first two attributes, but the last one can be more elusive. It's easy to gravitate toward task completion (such as securing a fellowship or completing a project), and for some residents this may be sufficient. But the development of an individual so that he or she can successfully tackle the multiple tasks and opportunities necessary for professional development is the essence of mentorship.

Developing a Skill and Completing a Project Versus Developing an Individual

Mentors serve a variety of roles, including being a guide, counselor, motivator, sponsor, coach, challenger, and facilitator (2). Ideally, mentors meet the residents where they "are at" and join them on a journey that will benefit both. This means understanding where the residents want to go and challenging them with regard to the choices they are making to get there. Only then can a mentor meaningfully contribute to helping to shape the direction and approach. The "hook" that gets this process started may be a shared activity or task, such as a research project, fellowship selection, or securing a first job. But this activity provides the vehicle for deeper conversations that will shape personal and professional growth.

Residents may perceive that some forms of mentorship are directed less at their own development and more at recruitment into a particular discipline. They may see that mentorship is often linked to the goal of building up a particular dimension of the profession (such as attracting more residents into general medicine or laboratory-bench research) or enhanced representation (such as increased diversity or improved gender balance) (3). Residents may be appropriately wary if they feel that a particular agenda is being served or their own personal exploration of what is best for them is limited.

Reported Benefits of Mentorship for Residents

The literature on mentorship for physicians is more focused on faculty and less so on medical students (4). Information on the benefits of mentorship for residents, though limited, is quite positive. Several studies have addressed the development of research skills and preparation for academic careers. For example, internal medicine residents have identified the lack of mentorship as a barrier to completing a scholarly project (5). Several observational studies on the reported availability or desirability of mentorship for trainees have also been published (4).

In a survey of 329 residents from five internal medicine residency programs, 93% of respondents reported that it was important to have a mentor during residency (6). Although 57% of residents reported that their program encouraged the development of mentoring relationships, only 42% were satisfied with the mentoring they received during residency. Among residents who were mentored, the value to personal development and advice on research were cited as particularly important qualities of the relationship. For those who responded to questions about barriers to mentorship, 50% reported that they never considered approaching someone about mentorship, 26% noted that they were hesitant to approach someone, and 19% reported that they had not met someone whom they trust. This implies that a stronger case must be made for the value of mentorship, as well as mechanisms to help establish effective relationships.

❖ Preparing Residents for Mentoring Relationships

Once the case for mentorship has been established within the residency programs, individual residents need guidance on how to construct a successful mentoring relationship. Ideally, they should be groomed to be sophisticated consumers of formal as well as informal mentorship. Not uncommonly, residents can find this to be very challenging, particularly when overwhelmed with other duties. For some, the major barrier is not knowing how to start the process.

Often a pre-mentorship interview or exploratory discussion with a program director or interested faculty member is useful to determine some key areas of focus for an optimal mentorship. This approach is often viewed as less daunting to busy residents. Instead of "picking a mentor," the focus is more on exploring the optimal ingredients of a pertinent mentorship. This pre-mentorship interview will arm the resident with an approach to selecting an appropriate mentor or set of mentors. They will also gain a better sense of how to construct a relationship that will guide their own development. Faculty who are holding this pre-mentorship interview can then perhaps recommend specific faculty whom the resident can meet with to explore the possibility of a mentoring relationship.

Ideally, a pre-mentorship interview will help to locate the resident around specific questions that are most relevant to their current stage of development. The faculty member poses some probing questions whose answers are ideally guided by the resident's self-reflection. While asking about current career plans, the faculty member is often listening for the answer to the following question: *Do you need more help figuring out what you want or more help trying to figure out how to get what you want?"* The interviewer is also listening for what residents are saying to help answer the question, *"Are you looking for exploration, critique, direction, or reaffirmation?"*

Another approach is to ask residents to rank-order questions that they are wrestling with (Box 6-1) to determine where focused mentorship may help. While it is crucial for the faculty member to understand the apparent needs of the resident, it is useful to also point out the opportunities of men-

---

Box 6-1. Potential Questions for Residents to Answer

- ▶ Am I in the right discipline?
- ▶ Am I at the right institution?
- ▶ How do I choose my next career move after residency?
- ▶ How do I fit my professional activities with my life?
- ▶ How much patient care do I want to do relative to research, administration, teaching?
- ▶ How can I investigate and prepare for these other dimensions?
- ▶ How can I investigate or pursue combined career tracts (e.g., public health, business, law)?
- ▶ Should I continue with training (e.g., fellowship) or seek a job after residency?
- ▶ What are my job options and which make the most sense for me?
- ▶ What types of fellowships should I consider?
- ▶ Which are the best fellowships for me in my field of interest?
- ▶ How do I maximize my chances for securing the fellowship I want?
- ▶ How do I choose the right research experience and research mentor?
- ▶ How can I be successful at research? Where does it fit in my career?
- ▶ How can I prepare for a faculty position where I'm valued as a teacher?
- ▶ How can I get some assistance with technical solutions for a specific problem?

torship that may not be obvious to the resident. The listener should be alert to decisions made on the basis of incomplete or erroneous information. When appropriate, these may be identified as potential focus points that could be explored through mentorship.

The interviewer needs to be aware that personal exploration can make residents uncomfortable. Some have been "running with the pack" and haven't had the need or the opportunity to be reflective. They may feel genuinely stuck by questions regarding the future or next steps. For these, more pragmatic questions may be a safer place to start the inquiry. Opening questions include: *"Who are some of your current role models and why?"* and *"What day-to-day activities are the most rewarding?"*

Once the right focus is identified, along with some desired key attributes of an optimal mentor, potential mentors should be listed. Residents should be informed that they may benefit from several different mentors to serve specific needs (7). However, it is important that residents actively help construct a mentoring relationship or network.

The ultimate goal is to help individual residents see that having a mentor is an essential component of their professional development. They will then be prepared to create these relationships at different junctures in their career. The hope is that residents will also learn the values, skills, and attributes that will make them successful mentors themselves in their future careers.

Preparing Residents to Be Successful Mentees

Residents often benefit from explicit guidance on how to be a mentee so as to maximize the relationship with their mentor (7) (Box 6-2). Residents who are passionate, driven, and resilient are typically destined for success. But simple traits such as staying organized, being responsible, and remaining committed to fulfilling agreed-upon next steps (such as making and keeping appointments) are at times overlooked, to the detriment of a productive professional relationship. Honesty and receptiveness to feedback are essential. Residents who reflect out loud on the basis for their thinking or questions open themselves up in a way that allows mentors to be helpful. A humble and appreciative demeanor will typically attract even more investments on the mentor's part.

❖ Selecting the Right Mentor and Managing the Relationship

Once oriented to the personal goals of mentorship, residents will benefit from coaching on how to identify and select the mentor that best suits their needs. It is important to understand the match-up between what

Box 6-2. Expectations of the Mentee

▶ Takes greater responsibility in setting the agenda over time

▶ Seeks to initiate new ideas

▶ Is respectful of mentor's time and availability

▶ Communicates with mentor on concerns

▶ Provides status of activities and projects

▶ Accepts new challenges

▶ Seeks feedback and takes responsibility to give feedback to mentor

▶ Knows personal limits and when to ask for help

▶ Personally reassesses goals over time

▶ Doesn't overstep boundaries (e.g., overuse of time, dependency on mentor for answers)

Based on Drossman DA. On mentoring. Am J Gastroenterol.2007;102: 1848-52.

residents want, what they need, and what the mentor might be able to contribute. Mentees and mentors alike are seeking the "right chemistry" from the relationship (8). Studies on mentorship suggest that most successful relationships result from having a mentee choose the mentor (rather than having one that is assigned or set up by someone else) (3).

Empowering Residents to Find a Mentor

The outcomes of the prementorship interview or from the residents' self-identified needs should result in a list of at least several faculty who could be approached about a mentoring relationship. The resident should then set up an appointment for initial conversations that involve some probing questions. Often, it is difficult for a resident to conclude from one meeting, or even several conversations, that one individual is going to be *the* mentor. Several different mentoring models may be considered (3), including:

- Classic one-to-one mentoring between mentor and mentee
- Group mentoring, in which a small group of mentees is supervised by a mentor
- Individual or group mentoring with many mentors (the multiple-mentor experience model)
- Mentoring among co-equals (peer mentoring).

But perhaps the most common outcome for residents is to have one formal mentor and perhaps several key individuals who provide strategic advice on more focused issues (that is, informal mentors).

Residents may benefit from guidance on how to develop the right conversations with potential mentors. They may worry about the faculty members' expectations and be unsure about what they are asking for. At times, residents are nervous about committing to something before they are ready and getting stuck in a bad relationship.

Residents often appreciate having a script or an approach to use in their search for mentorship. They may understand the concepts but struggle with what to actually say. A few pointers may be helpful. First, they should identify several faculty who, perhaps only from a distance or only on the basis of reputation, might be potential mentors. Often, residents are attracted to prominent or well-known faculty, many of whom may make great mentors. But residents need to be informed that this is not always the case. Such faculty may have been excellent at developing themselves but may not be as adept at developing others. Next, residents should schedule an appointment with a prospective mentor to explore the possibilities. This should be a deliberate conversation rather than a spontaneous hallway encounter. When calling to arrange the appointment, the residents should state that the purpose is to "get some advice." Residents need to be reassured that most faculty are flattered to be asked advice, particularly when it comes from a trainee. Often, residents suspect that faculty are too busy for this. However, it is the rare faculty member who doesn't want to be viewed as a source of valued opinions.

When it comes to the meeting itself, residents struggling with the right words to say may try the following:

> *"Thanks for meeting with me. _____ suggested that I might find it useful to meet with you and get some advice. As you (may) know, I'm _____ [brief statement about your stage in the program (for example, a second-year resident)] interested in _____ [few words about your interest or goal]. I'm trying to identify or wrestle with the following questions _____. I'd be grateful if you could help me to explore what the next steps might be."*

Obviously, more details will be required, but faculty will appreciate an opening "orienting statement"; in addition, residents will feel more comfortable with something brief to launch the conversation in the right direction. Ideally, the faculty will then start asking some probing questions to better understand the resident's needs and questions in a manner that is respectful, collegial, and nondictatorial.

The resident should get a sense of perhaps another conversation or set of questions that might follow for a later meeting. Or, depending on the situation, some shared activities (such as a project or clinical experience) may emerge. But ideally, the resident will be speaking with several potential mentors and shouldn't "lock in" prematurely. A wrap-up script may sound like this: *"This has been helpful. Could we chat again?"* or *"I appreciate this. You've given me a lot to think about."*

The goal from this first session is to evaluate the chemistry (8). Again, it is often premature to enter into a mentoring relationship after only one encounter. Doing so implies more commitment than either party is ready for at this stage. Only after another meeting or two can the resident than move it to the next level. Residents can use these initial conversations to evaluate the style, commitment, and availability of the faculty member. Does the potential mentor appear to be sufficiently organized? Are meeting times protected (or at least responsibly rescheduled)? Have next steps been honored, and does the dialogue progress (or are the same things rehashed at each session)? Meanwhile, the resident can try to learn more about experiences that other mentees have had with this mentor.

Once the resident has decided on a particular faculty member, other scripts to consider are the following: *"I can tell from our discussions that your mentorship is something that would really benefit me,"* or *"Where I think I need the most guidance is ____. Is that an area you would feel comfortable providing mentorship for?"*

This can be followed by: *"Could we set up a more regular set of meetings? What works best for you?"* or *"Any examples or characteristics of mentoring relationships that have worked well for you? Or things that have not?"*

Making the Meetings Happen

It is crucial to meet regularly, and residents should take ownership for making these happen. The frequency of meetings should in part be determined by the goals and activities that are being discussed. But a relationship requires regular contact. In a study of five internal medicine residency programs, 177 residents responded to a survey on the nature of their mentoring relationships. Fifteen percent reported having contact with their mentors "at least once a week," 30% "at least once a month," 41% "at least twice a year," and 10% "at least once a year" (6). It is often best to start out with more frequent meetings (weekly or monthly) until the relationship has solidified and a rhythm that promotes development can be established.

Managing the Relationship

Successful mentees learn to manage the relationship. However, typically the mentor needs to model this practice, at least at the beginning. One suggested structure for each mentoring meeting begins with a social opening, followed by agenda negotiation, goal-setting, discussion of two to three topics, and a closing, including a summary and plans for the next meeting (9). A checklist for "managing up" by which mentees can promote a successful mentoring relationship has been proposed (7). Residents should be encouraged to write down their goals and a proposed timeline. This can be referred to periodically and will probably change as the residents mature. But it is an important component of active reflection that provides the mentor with opportunities to critique.

Residents should be familiar with potential barriers to an effective mentoring relationship (described later in this chapter). Not uncommonly, initial enthusiasm and passion for the mentoring experience can evolve into tedium. Perhaps the most common reason mentee–mentor relationships become stale pertains to distractions from day-to-day activities that limit a resident's ability to maintain momentum toward their goals. Mentees can feel uncomfortable when they don't perceive progress and don't have anything new to report. The resident feels stuck, but takes it personally and anticipates that the mentor views this as a sign of failure. Therefore, the resident stops engaging. Mentors would prefer that residents bring these problems forward so they can help navigate and manage expectations. This represents a wonderful learning opportunity by which residents can learn how to maintain forward motion on their goals (7). The mentor must emphasize that talking about blocks and loss of momentum are all part of the process, and should not be hidden. If the resident perceives that the relationship isn't fruitful, it is important to recognize the impasse and get some advice from their program director on how to start over. It would be unfortunate if residents confused a particular dysfunctional relationship with a lack of value to mentorship in general (10).

❖ Faculty Recruitment and Development as Mentors

It is in the nature of many physicians and academic faculty to nurture the next generation. Although the concept may be attractive, many will not have had the benefit of an effective mentoring relationship during their own development from which to draw. Residency programs should encourage faculty to serve as mentors and facilitate the development of effective mentorship skills.

Why Mentor Residents? Making the Case for Faculty

Whereas mentees benefit from personal and professional development, mentors benefit by gaining professional stimulation, personal enrichment, satisfaction, and a sense of giving back to their profession (7). Participating in the growth and success of a resident can be particularly rewarding. Typically, residents are starting to focus their development in areas that align with the faculty's own interests. Mentors are often challenged to stay up to date in their field by more junior colleagues who ask probing questions that test assumptions (11). These relationships often reignite in faculty their own initial attraction to their field. Through shared projects and collaborations, residents often bring their mentors into new arenas and new professional relationships. A certain amount of "reflected light" also comes back to the mentor when a mentee does well. In addition, residents can extend the productivity of mentors through shared activities in research, teaching, or patient care.

One of the most satisfying parts of mentoring is the frequency with which learners surprise faculty with their accomplishments. While some relationships will not produce the desired growth or output, others will lead to residents' reaching heights that were not initially envisioned by the faculty. These relationships often reshape and inform the mentors' ability to forecast the potential they envision in others (9).

While the benefits of mentoring residents are often implicit, making them explicit can help attract faculty and build a community of mentors. More successful or visible mentors are often flattered to be asked to help recruit and develop other faculty. Personal recognition from departmental or institutional leadership by highlighting individual contributions to the learning community or through award mechanisms (see chapter 8 of this book) can be a very effective strategy to encourage faculty as mentors. Few things are as powerful as testimonials from residents about the contributions a mentor has made to their growth and development (9).

What Are the Rules of Good Mentorship?

For most, mentoring is an acquired skill that is the result of accumulated life experiences. But it is useful for faculty to share a common understanding of good mentorship (8, 12–14).

Effective mentors balance three different dimensions of their relationships with mentees: support, challenge, and a vision of the mentee's future (15). Perhaps most important is the role that mentors play in helping residents to see the possibilities and instilling confidence by having faith in their success.

The following 10 attributes of good mentorship are particularly important for residents (Box 6-3):

1. Good mentors are *goal-oriented*. They help frame a vision for what the resident can become and provide direction on reaching goals. This requires faculty to be perceptive, listening to both what is said and what is often left unsaid. They are "resident-centric" and reluctant to impose their own expectations or advice prematurely, particularly if inconsistent with the needs of their mentee (16). Good mentors model exploration rather than mere skill or knowledge transfer (11).

2. Good mentors are *credible, with special knowledge or expertise*. At some level, the mentor should serve as a role model for the resident. However, a mentor can rarely serve as the complete role model. As such, good mentors can help residents identify others who may also complement their own strengths.

3. Good mentors *inspire excellence*. The mentor's integrity and professionalism should transcend the message. Good mentors have a positive, optimistic outlook—for themselves and for the resident. Their presence in the profession and in the relationship with the resident should motivate residents to grow and extend their reach. Residents should yearn to be "better" as a result of the relationship and become more confident that their goals can be accomplished.

Box 6-3. Ten Desirable Attributes in Faculty Who Mentor Residents

Good mentors:

1. Are goal-oriented
2. Are credible, with special knowledge or expertise
3. Inspire excellence
4. Reveal aspects of their own personal journey
5. Are honest and thoughtful
6. Are trustworthy, reliable, and committed
7. Develop time management skills in their mentees
8. Promote information management
9. Enable residents to navigate the professional community
10. Promote independence

4. Good mentors *reveal aspects of their own professional journey*. They highlight their own story, both the stumbles and the "turning point" successes. Residents often assume that a mentor's current position was the careful result of very deliberate, reasoned decisions that were calculated from the beginning to achieve the position they now hold. Most faculty realize this is rarely, if ever, the case. Residents need to hear how struggles or uncertainties were managed and see their mentors' active reflection. The processing of disappointments and missteps helps reduce the psychological size of mentors while showing how residents should be anticipating and interpreting their own journey.

5. Good mentors are *honest and thoughtful with residents*. While being respectful, nurturing, and supportive, they are constructive and nonjudgmental. They find a way to tell their mentees what others may find hard to say (or what some residents may find hard to hear). While quick to point out opportunities and next steps, good mentors also don't hesitate to explore inconsistencies and overlooked possibilities. They help summarize and synthesize what residents are saying while challenging assumptions. Good mentors help residents to explore doubts and fears while providing the security to develop new ideas and take risks. They are also adept at teasing out emotional components (such as frustration, anger, or envy) so that those emotions can be properly identified. Good mentors help to interpret and manage disappointments. They promote the value of resilience.

6. Good mentors are *trustworthy, reliable, and committed to residents and their growth*. They make themselves available and responsive. Good mentors establish and honor "protected time" with their mentees. They reaffirm, enable, and empower while helping to advocate and protect. When applicable, they help connect residents to resources and new opportunities.

7. Good mentors *develop time management skills in their mentees*. Residents often need assistance in managing their ambitions and ideals. If expectations are not appropriately managed, disappointments can signal to residents that they have taken the wrong path rather than miscalculated the steepness of the climb. Good mentors help residents to set time frames and break up large tasks into attainable goals. They are instrumental at helping the resident to realize satis-

faction from sequential accomplishments rather than waiting to attain goals so far off in the future that accomplishing them may seem impossible (14).

8. Good mentors *promote information management.* They help residents learn how to gather, sort, and interpret relevant information. Good mentors model the art of professional decision-making. They also model optimal communication styles in writing and in speaking so that residents can be properly understood. Most residents are anxious about giving talks and initially clumsy with their writing skills. Mentors are in a unique position to provide an approach and learning plan that will help residents to find these activities rewarding. Developing or using materials to nurture these skills can be useful (9, 17).

9. Good mentors *enable residents to navigate the professional community.* Residents can be a bit mystified about the rules of the profession or assume that they can rely on their intuition for how best to proceed (14). Good mentors help explain the culture of the profession, pointing out which behaviors promote success and which are more inhibitory. Potential conflicts or misunderstandings provide particularly rich material for learning professional "codes." Good mentors try to create shared activities, which can provide the venue for a relationship in which to express the values of the profession. These activities have often focused on a scholarly project. However, opportunities to discuss a paper, a book, learning materials, health policy, or a shared lecture should also be pursued. Good mentors also strive to promote residents within the profession by providing introductions and opportunities for development (such as presentations, nominations, and committee work) (8).

10. Good mentors *promote independence.* They enable self-challenge and engender self-sufficiency. Through the art of self-reflection, good mentors help residents to develop the insight they need to steer their own course (16). They help residents to understand the concept of intellectual property. Residents benefit from explicit instruction on what justifies authorship (18), including the role of authorship "position" in a publication. Inappropriate inclusion or exclusion can be at odds with the standards of the profession (10).

Practical Pointers and Technical Suggestions for Mentors

Following are six tips to get the relationship going in the right direction (Box 6-4).

1. *Make the resident feel comfortable.* Initially, one of the greatest sources of discomfort among residents is not knowing what to talk about. Get them talking through the use of focused questions to better understand the residents path to date (for example, *"Tell me about your previous education and training"*). Understand the basis of some of their decisions to date. Talk about yourself. Sharing your own stories, particularly if seasoned with some humor or self-deprecation, will make them more comfortable at opening up.

2. *Maintain contact; build the relationship.* Some mentors may wish to rely on "as-needed" mentorship, with an "open-door" policy and admonitions of "please don't hesitate to contact me if I can be of help." While necessary, this approach is insufficient. A more structured, agreed-upon schedule is recommended. Scheduled appointments highlight the importance of the relationship. This also allows the establishment of a regular agenda by which progress on items previously discussed can be monitored (7). Asking residents to determine the frequency while providing feedback on what works best from your perspective is advised (see the following section on managing the relationship). Nurturing the relationship with quick e-mails, phone calls, or "hallway" discussions is also helpful (19).

3. *Stimulate self-reflection.* Try to help residents see themselves and how they look to others. Answers to questions such as *"What was your interpretation?" "What else did you consider?" "What do you see as your options?"* or *"What would someone*

Box 6-4. Six Practical Pointers for Faculty

1. Make the resident feel comfortable
2. Maintain contact; build the relationship
3. Stimulate self-reflection
4. Avoid preaching and telling the resident what to do
5. Encourage other mentoring relationships
6. Manage transitions explicitly

who is close to you say about this?" will also help mentors to gauge a resident's skill at self-reflection.

4. *Avoid "preaching" and telling the resident what to do.* It's best to help residents by framing the right questions as opposed to providing your answers. At times, faculty may find it helpful to cite similar examples from their own life and how they arrived at a decision. Residents value the opportunity to see how faculty make decisions. Mentors must distinguish between a mentee's request for advice or critique from a request for acceptance of a decision that has already been reached (10).

5. *Encourage other mentoring relationships.* Be a good broker. Connect the resident with others that may be of help. Residents also benefit from peer mentoring, particularly from those who may be closer to the residents in terms of their developmental stage but further along to be able to share some lessons learned (15).

6. *Manage transitions explicitly.* At times the relationship may be a bad fit or just not fruitful. In these cases, it is critical to recognize the impasse, learn what you can from the experience, and then move on (10). Seeking guidance from the program director can help structure a conversation that will set up the resident for a more successful mentoring relationship in the future.

Potential Barriers and Pitfalls of Mentorship

Well-meaning faculty may at times have alternative agendas that conflict with good mentorship. Residents commonly spend time with faculty who often have missed out on the value of mentorship or, worse, had experiences that didn't provide the desired benefit. In some fields, less than 20% of faculty have had a mentoring relationship (4). Some faculty were mentored only on specific academic skills, such as research. This may have taken place with faculty who had a more paternalistic view of mentorship, which was more common in the past and largely focused on the "cloning" of the "ideal" academic physician. These faculty may have a more difficult time mentoring residents who are exploring other careers or alternative pathways.

Faculty usually enter mentoring relationships with experiences that share at least some of the attributes of good mentorship, but these experiences may hinder, not help, their success as mentors. For example, many faculty are parents, and should be cautious about making residents feel as if they are children. Many mentors are clinicians but should not make residents feel like they are patients. This is particularly true should the resident require clinical care. Assuming care for a resident or obviating the need to seek proper attention is inappropriate. Psychological problems may emerge in the context of a trusting relationship. Mentors should be quick to show concern, which can be best expressed by directing the resident to seek appropriate care. These are opportunities for faculty to model self-care.

Mentors should not be placed in the role of academic supervisors. If residents feel they are being "graded," they may hesitate to take risks or share struggles for fear such actions will reflect poorly on them (16). Finally, while mentors should be friendly, they need to be vigilant about the boundaries of their relationship and cautious about constructing the relationship around the dynamic of being "best friends." Many faculty find that a deep personal friendship can interfere with the professional authority that mentees require (10). While an element of shared social activities should be encouraged, extraneous favors (such as housesitting, babysitting, or help with nonacademic chores) might contaminate the true nature of a mentoring relationship (15).

Faculty mentors should keep in mind common attitudes or misperceptions among residents that often impede a productive mentoring relationship. Explicitly disarming residents of these misperceptions can help facilitate a more effective relationship. Some of these resident viewpoints include:

- "I don't want to bother you." Residents are often intimidated by faculty whom they admire. They don't see the value that faculty have in this relationship, and they don't want to come across as overly needy (2). Mentors should frequently remind residents why they value this relationship.
- "I don't want to seem uncertain." Certainty is a valued commodity in medicine. Residents are often reluctant to share hesitancy or a changing opinion. As such, they may tend toward premature closure with opinions and decisions. The mentor can reassure residents while pointing out that exploration and a "changing mind" are part of the process.
- "I sure would like to please you." Residents have survived by responding to external expectations. They may find it easier to identify what mentors would like them to do and perform to that end rather than identifying their own goals. They may be hoping that you will be "writing a good letter" for them, and this may unfortunately bias the relationship. Coach residents on how to disagree without being disagreeable.
- "I don't want to look like my values are different from yours." Not uncommonly, a culture or generational gap may exist

between residents and faculty. Role-modeling on how to express these differences in a value-neutral way is required. Residents are often more sensitive to work-life balance than many of the faculty who might be their mentors. This may naturally leave them feeling that they aren't "working hard enough" in the eyes of their mentor (20).

Helping Residents With Decisions Regarding Subsequent Training

Residents often wrestle with decisions regarding continued training (such as fellowships). Preferences for any given subspecialty fluctuate during residency, and this has been best documented with internal medicine residents (21). Residents would benefit by hearing this from their mentors and knowing that such instability is more the rule than the exception. Mentors can pose some guiding questions to help residents think through what type of discipline or future training pathway may best fit their needs. Potential questions for internal medicine residents who are considering fellowship training in a subspecialty may include the following (22):

- *"Do you want to focus on a specific organ system (such as cardiology or gastroenterology) or disciplines that are multi-systemic (such as infectious diseases or oncology)?"*
- *"Do you derive more satisfaction from dealing with acutely ill patients or the long-term management of chronic diseases? Are you interested in procedures?"*
- *"Do you enjoy focusing on the provision of comprehensive care to patients or more focused consultation around a specific disease or set of problems or emphasis on procedures?"*
- *"Do you prefer to have a prominent inpatient component to your practice or an outpatient focus? What kind of patient mix do you prefer?"*
- *"What are the 'hot areas' for scholarship in the discipline under consideration? If you are interested in a future faculty position, what academic niche do you see yourself filling?"*
- *"Where geographically are you hoping to settle, and what is the job market in that region?"*

Residents should be encouraged to talk through the critical factors influencing their answers with several people who can provide them feedback on the consistency of their reasoning, as well as a realistic assessment of what it takes to secure a position. For example, the subspecialties of internal medicine vary widely in terms of their competitiveness (23) and prospects for future academic appointments.

Guiding Residents on the Role Research and Scholarship Might Play in Their Careers

Historically, mentorship has focused on preparing for academic careers that include a substantial research component. However, mentorship is perhaps even more necessary for residents who are seeking nontraditional pathways or positions outside of academia.

Scholarship is an important requirement for most fellowship programs and traditional academic positions. In the absence of scholarly productivity, it is essential that residents understand academic values and scientific inquiry. They must be prepared to explain what scholarship means to them. Fellowship directors may overlook the lack of a track record of rigorous research, but they rarely ignore misperceptions of why academics are based on investigation.

Good mentors will help residents explore whether scholarship is a desirable, potentially attractive option, or only a "requirement" that is necessary to pursue the type of clinical position they truly desire. For the latter, it can be particularly difficult to stay genuine while knowing that the lack of a profound interest in scholarship and an academic career may hurt their chances to succeed. A common mistake is to prematurely close the door to scholarship on the basis of negative experiences with or perceptions of research. To continue with fellowship training or a potential academic position, residents should become excited about some form of inquiry. A good mentor will help the resident explore the possibilities to see where this inquiry would be best directed.

To begin, a few probing questions from a thoughtful mentor will often help. It is important to better understand the basis of a resident's opinion on scholarship. Is it based on experience or on perceptions from a distance? Most residents who are wary of research would benefit from a wider introduction to the concept of scholarship, which, in addition to new discoveries, encompasses the scholarship of integration, application, and dissemination of new knowledge (24). Residents should be alerted to the fact that discovery can take place at the laboratory bench, at the bedside, through clinical trials, or through work with populations (for example, epidemiology). Residents sometimes develop their own research questions, but more commonly, they will join an ongoing project, perhaps carving out a piece that they can later make their own. Hypothesis-based research is, in general, more valued than descriptive projects or case reports. But these latter opportunities are useful starting points that can often lead to deeper lines of inquiry. The recent emphasis on health services research, safety, and quality improvement also opens many possibilities for scholarship that can be compatible with clinical careers. Residents should be encouraged to explore and "stay open" to the possibilities, particularly if this is required for their next goal. However, they may need to explore with their mentors the common fear that they will be trapped working in an environment that takes them away from clinical work.

Often residents enjoy the environment in which they've trained and would like to consider a role in which they could focus on teaching and medical education. In most traditional academic settings with tenure track positions, being a "good teacher" is considered similar to being a "good doctor"; they are assumed prerequisites that don't in and of themselves speak to scholarship or result in promotion. Yet, there are multiple scholarly approaches to new methods of teaching, learning, and evaluation that can be subject to peer review. When residents claim that their scholarship will manifest itself primarily in the form of teaching, they should be cautioned that many fellowship directors do not intuitively consider this to be a type of scholarship that is required in their program or in their discipline. These directors will wonder what the candidates will bring to the program and how will they know whether that work is being done in a scholarly way. Opportunities for scholarship in medical education are ripe, but educational outcomes and approaches to creatively enhance learning should be emphasized. Postresidency training pathways that stress skill-building in education research, such as some chief residency positions or master's programs in medical education, could also be considered.

Guiding Residents for Careers in Clinical Practice

Mentorship for residents seeking positions in clinical practice upon completion of their residency often doesn't receive the attention it deserves. This is particularly true in training programs that pride themselves on their academic nature and hope that their graduates will continue with training and choose to stay in the scholarly environment. The need for general internists to provide first-line and coordinated care has never been greater. It is hoped that health care reform and initiatives such as the patient-centered home will reinvigorate this important career path.

In counseling residents about career paths in general medicine, three questions come to the forefront sooner than others. First, how much of an inpatient practice does the resident desire relative to an outpatient practice? Hospitalist positions have been growing in popularity in part because of their defined hours, the ability to work in concentrated blocks that are interspersed with more protected time, and a relative familiarity to the residents' training environment (which is weighted toward inpatient medicine). At times, the outpatient clinics that are used for training are often not as functional as practices in the community. The hope is that residents will have a chance to experience a variety of clinic settings and a diversity of patient populations before deciding on the best inpatient-outpatient mix.

A second question to ask is the desired geographic setting or community in which the resident would like to practice. The larger the city, the more opportunities there are to work in larger group practices that are shared with other general internists. These individuals will often have more latitude to develop a niche or area of special interest. General internists in smaller communities often are called upon to provide more comprehensive care while serving as the consultant to other primary care physicians.

Third, what is the resident's interest in working with medical students and residents? General internists can often secure a clinical faculty position at a medical school because of their willingness to teach residents and medical students in the context of their own practice. These are rich learning environments, and the opportunity to teach provides a welcome diversity to a practitioner's day. Similarly, many academic medical centers rely on a large group of general internists, both tenure and nontenure track, to help provide care and serve the teaching mission of the institution.

Organized Faculty Development Programs in Mentoring

Mentors are not born but developed (15). However, most do not receive any formal training on the mentoring process, and few have witnessed the intimacy of successful relationships between other mentors and their mentees. New mentors are often ill-equipped to face challenges when taking on major mentoring responsibilities. Residency programs and other learning communities should consider developing workshops and venues for discussion among faculty about perspectives on mentoring. Ideally, workshops would include seasoned mentors, who could speak to lessons learned, and more senior residents, who could collate some of the collective experiences of their colleagues. Special attention should be given to the development of skills in active listening, nondirective facilitation of change, and problem management (16). Shared activities, such as work on a mentoring curriculum, pursuit of research questions on mentorship, or the development of evaluation tools for mentorship, may be useful faculty development exercises (9, 12, 15). A case-based approach to promote mentorship in scientific inquiry (9) could also be incorporated into faculty development workshops for mentors of residents. Discussion questions that might be pursued in a faculty discussion group (9) include:

- *"What barriers might affect the relationship between you and your mentee?"*

- *"How can you help your mentee learn to solve problems without solving them yourself?"*
- *"What have you as a faculty member learned from working with your mentee?"*

An explicit program to promote and develop faculty in the skills of mentorship sends a message that this is valued and that the skills of mentorship can be cultivated.

❖ Conclusion

In conclusion, program directors and faculty who work with residents need to explicitly articulate the value of mentorship and ensure that despite other demands placed on residents, they should use this important resource for professional and personal development. Both residents and faculty benefit from coaching on how best to structure the mentoring interaction for a mutually productive and rewarding relationship, which can shape personal and professional growth.

While most residents seek and value mentoring, it is clear that residents might avoid mentoring that does not have their personal best interests at heart but might instead serve the institution's or the faculty member's purposes. In addition, many institutions do not have mechanisms for identifying a mentor and establishing a relationship, leading to the lack of satisfaction with mentoring that many residents report.

Helping residents find mentors requires personal exploration with the resident as well as structured guidance on how to develop and manage such relationships with faculty. Conversely, faculty will also need support and guidance on attaining excellence as mentors and on the factors and characteristics associated with outstanding mentorship. They also must have practical pointers and technical advice for developing a strong mentoring relationship with residents. Finally, mentors are developed, not born, and creating an institutional culture of mentoring involves faculty development and ongoing support for this vital aspect of medical education.

REFERENCES

1. **Carr P, Bickel J, Inui T.** Taking Root in a Forest Clearing: A Resource Guide for Medical Faculty. Boston: Boston Univ School of Medicine; 2003.
2. **Omary MB.** Mentoring the mentor: another tool to enhance mentorship [Editorial]. Gastroenterology. 2008;135:13-6.
3. **Buddeberg-Fischer B, Herta KD.** Formal mentoring programmes for medical students and doctors—a review of the Medline literature. Med Teach. 2006;28:248-57.

4. **Sambunjak D, Straus SE, Marusic A.** Mentoring in academic medicine: a systematic review. JAMA. 2006;296:1103-15.

5. **Rivera JA, Levine RB, Wright SM.** Completing a scholarly project during residency training. Perspectives of residents who have been successful. J Gen Intern Med. 2005; 20:366-9.

6. **Ramanan RA, Taylor WC, Davis RB, Phillips RS.** Mentoring matters. Mentoring and career preparation in internal medicine residency training. J Gen Intern Med. 2006; 21:340-5.

7. **Zerzan JT, Hess R, Schur E, Phillips RS, Rigotti N.** Making the most of mentors: a guide for mentees. Acad Med. 2009;84:140-4.

8. **Jackson VA, Palepu A, Szalacha L, Caswell C, Carr PL, Inui T.** "Having the right chemistry": a qualitative study of mentoring in academic medicine. Acad Med. 2003;78:328-34.

9. **Handelsman J, Pfund C, Miller Lauffer S, Maidl Pribbenow C.** Entering Mentoring: A Seminar to Train a New Generation of Scientists. The Wisconsin Program for Scientific Teaching. Accessed at www.hhmi.org/grants/pdf/labmanagement/entering_mentoring.pdf.

10. **Detsky AS, Baerlocher MO.** Academic mentoring—how to give it and how to get it. JAMA. 2007;297:2134-6.

11. **Chan J, Fortunato M, Mandell A, Oaks S, Mann D.** Reconceptualizing the faculty role: alternative models. In: Smith BL, McCann J, eds. Reinventing Ourselves: Interdisciplinary Education, Collaborative Learning, and Experimentation in Higher Education. Bolton, MA: Anker; 2001.

12. **Drossman DA.** On mentoring. Am J Gastroenterol. 2007;102:1848-52.

13. **DeLong T, Gabarro J, Lees R.** Why mentoring matters in a hypercompetitive world. Harvard Business Review. January 2008:115-21.

14. **Ludwig S, Stein RE.** Anatomy of mentoring [Editorial]. J Pediatr. 2008;152:151-2.

15. **Ramani S, Gruppen L, Kachur EK.** Twelve tips for developing effective mentors. Med Teach. 2006;28:404-8.

16. **Taherian K, Shekarchian M.** Mentoring for doctors. Do its benefits outweigh its disadvantages? Med Teach. 2008;30:e95-9.

17. **Gray T.** Publish & Flourish: Become a Prolific Scholar. Las Cruces, NM: The Teaching Academy, New Mexico State University; 2005.

18. **International Committee of Medical Journal Editors.** Uniform requirements for manuscripts submitted to biomedical journals: writing and editing for biomedical publication. Accessed at www.icmje.org.

19. **Macafee DA.** Is there a role for mentoring in Surgical Specialty training? Med Teach. 2008;30:e55-9.

20. **Straus SE, Chatur F, Taylor M.** Issues in the mentor-mentee relationship in academic medicine: a qualitative study. Acad Med. 2009;84:135-9.

21. **West CP, Popkave C, Schultz HJ, Weinberger SE, Kolars JC.** Changes in career decisions of internal medicine residents during training. Ann Intern Med. 2006;145:774-9.

22. **Kolars J, Clayton C.** A Textbook for Internal Medicine Education Programs. 9th ed. Washington, DC: Assoc of Program Directors of Internal Medicine; 2007:242-6.

23. Match Results Statistics. Medical Specialties Matching Program. Accessed at www.nrmp.org/fellow/match_name/msmp/stats.html.

24. **Boyer E.** Scholarship Reconsidered: Priorities of the Professorate. Princeton, NJ: Princeton Univ Pr; 1990.

7

Mentoring of Faculty in Academic Medicine: A Review of Best Practices and Policies

Thomas R. Viggiano, MD, MEd

> We don't accomplish anything in this world alone ... and whatever happens is the result of the whole tapestry of one's life and all the weavings of individual threads from one to another that creates something.
> —*Sandra Day O'Connor*

Faculty in academic medical centers play a critical leadership role in improving the public's health, advancing knowledge in life sciences, training future physicians and scientists, reforming the delivery of health care, and engaging in community service. In recent years, diminished reimbursement for health care services has resulted in clinical faculty spending more time in clinical service activities and less time in scholarly activities (1). Research funding has also decreased and intensified the competition for investigators. The challenge for faculty to succeed in academic medicine has become much more formidable. In 2000, a survey conducted by the Association of American Medical Colleges reported that no academic medical center in North America had a comprehensive program for faculty development (2).

Nonetheless, mentoring has long been considered an essential activity to facilitate the career advancement of faculty in academic medical centers. Many faculty members have experienced the benefit of mentoring relationships, and this has contributed to what Wrightsman has described as "a false sense of consensus" about the nature and value of these relationships (3). Mentoring relationships vary widely, and the characteristics of effective ones have not been well defined (4–6). Mentoring has not been rigorously studied, and although there is significant anecdotal support for mentoring, there is

KEY POINTS

- Despite a considerable body of literature, mentoring academic faculty has not been well studied.
- Mentoring relationships do create unique, deeply personal, complex, and important developmental relationships that can be meaningful and lead to mutual benefits.
- Mentoring is particularly vital for faculty in academic medicine because they need to develop a wide range of skills and competencies to execute the clinical, educational, research, and service missions of the academic health center.
- However, only one third to one half of faculty in academic medicine report having received mentoring, and women and clinician-educators have more difficulty finding mentors.
- Successful mentoring relationships can influence personal development, career satisfaction of faculty, selection of specialty, interest in a career in academic medicine, research productivity, and retention.
- Guidelines for faculty mentors and mentees, as well as suggestions for furthering institutional commitment to mentoring, are provided.

little empirical evidence of its effectiveness (3–8). Faculty in academic medical centers usually do not have protected time for mentoring activities, and many institutions undervalue mentoring service for academic promotion (9).

This chapter reviews the literature in order to examine what is known about mentoring in general and in academic medicine. Then, practices that maximize the effectiveness and outcomes of mentoring relationships in academic medical centers are considered.

❖ What Is Known About Mentoring: A Review of the Literature

While the craft guilds and apprenticeships of the middle ages were not described as mentoring relationships, they nonetheless can serve as prototypes for mentoring in academic medicine (10, 11). Academic medicine can be considered an apprenticeship system in which clinicians, investigators, educators, and leaders learn "on the job" from more experienced physicians, scientists, and administrators. Scholarly interest in mentoring in academic medicine gained momentum only in the 1980s (5). In fact, interest in mentoring throughout society did not even take hold until the 1970s, when several seminal publications were released. Among these was *The Seasons of a Man's Life,* Levinson's qualitative study of the adult development of 40 men (12). Levinson concluded that a mentoring relationship was the most important relationship young men experience. It was also during this period that *Harvard Business Review* published an article titled "Everyone Who Makes It Has a Mentor" (13), which reported greater satisfaction from career and work in business executives with mentors (14). In *Men and Women of the Corporation,* Kanter discussed the importance of corporate structure on behavior and relationships, and emphasized the importance of a sponsor (mentor) in the career advancement of women and minorities (15).

Many different types of relationships in a variety of educational, professional, and corporate contexts became commonly referred to as mentoring relationships. Several types of mentoring relationships, distinct and occurring at different life stages, have been the subject of numerous reports and studies and have yielded three domains of mentoring scholarship (6). *Youth mentoring* is concerned with the personal, psychological, emotional, and cognitive growth of children and adolescents. *Mentoring for academic success* usually describes a faculty–student relationship in which the faculty mentor may provide support and guidance for both academic and personal concerns so the student succeeds academically. *Workplace mentoring* occurs in an organizational setting and focuses on the personal and professional growth of the mentee. Mentoring of faculty is characterized as workplace mentoring (6), but most mentees in academic medicine are junior faculty. Because the goal of mentoring is to achieve and sustain academic success, mentoring faculty is a hybrid of workplace and academic mentoring. Healy and Welchert (16) proposed the following definition of general mentoring, grounded in contextual development theory: "Mentoring is a dynamic, reciprocal relationship in a work environment between an advanced career incumbent (mentor) and a beginner (mentee) aimed at promoting the career development of both."

This definition emphasized the reciprocal nature of the mentoring relationship and has been frequently cited in the mentoring literature over the past two decades.

Other scholars chose to delineate the roles and responsibilities of mentors. Kram described two broad categories of mentor functions: career development and psychosocial functions (17). Career development functions include promoting and sponsoring, coaching, challenging, protecting, and enhancing visibility and exposure of the mentee. Psychosocial functions include the interpersonal aspects of facilitating personal and professional development and enhancing the mentee's competence and self-efficacy. Similarly, Jacobi delineated three components of mentoring relationships in an academic setting: emotional and psychological support, direct assistance with career or professional development, and role-modeling (5).

Mentoring relationships can be either formal or informal (7). Informal mentoring relationships develop spontaneously on the basis of mutual identification, interpersonal comfort, and perceived competence to fulfill career needs. Informal mentoring usually occurs over 3 to 6 years, meetings are scheduled flexibly, and the goals of the relationship evolve and adapt over time. Formal mentoring relationships are usually assigned by a program coordinator, occur over 6 months to 1 year, entail regularly scheduled meetings, and involve specified goals. In informal relationships, it is much more likely that mentors will provide the career development and psychosocial functions of a mentor (17). Informal relationships are evaluated by both mentors and mentees as being meaningful and effective; however, there is little evidence on whether formal and informal mentoring relationships differ in the outcomes the mentee obtains (7).

Despite the considerable body of literature on mentoring relationships, mentoring scholars agree that these relationships have not been well studied (3–8). Most of the reported studies are cross-sectional, self-reported surveys of mentees in dyadic (one-on-one) mentoring relationships. These reports are limited by the availability of extractable data, and it is difficult to determine whether the reported mentoring relationships had anything in common. Descriptions of important details of the relationships are insufficient, including whether the relationships were formal (assigned) or informal (self-identified), the duration, the frequency of meetings, the intensity of interactions, and the amount of administrative support. Assessments of the overall effectiveness of mentoring relationships are not reported or are difficult to quantify, and there is little input on assessment from mentors. The frequent lack of comparison groups in the reported studies makes it unclear whether beneficial outcomes are the result of the mentoring relationship or individual characteristics of the mentee.

Nonetheless, mentoring continues to be seen as a vital and important aspect of academic career development. In 1997, a joint committee of the National Academy of Sciences, the National Academy of Engineering, and the Institute of Medicine published a consensus statement on mentoring students in science and technology (18). This statement, titled "Adviser, Teacher, Role Model, Friend," categorized characteristics of the mentoring relationship into five domains: personal communication, professional development, skill development, academic guidance, and research. A useful and eloquent description of the roles of a mentor in science and technology was written by an internist, Dr. Jeremiah Barondess (19). This description was largely derived from important social science research in this area (12):

> The mentor, ordinarily several years older, with greater experience and seniority in the world the mentee is entering, serves variously as teacher, sponsor, advisor and model: as teacher in enhancing the younger individual's skills and intellectual development; as sponsor in using his or her influence to facilitate the mentee's entry and early advancement in the field they both inhabit; as host and guide, in helping to initiate the younger person into a new occupational and social world, acquainting him or her with its values, customs, resources, and cast of characters; as advisor, providing counsel, moral support and direction; and through his or her own virtues, achievements and lifestyle, serving as an exemplar whom the mentee can seek to emulate (19).

This summary of the scholarship of mentoring suggests that concepts of mentoring relationships are multidimensional. Not surprisingly, the nature of mentoring relationships is elusive. As a result, defining and characterizing these relationships can be challenging. Nevertheless, evidence that supports the value of mentoring should not be dismissed as merely anecdotal just because there is a lack of rigor. Mentoring creates unique, deeply personal, complex, and important developmental relationships that are formed for meaningful purposes and mutual benefits. The relationship itself is a source of fulfillment for both mentees and mentors. The mentee achieves self-efficacy and becomes a full member of a profession. The mentor assists in the realization of a dream and experiences the sense of generativity.

❖ Mentoring of Faculty in Academic Medicine

Faculty in academic medicine must develop a wide range of competencies to execute the clinical, educational, research, and service missions of the academic medical center. Essential skills for faculty in academic medicine (20), which should be addressed via faculty development, have traditionally included:

- Education
- Research
- Administration
- Written communication
- Professional academic skills

In 2007, Harris and colleagues updated these core academic competencies to reflect the changing roles and responsibilities of faculty as the needs of patients and society evolved (21). The revised list of compentencies was extended to include the following:

- Medical informatics
- Care management
- Multiculturalism

If mentoring was important for faculty development in the past, recent years have brought an even greater appreciation of mentoring as a key strategy for faculty success (22–24).

A recent systematic review revealed many important insights about mentoring in contemporary academic medicine (25). Overall, approximately one third to one half of faculty report receiving mentoring. Women perceive having more difficulty finding mentors than men, and clinician- educators have more difficulty finding mentors than clinician investigators. Personality characteristics of the mentee, such as good internal control, self-monitoring skills, and emotional stability, can affect the likelihood of receiving mentoring. Again, while evidence is not strong, mentoring relationships were reported to have a positive influence on personal development, career satisfaction, selection of specialty, interest in a career in academic medicine, research productivity, and retention of faculty. Other studies addressing factors associated with having a mentor and satisfaction with being mentored demonstrate that faculty who are committed to a career in academic medicine were more likely to have a mentor than those not committed (85% vs. 15%) (26). Faculty identified the seven specific qualities outlined in Box 7-1 as being associated with their overall satisfaction with their mentors.

Box 7-1. Seven Qualities Associated With Faculty's Overall Satisfaction With Their Mentors

Faculty are satisfied with a mentor who:

1. Keeps in touch regarding progress
2. Does not abuse power
3. Provides advice on goals and career plans
4. Provides opportunities to develop communication skills
5. Provides thoughtful advice on research
6. Provides counsel on professional decisions
7. Is instrumental in building professional networks

Qualitative analysis of faculty's experiences with mentoring relationships demonstrates the value that faculty themselves place on attaining mentors (27). In overwhelming numbers, faculty described lack of mentoring as the first or second most important factor hindering career progress in academic medicine. To compensate, mentees often enlisted the aid of more than one mentor, with the idea that perhaps the specific person who serves as a mentor is less important than obtaining the functions mentors provide. Participants repeatedly emphasized the critical importance of interpersonal factors, such as "having the right chemistry" or "being on the same wavelength."

One reason for the perceived dearth of mentors is lack of support for mentoring them in the current academic environment. Level of support for mentoring at multiple institutions was examined among leaders from the Society of General Internal Medicine (28). Supported time for mentoring activities ranged from 0% to 60% (median, 15%). Only 17% of faculty received institutional support for mentoring. Mentors worked with a mean of 6.7 mentees, and many mentors reported that their current number of mentees was greater than or equal to the maximum number they could supervise. Eighty-five percent of mentors reported co-mentoring mentees, and many expressed the belief that co-mentoring was less demanding and more fulfilling and resulted in a better experience for the mentee.

Not only mentors support the idea of co-mentoring. Interestingly, faculty (as mentees) who reported having multiple mentors were more satisfied than those who had one mentor (29). Another approach to the limited number of mentors available for long-term relationships is to use a mentor who has specific skills and expertise over a limited period of time to accomplish a defined project (30). This approach, described as "functional mentoring," centers the mentoring relationship on the project, and the objectives of the project are used as outcome measures. This model was shown to enhance the recruitment of mentors because projects were aligned with the mentor's expertise and the mentors' time commitment was limited.

The limited number of mentors and the positive aspects and outcomes of multiple mentor relationships suggest looking beyond the traditional dyadic mentoring relationship to different types of mentoring relationships (31, 32). *Group mentoring* involves a group of individuals who engage in mentoring relationships to achieve specific goals. In facilitated group mentoring, a mentor or mentors simultaneously facilitate a group of mentees. *Peer-group mentoring* brings together self-directed and self-managed peers who set the learning agenda and regulate the learning process to meet the group's interests and needs. Group mentoring can extend mentoring efforts within an organization that has limited available mentors. Proponents of group mentoring believe that bringing together individuals with different perspectives contributes to diversity of thinking, a feeling of inclusion, sharing of knowledge, networking, and psychosocial support within an organization (31).

Several faculty groups have important and unique mentoring considerations, including women (33–36) and underrepresented minorities (37, 38). Chapters 10 and 11 of this book address these important topics. Two additional populations deserving of special attention are clinician-educators and midcareer faculty.

Faculty in traditional tenure tracks are more likely to have a mentor than faculty in clinician-educator tracks (39, 40). However, feedback from clinician-educators speaks strongly to the value they place on mentoring as an important component of their career development and the impact that mentoring has on scholarly activity and output (40, 41). Because the "job description" for clinician-educator faculty may vary considerably from one institution to another and expectations for faculty performance and promotion may be unclear, clinician-educators have a great need for mentoring (42). Clinician-educators often spend 50% to 90% of their time caring for patients. The remaining time may be spent teaching and supervising medical students and residents, leading quality initiatives, or serving on hospital committees. Because clinician-educators spend so much time teaching, supervising, and providing direct clinical care, clarifying how they will be evaluated and assessed is critically important for their own careers as well as for the vibrancy of the department and the institution.

Mentoring clinician-educator faculty demands an understanding of the institution's promotion and tenure criteria. Many institutions are using "teaching portfolios" to more comprehensively record teaching activities and contributions. Getting started with this activity from the outset of a faculty appointment, rather than trying to develop a portfolio retrospectively, is critical. Institutions differ in how they evaluate clinical excellence. A recent report from Johns Hopkins Bayview Medical Center, which used in-depth semi-structured interviews, described eight domains (Box 7-2) of clinical excellence in academic departments of medicine (43). Mentors should be aware of these expectations and should be concerned with the resources provided for their clinician-educator mentees to accomplish clinical work.

Even for clinician-educators, promotion may depend heavily on academic reputation and scholarly work. In his book *Scholarship Reconsidered: Priorities of the Professoriate*, Boyer wrote that scholarship included application, integration, and teaching (44). Some have interpreted this to mean

Box 7-2. Eight Domains of Clinical Excellence in Academic Departments of Medicine

1. Clinical reputation
2. Communication and interpersonal skills
3. Professionalism and humanism
4. Diagnostic acumen
5. Skillful negotiation of the health care system
6. Knowledge
7. Scholarly approach to clinical care
8. Passion for clinical medicine

scholarly teaching, linking teaching with learning. Others have indicated that the scholarship of teaching may advance the field, not just individual students' learning (45). This includes subjecting teaching materials to peer review and public dissemination. Today, an increasing number of venues do just that, including MedEd-Portal, HEAL (Health Education Assets Library), and MERLOT (Multimedia Education Resource for Learning and Online Teaching) (45).

The Association of American Medical Colleges Group on Educational Affairs convened a Consensus Development Conference on Education Scholarship in 2006. Five categories of education activities were identified as education scholarship: 1) direct teaching, 2) curriculum development, 3) mentoring and advising, 4) assessment of learners, and 5) education leadership and administration (46). The consensus conference also proposed a framework for documenting and rewarding scholarly contributions in the five education activities (47). The extent to which these guidelines will be adopted by academic health centers and result in advancing educators in academic rank is not known.

Often, the most important role that the mentor will play is to remind clinician-educators that their work matters and is valued by the department. A "universal sentiment" frequently identified as a threat to the careers of clinician-educators is that they do not feel that they or their work really matters (48). Mentors can serve an important role in helping clinician-educators feel validated and valuable and in blazing new paths in academic medicine.

Another faculty cohort in specific need for mentoring is the large proportion of faculty in the middle of their careers. There are very real challenges for mentoring in this category (48). Midcareer faculty are expected to be highly productive. However, after promotion and achievement of stature as a professional, there are fewer external motivators. Midcareer faculty frequently experience a career plateau, and may develop burnout and confusion. Midcareer can be a time of reassessment of career goals and redistribution of the time and effort devoted to clinical care, research, teaching, and service, yet there is less mentoring and satisfaction with mentoring among midcareer faculty. Midcareer faculty are expected to assume new responsibilities as mentors, committee chairs, department chairs, and leaders in various administrative roles. Some institutions provide leadership training, and education and training programs are offered by professional organizations, associations, and societies (50). Informal mentoring occurs in academic health centers as "grooming successors," but no available reports of mentoring programs specifically address midcareer faculty needs.

❖ Effective Practices for Mentoring Faculty

Although there are limited data establishing the most effective practices for mentoring faculty (and likewise, limited data guide faculty mentees), the literature does identify behaviors—for both members of the mentoring relationship—that contribute to effectiveness. For mentors, behaviors associated with effectiveness are listed in Box 7-3 and are described more fully in the following paragraphs. These behaviors need to be supported by the administrative structures of academic medical centers, as has been described in the literature (17, 50–55).

Box 7-3. Eight Behaviors of Effective Mentors

An effective mentor:
1. Is committed to the mentee's career advancement
2. Is respectful of the mentee as a person
3. Engenders trust
4. Partners with the mentee to set and monitor goals
5. Inspires and motivates the mentee
6. Fosters reflection
7. Provides encouragement and support
8. Is magnanimous

Behaviors of Effective Mentors

1. *A good mentor is committed to the mentee's career advancement.* The mentor consistently communicates a sincere interest in the mentee's professional development by being readily accessible and by teaching and offering guidance to enhance learning and professional skills. The mentor provides career advice and connects the mentee to other mentors and to the larger academic community and helps the mentee advance.

2. *A good mentor is respectful of the mentee as a person.* The mentor treats the mentee as a genuine collaborator, does not try to produce a clone of herself or himself, and accepts the mentee's different ways of doing things. The mentor is sensitive to the personal circumstances of the mentee, including matters that involve gender, race, culture, and work–life challenges.

3. *A good mentor engenders trust.* The mentor communicates in a direct, honest, and thoughtful manner and maintains confidentiality of the mentees affairs. The mentor is an exemplary role model for integrity and professionalism.

4. *A good mentor partners with the mentee to set and monitor goals.* The mentor helps the trainee formulate goals that are specific, measurable, and realistic within the available time. The mentor and mentee discuss progress on goals, identify barriers to achievement of goals, and revise strategies or reformulate goals. The mentors' and mentees' goals and expectations are continually aligned.

5. *A good mentor inspires and motivates the mentee.* The mentor inspires the mentee by being enthusiastic about the mentee's work and helping the mentee envision new possibilities. The mentor motivates the mentee by setting high standards and by balancing the mentee's challenges with a commensurate level of support.

6. *A good mentor fosters reflection.* The mentor asks probing questions that prompt the mentee to come up with ideas and theories. The mentor encourages the mentee to share ideas and gently reigns in the mentee when he she goes off track. The mentor offers advice as suggestions and follows up with conversations to explore and enrich the mentee's thinking.

7. *A good mentor provides encouragement and support.* The mentor creates a safe environment by turning small mistakes by the mentee into learning opportunities. The mentor helps

the mentee troubleshoot problems, analyze failures, and prevent big mistakes. The mentor conveys optimism and provides support when it is most needed—when the mentee experiences setbacks. Appropriate self-disclosure of some of the mentor's struggles as a mentee can be helpful.

8. *A good mentor is magnanimous.* The mentor readily shares her or his ideas, information, and resources. The mentor invites the mentee to be a coauthor or presenter when appropriate. The mentor celebrates the mentee's progress and accomplishments and is genuinely happy to see others succeed.

Behaviors of Productive Mentees

The literature also describes mentee behaviors that increase the likelihood of receiving effective mentoring and enhancing the productivity of a mentoring relationships (56–60) (Box 7-4).

1. *The mentee takes responsibility for the mentoring relationship.* The mentee demonstrates a commitment to learning, achieving the desired goals, and becoming an independent professional. The mentee does not prevail on the mentor for support and takes responsibility for decisions, actions, and results achieved.

2. *The mentee engages in self-assessment, -monitoring, and -reflection.* The mentee tracks progress on goals and engages in critical self-assessment to identify barriers, learning needs, and opportunities to improve performance. The mentee asks for feedback and advice, and is very specific when asking for needed assistance.

3. *The mentee respects and appreciates the mentor's time and advice.* The mentee is prompt for appointments, does not

---

Box 7-4. Four Behaviors of Productive Mentees

A productive mentee:

1. Takes responsibility for the mentoring relationship
2. Engages in self-assessment, -monitoring, and -reflection
3. Respects and appreciates the mentor's time and advice.
4. Cultivates an appropriate personal relationship with a mentor and demonstrates professionalism.

abuse the mentor's open door policy, and is flexible if the mentor has to reschedule meetings. The mentee is well prepared for meetings and listens carefully to the mentor's advice with an open mind. The mentee follows through on the mentor's advice and reports on progress at subsequent meetings. The mentee communicates appreciation for the mentor's guidance.

4. *The mentee should cultivate an appropriate personal relationship with a mentor and demonstrate professionalism.* The mentee will learn personal and professional values and behaviors from the mentor, and can learn how to make judgments, manage interpersonal relationships, and handle career–life challenges. The mentee should respect boundaries in the mentoring relationship and remember that personal and professional behaviors reflect on the mentor.

❖ Developing and Administering a Mentoring Program

The literature on mentoring focuses on relationships, and few reports have examined administrative processes that underlie effective mentoring. Some observations from published reports about effective mentoring programs suggest practical considerations in administering a mentoring program (60, 61). Involvement of institutional leadership, including the dean, department chairs, and key faculty, and appointment of a coordinator with dedicated staff and support resources make a strong statement to the faculty that their personal career growth is essential to the institution's mission. A mentoring program should articulate clear goals that are aligned with the institution's missions, culture, and strategic priorities. Events such as orientation, faculty development activities, regular communications about activities and accomplishments, celebrations, and awards bolster the academic community. The program should be evaluated with assessment metrics that evaluate faculty participation and satisfaction, faculty learning, effect on faculty behaviors, competencies and performance, and impact on the organization, including return on invested resources (62).

❖ Case Studies

Following are two examples of common issues that a faculty mentor might address and examples of how a mentor might work with the faculty member to work through these problems and concerns.

Scenario 1: Translating Teaching Interest Into an Academic Career

A young woman recently returned from part-time work as a clinical associate and is interested in jump-starting her career on the clinician-educator track. For the past 2 years she has been closely involved with the clinical skills class for second-year students. Although she has only been working part-time, she is known among other faculty as an innovative and enthusiastic faculty member. She is unclear about what steps she should take to translate her teaching and education experience into an academic career and scholarly publications.

The following are suggestions for how to proceed:

- The mentor and mentee should discuss and focus the mentee's interests, assess the mentee's professional development needs, and identify opportunities for the mentee to engage in education roles and responsibilities and develop related skills and competencies.
- After reflection, the mentor and mentee should formulate specific, measurable, and meaningful goals that consider the mentee's part-time status and are both realistic and respectful of the mentee's personal circumstances.
- The mentor and mentee should establish a time frame for achieving the goals and schedule regular meeting to monitor progress on the goals.
- At the regular meetings, the mentor and mentee should assess progress on goals, identify funding streams and venues for presenting scholarly work, identify strategies to surmount any barriers that arise, and continually align expectations and, if appropriate, revise the goals or strategies to achieve them.

Scenario 2: Building a Research Career

A junior faculty member is eager to begin his career as a clinician investigator. He knows his research is not yet competitive for a K award or National Institutes of Health R01 grant but wonders whether other sources of funding may lay the groundwork for future proposals. He collaborates extensively with other faculty members but complains that he is struggling to find time to do his own research, which could lead to a first-author publication and presentations at national meetings. One issue is that his research interests (medical ethics and the psychosocial impact of disease) do not have clear avenues for obtaining extramural support.

The following are suggestions for how to proceed:
- The mentor should assess the mentee's interests and professional development needs, to more sharply identify a focus for investigation.
- The mentor and mentee should identify interested professional organizations and explore potential funding sources and professional development opportunities.
- The mentor and mentee should set specific, realistic goals that include plans for the mentee to develop as a scholar and evolve to independent authorship.
- The mentor should meet regularly with the mentee to monitor progress on goals and help the mentee to achieve them.
- The mentor should share ideas, connect the mentee to the professional community, and help identify opportunities to disseminate scholarly work through presentations and publications.

❖ Next Steps

Over the past decade, offices for faculty affairs have proliferated in North American medical schools, and many clinical departments in academic medical centers have implemented mentoring programs (2). In 2007, the Association of American Medical Colleges instituted a formal Group on Faculty Affairs. The Association of American Medical Colleges Group on Educational Affairs has included advising and mentoring as a component of education scholarship and has proposed methods for documenting these developmental relationships so they can be evaluated as evidence for academic promotion (46). The Society of General Internal Medicine also sponsors a very active one-on-one mentoring program, as well as awards and grants to support mentoring for junior and midcareer faculty (63). The academic medicine community has an opportunity to collaboratively study mentoring across all stages of a faculty member's career, across disciplines, and across multiple institutions. Much remains to be learned. By collaboratively studying mentoring, important best practices may be identified on how to develop, support, and reward all faculty; use institutional resources effectively and efficiently; and enhance the performance, well-being, and career satisfaction of faculty who execute and lead the missions of the academic medical center.

REFERENCES

1. **Kuttner R.** Managed care and medical education. N Engl J Med. 1999;341:1092-6.
2. **Morahan PS, Gold JS, Bickel J.** Status of faculty affairs and faculty development offices in U.S. medical schools. Acad Med. 2002;77:398-401.
3. **Wrightsman LS.** Research Methodologies for Assessing Mentoring. Presented at the Annual Conference of the American Psychological Association, August 1981, Los Angeles, California. ERIC Document Reproduction Service No. ED 209 339.
4. **Allen TD, Eby LT, O'Brien KE, Lentz E.** The state of mentoring research: a qualitative review of current research methods and future research implications. J Vocat Behav. 2008;73:343-57.
5. **Jacobi M.** Mentoring and undergraduate success: a literature review. Review of Educational Research. 1991;61:505-32.
6. **Eby LT, Allen TD, Evans SC, Ng T, Dubois D.** Does mentoring matter? a multidisciplinary meta-analysis comparing mentored and non-mentored individuals. J Vocat Behav. 2008;72:254-267.
7. **Ragins BR, Cotton JL.** Mentor functions and outcomes: a comparison of men and women in formal and informal mentoring relationships. J Appl Psychol. 1999;84:529-50.
8. **Chao GT.** Mentoring Phases and Outcomes. J Vocat Behav. 1997;51:15-28.
9. **Carr P, Bickel J, Inui T.** Taking Root in a Forest Clearing: A Resource Guide for Medical Faculty. Boston: Boston Univ School of Medicine; 2004.
10. **Roberts A, Chernopisakaya A.** A historical account to consider the origins and associations of the term mentor. History of Education Society Bulletin. 1999;64:81-90.
11. **Sox HC.** The ethical foundations of professionalism: a sociologic history. Chest. 2007; 131:1532-40.
12. **Levinson D, Darrow C, Klein E, Levinson M, McKee B.** The Seasons of a Man's Life. New York: Knopf; 1978.
13. **Lunding FJ, Clements GE, Perkins DS.** Everyone who makes it has a mentor. Harvard Business Review. 1979;56:89-101.
14. **Roche GR.** Much ado about mentoring. Harvard Business Review. 1979;57:14-20.
15. **Kanter RM.** Men and Women of the Corporation. New York: Basic Books; 1977.
16. **Healy CC, Welchert AJ.** Mentoring relationships: a definition to advance research and practice. Education Research. 1990;19:17-21.
17. **Kram KE.** Mentoring at Work. Developmental Relationships in Organizational Life. Glenview, IL: Scott Foresman; 1985.
18. Advisor, Teacher, Role Model, Friend. Washington, DC: National Academy Press; 1997.
19. **Barondess JA.** A brief history of mentoring. Trans Am Clin Climatol Assoc. 1995;106: 1-24.
20. **Bland CJ, Schmitz CC, Stritter FT, et al.** Successful Faculty in Academic Medicine: Essential Skills and How to Acquire Them. New York: Springer; 1990.
21. **Harris DL, Krause KC, Parish DC, Smith MU.** Academic competencies for medical faculty. Fam Med. 2007;39:343-50.
22. **Jotkowitz AB, Clarfield AM.** Mentoring in internal medicine. Eur J Intern Med. 2006; 17:399-401.
23. **Saha S, Christakis DA, Saint S, Whooley MA, Simon SR.** A survival guide for generalist physicians in academic fellowships part 1: getting started. J Gen Intern Med. 1999;14: 745-9.
24. **Hazzard WR.** Mentoring across the professional lifespan in academic geriatrics. J Am Geriatr Soc. 1999;47:1466-70.

25. **Sambunjak D, Straus SE, Marusic A.** Mentoring in academic medicine: a systematic review. JAMA. 2006;296:1103-15.
26. **Ramanan RA, Phillips RS, Davis RB, Silen W, Reede JY.** Mentoring in medicine: keys to satisfaction. Am J Med. 2002;112:336-41.
27. **Jackson VA, Palepu A, Szalacha L, Caswell C, Carr PL, Inui T.** "Having the right chemistry": a qualitative study of mentoring in academic medicine. Acad Med. 2003;78:328-34.
28. **Luckhaupt SE, Chin MH, Mangione CM, Phillips RS, Bell D, Leonard AC, et al.** Mentorship in academic general internal medicine. Results of a survey of mentors. J Gen Intern Med. 2005;20:1014-8.
29. **Wasserstein AG, Quistberg DA, Shea JA.** Mentoring at the University of Pennsylvania: results of a faculty survey. J Gen Intern Med. 2007;22:210-4.
30. **Thorndyke LE, Gusic ME, Milner RJ.** Functional mentoring: a practical approach with multilevel outcomes. J Contin Educ Health Prof. 2008;28:157-64.
31. **Zachary LJ.** Creating a Mentoring Culture: The Organizations Guide. San Francisco: Jossey-Bass; 2005:192-210.
32. **Moss J, Teshima J, Leszcz M.** Peer group mentoring of junior faculty. Acad Psychiatry. 2008;32:230-5.
33. **Bickel J, Wara D, Atkinson BF, Cohen LS, Dunn M, Hostler S, et al; Association of American Medical Colleges Project Implementation Committee.** Increasing women's leadership in academic medicine: report of the AAMC Project Implementation Committee. Acad Med. 2002;77:1043-61.
34. **Mark S, Link H, Morahan PS, Pololi L, Reznik V, Tropez-Sims S.** Innovative mentoring programs to promote gender equity in academic medicine. Acad Med. 2001;76:39-42.
35. **Morahan PS, Voytko ML, Abbuhl S, Means LJ, Wara DW, Thorson J, et al.** Ensuring the success of women faculty at AMCs: lessons learned from the National Centers of Excellence in Women's Health. Acad Med. 2001;76:19-31.
36. **Nonnemaker L.** Women physicians in academic medicine: new insights from cohort studies. N Engl J Med. 2000;342:399-405.
37. **Lewellen-Williams C, Johnson VA, Deloney LA, Thomas BR, Goyol A, Henry-Tillman R.** The POD: a new model for mentoring underrepresented minority faculty. Acad Med. 2006;81:275-9.
38. **Mahoney MR, Wilson E, Odom KL, Flowers L, Adler SR.** Minority faculty voices on diversity in academic medicine: perspectives from one school. Acad Med. 2008;83:781-6.
39. **Wasserstein AG, Quistberg DA, Shea JA.** Mentoring at the University of Pennsylvania: results of a faculty survey. J Gen Intern Med. 2007;22:210-4.
40. **Chew LD, Watanabe JM, Buchwald D, Lessler DS.** Junior faculty's perspectives on mentoring. Acad Med. 2003;78:652.
41. **Marks MB.** Academic careers in medical education: perceptions of the effects of a faculty development program. Acad Med. 1999;74:S72-4.
42. **Levinson W, Rubenstein A.** Mission critical—integrating clinician-educators into academic medical centers. N Engl J Med. 1999;341:840-3.
43. **Christmas C, Kravet SJ, Durso SC, Wright SM.** Clinical excellence in academia: perspectives from masterful academic clinicians. Mayo Clin Proc. 2008;83:989-94.
44. **Boyer EL.** Scholarship Reconsidered: Priorities of the Professoriate. San Francisco: Jossey-Basse; 1997.
45. **Fincher RM, Work JA.** Perspectives on the scholarship of teaching. Med Educ. 2006; 40:293-5.

46. **Simpson D, Fincher RM, Hafler JP, Irby DM, Richards BF, Rosenfeld GC, Viggiano TR.** Advancing Educators and Education: Defining the Components and Evidence of Educational Scholarship. Proceedings from the Association of American Medical Colleges Group on Educational Affairs Consensus Conference on Educational Scholarship, 9-10 February 2006, Charlotte, NC. Washington DC: AAMC 2007.

47. **Simpson D, Fincher RM, Hafler JP, Irby DM, Richards BF, Rosenfeld GC, et al.** Advancing educators and education by defining the components and evidence associated with educational scholarship. Med Educ. 2007;41:1002-9.

48. **Manning KD.** The death of a clinician-educator. Ann Intern Med. 2008;149:281-2.

49. **Baldwin R, Dezure D, Shaw A, et al.** Mapping the terrain of mid-career faculty at a research university: implications for faculty and academic leaders. Change. 2008; September-October.

50. **Schwartz RW, Pogge CR, Gillis SA, Holsinger JW.** Programs for the development of physician leaders: a curricular process in its infancy. Acad Med. 2000;75:133-40.

51. **Daloz LA.** Effective Teaching and Mentorship: Realizing the Transformational Power of Adult Learning Experiences. San Francisco: Jossey-Bass; 1986:209-35.

52. **Bhagia J, Tinsley JA.** The mentoring partnership. Mayo Clin Proc. 2000;75:535-7.

53. **Rabatin JS, Lipkin M Jr, Rubin AS, Schachter A, Nathan M, Kalet A.** A year of mentoring in academic medicine: case report and qualitative analysis of fifteen hours of meetings between a junior and senior faculty member. J Gen Intern Med. 2004;19:569-73.

54. **Ramani S, Gruppen L, Kachur EK.** Twelve tips for developing effective mentors. Med Teach. 2006;28:404-8.

55. **Detsky AS, Baerlocher MO.** Academic mentoring—how to give it and how to get it. JAMA. 2007;297:2134-6.

56. **Lee A, Dennis C, Campbell P.** Nature's guide for mentors. Nature. 2007;447:791-7.

57. **Berk RA, Berg J, Mortimer R, Walton-Moss B, Yeo TP.** Measuring the effectiveness of faculty mentoring relationships. Acad Med. 2005;80:66-71.

58. **Rogers J, Monteiro FM, Nora A.** Toward measuring the domains of mentoring. Fam Med. 2008;40:259-63.

59. **Straus SE, Chatur F, Taylor M.** Issues in the mentor-mentee relationship in academic medicine: a qualitative study. Acad Med. 2009;84:135-9.

60. **Zerzan JT, Hess R, Schur E, Phillips RS, Rigotti N.** Making the most of mentors: a guide for mentees. Acad Med. 2009;84:140-4.

61. **Johnson WB.** The intentional mentor: strategies and guidelines for the practice of mentoring. Professional Psychology: Research and Practice. 2002;33:88-96.

62. **Kirkpatrick DL, Kirkpatrick JD.** Transferring Learning to Behavior: Using the Four Levels to Improve Performance. San Francisco: Berrett-Koehler; 2005.

63. **Society of General Internal Medicine.** Mentoring programs. Accessed at www.sgim.org/index.cfm?pageId=298.

8

Peer Mentoring: A Model for Development of Clinician-Educator Faculty in Academic Medicine

Stacy Higgins, MD, FACP

William T. Branch Jr., MD, MACP

Jada Bussey-Jones, MD, FACP

Mentoring frequently determines the success or failure of academic careers. Unfortunately, many institutions lack enough mentors to meet the needs of all young faculty members. Furthermore, because mentoring frequently requires service across a wide range of functions and roles, not all mentors can fulfill the entire spectrum of needs. One potential solution to these problems is peer mentoring, which has the potential to augment traditional mentoring in meaningful and significant ways. This chapter describes current experiences with peer mentoring and analyzes the strengths, weaknesses, and barriers to the implementation of peer mentoring programs. Peer mentoring should not be the only form of mentoring; it is provided for faculty, but it can be a useful component to supplement or complement a traditional mentoring program.

❖ Personalities and Practices of an Outstanding Mentor

The ability to mentor is not a single feature of a personality but an amalgam of many traits. Perhaps most essential are selflessness, respect for others, sensitivity to feelings, and an innate passion and enthusiasm for scientific or academic work. Great mentors deeply appreciate the unique gifts and abilities of each individual mentee and

KEY POINTS

- Peer mentoring is an emerging approach to faculty development that can advance career goals. The use of support group–like activities for the participants can be used to facilitate collaboration, peer feedback and critique, encouragement, and enhanced self-confidence.
- Potential drawbacks of peer mentoring include competition among mentees for limited resources and the lack of experience and contacts inherent to senior faculty.
- Although few published studies support the academic success of participants in peer mentoring programs, limited reports in business, education, nursing, and academic medicine suggest mostly positive outcomes.
- Peer mentoring may provide an alternative or a supplement for the many junior faculty in need of mentoring and the relatively few experienced faculty available for traditional dyad relationships.
- Peer mentoring offers a particularly promising avenue for clinician-educators whose professional development focuses on the science of application and integration rather than the generation of new knowledge.

strongly support their mentees (1). Patience, honesty, and open-mindedness are also traits of superb mentors (2).

While personality traits cannot be taught, key mentoring practices can, including accessibility and giving feedback. Other aspects of mentoring that can be learned through emulation and practice include the ability to promote personal growth by balancing advice with the mentee's self-direction. Good mentors are also good listeners and good questioners. When appropriate, they treat their mentees' discussions with them as confidential. They wisely choose projects for their mentees that are likely to succeed in a reasonable time frame. They have a knack for helping, without taking over the mentee's writing and research. They encourage their mentees to present at national and international meetings, and they use their widespread contacts to introduce mentees to a network of fellow scientists and colleagues. They celebrate their mentees' successes. A good mentor understands the importance of gradually increased independence as the mentee grows and becomes a valued colleague. Great mentors are personally interested in their mentees and assist with career decisions and opportunities.

They follow up to learn whether their mentees have flourished after "graduating" from the mentoring relationship. Finally, strong mentors move beyond the one-on-one relationship to build a community within their laboratories, services, or hospitals that is supportive and collegial for all mentees.

❖ What Is Peer Mentoring?

All students, residents, and junior faculty deserve the ideal, supportive mentoring relationship just described. Unfortunately, not everyone has access to such an individual, nor can a mentor provide all the supportive services and practices that a mentee might need. One possibility to supplement and complement the traditional dyad mentor–mentee relationship is peer mentoring.

Peer mentoring involves a group of individuals with similar backgrounds engaged in similar work, often at different stages of professional development, who meet regularly to mentor each other (3). Peer mentoring can be facilitated by an older mentor or self-facilitated by the group or a chosen leader. Groups range in size, but the average is six to eight members. Sometimes peer mentoring consists of a more experienced peer "showing the ropes" to a less experienced colleague. Peer mentoring is often implemented in situations where experienced faculty mentors and opportunities for traditional mentoring dyads are limited.

There are pros and cons to peer mentoring. For example, how can the characteristics of an individual mentor listed earlier be attributable to a group, and to what extent would a group fail to achieve such characteristics? What are the weaknesses and strengths of a group compared with a good senior faculty mentor? What are the barriers to peer mentoring versus traditional mentoring? This chapter explores these questions and provides examples of successful peer mentoring programs. The literature reports several examples of peer mentoring groups that consider their outcomes to be highly satisfactory, to have benefitted members, and to have helped the members develop their careers (3–6). These models will be described and assessed.

❖ Peer Mentoring Programs

Models From Other Disciplines

An examination of peer mentoring programs initially developed in fields outside of medicine, such as business, secondary education, and nursing, may yield important examples and pathways for peer mentoring in medicine.

Business
Peer mentoring in the business world came about because downsizing, the use of work teams, and flattening hierarchies led to a dearth of senior mentors. In business, employees may seek a mentoring relationship with someone who is at the same level in the firm but is a more experienced employee. Such an individual therefore can provide support and teach new knowledge and skills. Bryant and Terborg (7) assessed whether peer mentoring facilitates sharing of organizational knowledge or benefits only the members of the peer mentoring relationship. They found that using a peer mentoring model in business produced higher perceived levels of knowledge creation and sharing. Ultimately, such qualities are linked to a company's competitive advantage.

Secondary Education
In the K–12 educational setting, the opportunity for peer feedback for teachers is limited because of administrative burdens, the nature of the physical space in which teaching occurs, overlapping schedules, and the structures of most schools. However, teacher attrition is such that many schools are looking for ways to build on individual teacher excellence to support less experienced teachers. Positive and constructive coaching and feedback from a respected peer produce enhanced goal-setting, motivation to take risks, and implementation of challenging teaching strategies (8, 9). Teachers in peer coaching programs have been shown to be more successful than control group teachers in implementing new instructional strategies, using the new strategies in more appropriate ways, sustaining the use of new strategies, and understanding the purposes of instruction (10). Peer coaching also contributes to increased teacher efficacy or to the teacher's positive beliefs about his or her capacity as a teacher (8).

Nursing
Peer mentoring by senior nursing students can minimize the anxiety of new students being introduced to patient care (11). This approach also develops leadership skills in the senior students by increasing their sense of responsibility and confidence and improving interpersonal relationships and organizational skills. Younger students identified a decreased sense of anxiety as the major benefit of the peer coaching experience, along with increased confidence, improved organizational skills, and an enhanced sense of being a member of the health care team (11).

Common Themes
Several powerful common themes run through each of these nonmedical models, including transfer of skills and knowledge from a more experienced

to a less experienced learner, opportunity for leadership as well as fellowship among peers, and overall benefit to the organization. These same themes and principles drive peer mentorship in medicine.

Peer Mentoring Models in Academic Medicine

While the peer mentoring program at Emory University in Atlanta, Georgia, developed by the authors, constitutes the main example for discussion, other academic medical centers have used this model as well. These are also described below.

The Brody School of Medicine at East Carolina University

This institution piloted a collaborative mentoring program through the Faculty Development office, drawing on faculty from eight clinical departments (4). The program's goals were developed by senior faculty and included team-building, career planning, and a focus on oral and written presentations. To ensure that the program stayed on a track, a program director oversaw the experience while visiting facilitators handled specific content. On completion of the 2-year program, quantitative and qualitative evaluations were conducted. Overall, program attendance was high, and 27 manuscripts were submitted for publication over the 2-year period. Participants viewed the program positively, including the learning environment, content, and sense of community and connectedness to others in the school of medicine.

The University of Toronto Department of Psychiatry

A much different model for peer mentoring among junior faculty was developed by the Department of Psychiatry at the University of Toronto (5). In this much less formal and structured model, junior faculty were invited, via e-mail, to start a peer mentoring group. Once formed, the group determined their agenda and curriculum for the academic year. Meetings were held every 2 months for 2 hours in the evening. The department provided a minimal amount of financial support but no support for time. Invited guest speakers supplied content, and a senior faculty member was present at all meetings as an observer. Participant attendance over the year was 80%. Evaluation revealed that a key positive aspect of the program for the participants was their development of the curriculum as opposed to it being developed in a "top down" manner. Other positive aspects for the program included the peer support; reduced professional isolation; knowledge gains, such as creation of a teaching portfolio; and the opportunity for reflective time with peers.

Mayo Clinic in Scottsdale

Women and minorities in particular have described difficulty in finding senior mentors for the traditional dyad mentor relationship (12). One approach to addressing this imbalance can be seen in the implementation of a facilitated peer mentoring program at the Mayo Clinic in Scottsdale, Arizona. By using a senior mentor to provide structure, guidance, and support to the peer group, the program sought to amplify the limited resource of qualified senior minority and female mentors (7). In this pilot program, four female internists were recruited to participate; they then signed a contract committing them to 1-year involvement. Goals of the program and responsibilities of the peers and facilitators included starting a writing group for publications, establishing a peer mentoring curriculum, maximizing peer relationships, and focusing on work–life balance of female physicians. After completing 10 months of the program, participants indicated more satisfaction with their academic accomplishments, their attainment of necessary skills for desired academic advancement, and their belief that they had achieved the necessary writing skills.

Common Themes

Just as with the peer mentoring programs described in different fields, common themes emerge from comparing the peer mentoring programs from these academic medical centers:

- Peer mentoring groups were often formed as an alternative to traditional mentoring after surveys revealed a lack of senior mentors or lack of successful traditional dyad mentor pairings.
- Each group described benefit from collaborating with their peers, including social support from others at a similar stage in life; opportunities to collaborate across departmental or disciplinary divisions; and the passage of knowledge on teaching, research, or writing.
- Satisfaction ratings in each program were very high, assessed not only by surveys upon completion of the program but by the high participation rate over the entire program.

These descriptions also demonstrate how the model of "peer mentoring" can mean many different things. The Brody School of Medicine used a faculty development model for junior faculty. These faculty applied, were accepted, and were then provided with curriculum and specific expectations. Because of grant support, participants and mentors had their time "bought out" so that they could participate without feeling the pressure of competing responsibilities. This contrasts with the facilitated peer mentoring program at the Mayo Clinic in Scottsdale. New faculty were recruited into the program and given the curriculum by the facilitators, but senior mentors were available for the entire group. Finally, the program described in Toronto was completely self-generated. Members of this group met after hours, designed the curriculum, set internal expectations, and recruited expert content speakers.

Detailed Case Study: IMeRGE

A shortage of available traditional mentors in the Division of General Internal Medicine at Emory University School of Medicine's Grady Memorial Hospital, combined with a desire to enhance academic skills, was the primary driving force behind the formation of the peer mentoring group. The group named itself the Internal Medicine Research Group at Emory (IMeRGE) (3). IMeRGE included seven members who had been on faculty for 1 to 5 years when the group was formed. The members were united on the basis of a desire to develop research and other academic skills that would enhance their career advancement. Therefore, the primary goal of IMeRGE, beyond fostering a collaborative atmosphere, was to support the acquisition of experience in research, advanced teaching skills, and professional development. Figure 8-1 shows the program goals.

The IMeRGE program benefited from several structural elements. For example, members had division support for designated time and resources and were able to coordinate schedules such that all members would have the same half-day each week to dedicate to IMeRGE activities. Those senior faculty advisors, who were recruited to help the group, were compensated for their time by a faculty development grant. Finally, one of the initial activities

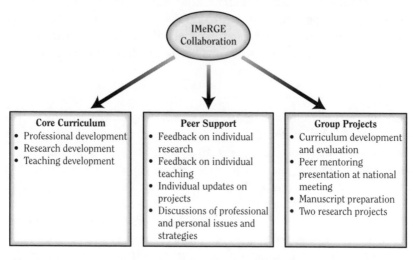

Figure 8-1 Design of the IMeRGE (Internal Medicine Research Group at Emory) peer mentoring group.

of IMeRGE was to specify member responsibilities and to develop a structured didactic curriculum. The elements of the program are described more
thoroughly below.

Didactic Curriculum

The curriculum alternated didactic sessions with collaborative work on
research projects and individual updates on works-in-progress. The didactic
curriculum included workshops on such topics as writing for grants and
peer review, research methods, public speaking, time management, negotiation, and navigating the promotion process. Sessions were led by
IMeRGE members, senior faculty from within the division, or faculty from
other departments in the university. The intimacy of the sessions allowed
for active discussion between the speakers and the audience. The curriculum was defined at the outset but also permitted flexibility: Over the course
of the year, the time allotted for exploration of self-directed areas of interest
was increased, as was sharing of individual strengths and areas of expertise.
Although resources were limited, a key asset of creating a visible and clearly
defined organization was that it attracted speakers to the group.

Peer Support

Throughout the mentoring process, the group supported each member's
ongoing successes. At dedicated sessions, members presented their
research, manuscript drafts, or teaching projects for group review. The
members also provided academic guidance to one another, using individual
experiences to provide insight into negotiations with senior faculty or
other common experiences. Perhaps the most enjoyable aspect of the
group was the opportunity to share and discuss personal issues, such as
balancing work and family life. In this aspect, IMeRGE was instrumental in
developing a collegial atmosphere and bolstering group morale within the
division.

Challenges

Although participating in IMeRGE was a rewarding experience, there were
several challenges in forming and maintaining the group. These offer
insight into some of the pitfalls that peer mentoring groups might
encounter: competing responsibilities, accountability to the group, and
melding diverse interests. Examples of how these challenges were
addressed are provided below.

   Competing responsibilities: IMeRGE members had multiple responsibilities that competed with their commitment to the group. Professionally,
members competed for grant support and had ongoing research projects,
clinical and teaching responsibilities, and administrative duties for the

school of medicine and the hospital. Because of their age, junior faculty tend to be making important changes in their family life, such as marriage or children. To address this issue, meetings for the entire year were set at the same time every week, when members were not scheduled for clinical or teaching responsibilities. In addition, real consequences for failing to live up to membership responsibilities were implemented; any IMeRGE member not on leave who missed more than four group sessions would have reduced participation in group projects. Finally, with the understanding that some conflicts were unavoidable, minutes were recorded and e-mailed to allow members to stay updated on the group's activities.

Accountability to the group: Because the mentor in formal mentoring relationship often holds a higher position than the mentee, there is an established power dynamic. This dynamic, whether good or bad, places pressure on the mentee to complete agreed-upon projects for fear of disappointing the mentor. In peer mentoring, this dynamic by definition does not exist; there are no fear-based motivations or "punishments" for unmet expectations. To counter this, members of IMeRGE agreed to adhere to work rules. The consequence of not adhering to these rules would be potential expulsion from the group. While not a perfect solution, it allowed for both self-discipline and group scrutiny.

Melding diverse interests: The mentor and mentee in the traditional mentoring model come together on the basis of similar areas of research or expertise, or the mentee often chooses the project while the mentor provides guidance and feedback. In a group of seven peers with equal voices, this level of consensus becomes much harder to achieve. To address the group goals for completing a research study, and in the spirit of working as a group, the IMeRGE members made a compromise. Members with no grant support were allowed to choose a project that was feasible and reflected the collective interests of the group. Authorship on conference abstracts and published manuscripts was determined in the order of level of involvement. Establishing these guidelines from the start made it possible to address diverse interests. It also permitted varying levels of individual involvement in projects based on a member's interest in the topic and his or her competing individual responsibilities.

Outcomes

The IMeRGE group worked together for 2 years and continued to meet periodically thereafter. The members subsequently enjoyed successful academic careers, obtaining key academic roles and leadership positions and successfully publishing work in peer-reviewed journals.

In addition, the initial success of IMeRGE led to duplication. Three peer mentoring groups were formed at Emory following the original

IMeRGE group. These groups were mostly composed of clinician-educators for whom peer mentoring would appear to be a promising strategy for supporting their academic development. As a result, faculty considered creating a peer mentoring group designed to address the development of faculty teachers as role models for humanism and professionalism, rather than a group that focused on mentoring for career development. Faculty drawn from five medical schools joined forces to develop such a peer mentoring group, overseen by a senior facilitator (13). Learning through critical reflection, including narrative writing and general discussion, was the basis for professional development. An evaluation of the program showed advantages for participants, indicating that supportive group dynamics and critical reflection are key components to promote professional growth in a group process (13). These are valuable lessons that can be applied to future peer mentoring efforts.

❖ Advantages of Peer Mentoring Compared With Traditional Mentoring

Although it is difficult to argue with the successes of traditional one-on-one mentoring, relying exclusively on this model has some inherent problems (Table 8-1). First, traditional mentoring is hierarchical and may not encourage creativity: The senior mentor maintains power and influence, usually until the mentee develops the skills to be an independent, powerful mentor. At that point the process repeats itself. This process promotes "sameness" within the institution (14) and may limit innovative approaches. Second, these hierarchical mentoring relationships can lead senior mentors to use junior faculty to further their own research and other career endeavors. There may also be overwhelming demands, personality clashes, and unrealistic expectations from both sides (14, 15). Third, traditional mentoring dyads may lack consistency: One mentor may be skilled at providing support and instruction, while another is better suited for providing career networking connections and provoking independent thought. Finally, a particular institution may lack suitable mentors for junior faculty. This may be especially true for minorities and women, as mentioned earlier (14–19). Because of these limitations, alternative approaches that augment traditional mentoring may be crucial for the career advancement of junior faculty. For these purposes, peer mentoring models show considerable promise.

In a peer mentoring model, a group of individuals who are essentially equal in age, experience, and rank mentor each other. Because of the inherent equality among group members, relationships are more mutual, and, ideally, each participant has something of value to contribute and gain.

Table 8-1. Advantages and Disadvantages of Peer Mentoring

Peer Mentoring	Traditional Mentoring
Advantages compared with traditional mentoring	
Comfortable reciprocal relationships— allows for bidirectional feedback	More formal relationships with a clear "leader"
Input from multiple sources	One viewpoint
Potential for innovative career approaches	Potential for homogeneity
Longer duration	Shorter duration
Increased opportunities for feedback and support on personal–work life issues	Focused primarily on professional issues
More personal support/friendships	More professional support
Increased availability for junior faculty, minorities, and women	Limited senior mentor resources to match junior faculty
Disadvantages compared with traditional mentoring	
Competition among colleagues at similar rank	Less competition with senior mentor who has already established career
Decreased professional experience and therefore limited advisory role	Long career with varied experiences, which enhances advisory capacity
Decreased ability to facilitate introductions and opportunities	Multiple contacts and knowledge of opportunities that can be readily passed to mentees
Less accountability to colleague regarding task completion	Possibility that senior rank may establish power dynamic that promotes performance and task completion

These relationships are likely to offer more personal feedback and friendship than traditional mentoring relationships (19). Peers may feel more comfortable sharing information with each other and may be less inhibited when discussing topics beyond a professional nature. As was noted with IMeRGE, one of the most satisfying aspects of the group was discussion of personal issues such as work–life balance (3). While the average length of a traditional mentoring relationship is 6 years, peer relationships often lead to much longer-lasting friendships and ongoing collegial relationships (15). Because peers are of similar rank and stature, peer relationships are often more flexible in everything from determining meeting times to defining expectations for the relationship. The inherent reciprocity of the relationship allows mutual feedback on issues such as career planning and even the mentoring relationship itself. Like traditional mentoring, peer mentoring is thought to enhance professional support, sense of well-being, and career development (14). This was demonstrated in the peer mentoring program at the University of Toronto, where participants reported reduced professional isolation and increased peer support as key aspects of the mentoring program (5). In short, because of all these qualities of peer mentoring, many faculty members find participating in a peer mentoring group to be tremendously supportive and empowering. Ideally, peer mentoring should occur in concert with traditional mentoring. This captures the advantages of both models and intensifies the mentoring process.

❖ Barriers to Peer Mentoring

Effective peer mentoring programs face many barriers. The most important ones relate to organizational resources and support, and to the motivations of peer mentoring participants. At a minimum, the organization adopting peer mentoring must provide a supportive environment. This goes beyond encouraging the junior faculty members who wish to organize and participate in such a program—it extends to making time for the peer mentoring group to meet, for its senior facilitator to work with the group, and for the junior faculty to develop the career goals being promoted by peer mentoring. As demonstrated by the peer mentoring program at the University of Toronto (5), this can be successful with very little departmental financial support. Although peer mentoring makes fewer demands on the senior faculty to be individual mentors, it does not replace the need for resources to protect the time of junior faculty.

In addition, not every junior faculty member is motivated to participate in peer mentoring. Peer mentoring succeeds best when the junior faculty request it and are enthusiastic about participating. As peer mentoring becomes more established, junior faculty members may expect to participate in such programs and will bring the same motivation as they do to developing their careers. Peer mentoring is likely to become an accepted component of academic faculty development when senior leadership demonstrates that they are ready to devote resources to ensure its success.

A common challenge faced in peer mentoring groups is competition between peers. Varying success in securing funding, publishing research, or developing relationships with departmental or institutional leaders may result in a competitive environment rather than a mutually supportive, collegial relationship. Another challenge is that members of peer mentoring groups may have fewer cumulative professional experiences and thus a more limited advisory role than would senior mentors. For example, a junior faculty member may not be able to introduce one of his or her peers to a more senior faculty member, whereas a more traditional mentor, by virtue of his or her seniority, may be better poised to facilitate that important connection. This disadvantage may be ameliorated when a senior faculty member facilitates the group (6).

The following scenarios illuminate some challenges that arise in peer mentoring programs and suggest how these challenges might be overcome.

❖ Case Studies

Case Scenario 1: Competition

A group of five faculty members belong to an internal medicine peer mentoring program focused on developing medical education portfolios. The first year of the program, the sessions were very collaborative and supportive. By the end of the year, two faculty members had earned intramural grants to pursue their project development. By the second year, it has become apparent that participants of the program are competing for the same resource and grant money. Members have stopped encouraging and supporting one another and the meetings have disintegrated into a show of one-upmanship between members. A member of the group has approached the section chief for advice.

Suggestions
- Enlist the section chief or other senior faculty advisor as a "mediator."
- Encourage the group to research/review multiple existing intramural and extramural funding sources. Group knowledge and discussions of funding opportunities could broaden perceptions of available resources and minimize the effect of competition.
- Reestablish a collaborative atmosphere by reviewing group members' pending grant applications. Funded group members could be asked to provide advice and examples of successful funding.
- Consider applying for grant funding as a group. Principal leadership roles may be given to members who remain unfunded. Those with funding will remain engaged in the process with a supportive and advisory role. Manuscripts resulting from this project could benefit all.
- Consider whether members of this group also need individual mentoring to ensure that each one receives maximum support and direction from a senior faculty mentor in the pursuit of their grant funding and research goals.

Case Scenario 2: Varying Degrees of Motivation

As a result of political turmoil in the Department of Medicine, several key senior faculty members left the institution. To boost morale and to make up for the loss of these physicians, several junior faculty members decide to institute a peer mentoring program. They hope to sustain and encourage each other. The program is initially well received, but attendance begins to drop off during the fourth and fifth months. The group considers disbanding, even though departmental morale remains low and mentors are in short supply.

Suggestions

- Enlist the section chief's support for the group. The recent "political turmoil" can be used to make the case that faculty satisfaction and stability are increasingly important. Resources such as time to meet regularly, administrative assistance, and food at meetings can be requested.
- Have a frank discussion to review the process of the group. Discuss the members' short- and long-term goals to determine why the group is no longer meeting the members' needs. Agree on solutions to make the group more productive.
- Invite and schedule senior faculty to occasionally attend meetings to advise or speak. This may help raise the profile of the meeting and increase attendance and participation.
- Have the group decide on changes, such as assignment of responsibilities to each group member. Establish a timeline for tasks with measurable outcomes, and hold members accountable for meeting deadlines (for example, Dr. "X" will present his grant application on January 1st).
- Consider adding a social event after hours to enhance work–life balance, improve cohesiveness, and increase the morale of the group.

❖ Summary and Conclusions

Peer mentoring can augment and complement the traditional mentoring process. When well-organized and fully supported by an academic unit, the peer mentoring process can further junior faculty members' career goals through collaborating, critiquing each other's work, and motivating each other. Even when less well-supported and -organized, peer mentoring efforts can still encourage the group and enhance self-confidence. Ideally, peer mentoring should complement and supplement, not replace, a traditional mentor. However, peer mentoring can add an energizing sense of collaboration and support, along with the additional motivation from meeting the expectations of one's colleagues. Peer mentoring provides many of the benefits gained from traditional mentoring. The group itself can be respectful, empathic, enthusiastic, generous, open-minded, and deeply appreciative of its individual members.

Peer mentoring is a relatively new form of faculty development. As such, it has not been tested rigorously or applied extensively in academic settings. Institutions that have tried peer mentoring have provided anecdotal reports of mixed, but mostly positive, outcomes from the process. For clinician-educators, a peer mentoring process may have the most beneficial impact. A group of colleagues working together and facilitated by a more experienced faculty member could fulfill the needs of clinician-educators, who are not expected to make original research contributions. Rather, the peer group can foster and promote the members' skills as advanced teachers and clinicians or educational leaders. Although clinician-educators have been around for years, a focus on developing their skills and fostering their professional careers is a relatively recent endeavor.

Medical schools are exploring ways to mentor the many clinician-educators now occupying important roles on their faculties. Peer mentoring offers a promising pathway that may overcome the problems of having large numbers of junior faculty in need of mentoring but relatively few senior faculty in the clinician-educator role. At five medical schools, a model similar to this was found to be effective for the development of teachers of humanism and professional values (13). Additional studies of outcomes related to peer mentoring should be undertaken if peer mentoring is to be widely adopted.

REFERENCES

1. **Lee A, Dennis C, Campbell P.** Nature's guide for mentors. Nature. 2007;447:791-7.
2. **Franko M, Ionescu-Pioggia M.** Making the right move: a practical guide to scientific management for post-docs and new faculty. In: Mentoring at Being Mentored. Burroughs Wellcome Fund and Howard Hughes Medical Institute; 2007:97-111.
3. **Bussey-Jones J, Bernstein L, Higgins S, Malebranche D, Paranjape A, Genao I, et al.** Repaving the road to academic success: the IMeRGE approach to peer mentoring. Acad Med. 2006;81:674-9.
4. **Pololi LH, Knight SM, Dennis K, Frankel RM.** Helping medical school faculty realize their dreams: an innovative, collaborative mentoring program. Acad Med. 2002;77: 377-84.

5. **Moss J, Teshima J, Leszcz M.** Peer group mentoring of junior faculty. Acad Psychiatry. 2008;32:230-5.
6. **Files JA, Blair JE, Mayer AP, Ko MG.** Facilitated peer mentorship: a pilot program for academic advancement of female medical faculty. J Womens Health (Larchmt). 2008; 17:1009-15.
7. **Bryant S, Terborg J.** Impact of peer mentor training on creating and sharing organizational knowledge. Journal of Managerial Issues. 2008;20:11-29.
8. **Bruce C, Ross J.** A model for increasing reform implementation and teacher efficacy: teaching peer coaching in grades 3 and 6 mathematics. Canadian Journal of Education. 2008;31:346-70.
9. **McLymont E, DaCosta J.** Cognitive coaching: the vehicle for professional development and teacher collaboration. Paper presented at the Annual Meeting of the American Educational Research Association. 1998. Accessed at www.eric.ed.gov/ERICDocs/data/ericdocs2sql/content_storage_01/0000019b/80/15/91/8b.pdf.
10. **Kohler F, Ezell H, Paluselli M.** Promoting changes in teachers' conduct of student pair activities: an examination of reciprocal peer coaching. Journal of Special Education. 1999;33:154-165.
11. **Broscious SK, Saunders DJ.** Peer coaching. Nurse Educ. 2001;26:212-4.
12. **Ramanan RA, Taylor WC, Davis RB, Phillips RS.** Mentoring matters. Mentoring and career preparation in internal medicine residency training. J Gen Intern Med. 2006; 21:340-5.
13. **Branch WT Jr, Frankel R, Gracey CF, Haidet PM, Weissmann PF, Cantey P, et al.** A good clinician and a caring person: longitudinal faculty development and the enhancement of the human dimensions of care. Acad Med. 2009;84:117-25.
14. **Angelique H, Kyle K, Taylor E.** Mentors and muses: new strategies for academic success. Innovative Higher Education. 2002;26:195-209.
15. **Phillip-Jones I.** Mentors and Proteges. New York: Arbor House; 1982.
16. **Levinson W, Kaufman K, Clark B, Tolle SW.** Mentors and role models for women in academic medicine. West J Med. 1991;154:423-6.
17. **Noe R.** Women and Mentoring: A review and research agenda. Academy of Management Review. 1988;13:65-78.
18. **Powell B.** Mentoring: one of the master's tools. Initiatives. 1999;59:19-31.
19. **Kram KE, Isabella LA.** Mentoring alternatives: the role of peer relationships in career development. The Academy of Management Journal. 1985;28:110-132

9

Mentoring Research Faculty in Academic Medicine: Opportunities, Challenges, and Best Practice

Thomas R. Hecker, PhD
Victoria A. Mulhern
Arthur H. Rubenstein, MD, MBBCh, MACP

Academic medicine is the foundation for scientific discovery, education, and clinical innovation that improves patients' lives. It is the unique context of this tripartite mission that provides a rich environment for faculty growth and development and that calls for the recognition of a fourth distinct mission—that appropriate values and principles in the conduct of patient care, education, and research are passed from one cohort of faculty to the next (1). As such, academic medical centers have a fundamental obligation to nurture the environment in which professional development occurs. A primary means of achieving this is through sustained commitment to a culture of mentoring.

Effective mentorship has long been acknowledged as central to the professional development process in institutions of higher learning. It is often described as a mutually reinforcing relationship in which the mentee further develops skills and confidence in his or her own work and one that can advance both career progression and career satisfaction for the mentee and mentor (1–3). Indeed, the relationship between mentor and mentee is ideally collaborative and collegial. A good mentor acts as a consultant who instructs as well as challenges the mentee toward developing the skills that the mentor has already achieved. Ideally, mentorship is a lifelong process in which the mentee eventually becomes the mentor.

KEY POINTS

- Mentoring faculty whose primary focus is research has become increasingly important in today's economic and clinical environment. Research faculty face increased pressure to generate funding and increased administrative burdens and regulations.
- Having access to an experienced and committed mentor can make or break a physician-scientist's career.
- A successful institutional strategy for mentorship should provide a balance between offering structured mentorship programs and the opportunity to develop informal mentoring relationships.
- Mentees benefit most from seeking out and engaging in relationships with multiple mentors.
- Mentors should guide mentees on how to actively assume control over their careers and develop a variety of networking and mentoring opportunities.

The need for proper mentoring of faculty who are focused on the research mission has become especially important in recent years. As Blixen and colleagues (4) aptly describe, there is enormous pressure on the traditional career model for physician-scientists and clinical investigators. The demand for clinical productivity (the primary source of revenue to support academic initiatives) has increased, as have the complexity of clinical investigation and the corresponding ethical guidelines and regulatory requirements for this research. These factors combine to produce an environment with fewer hours available to conduct ever more complicated scientific inquiry, higher expectations to generate funding to protect faculty time to conduct the research, and fewer funding sources. Added to these pressures is the desire for balance between professional careers and personal pursuits. Consequently, the number of physician-scientists and clinical investigators has declined; many of those faculty have instead chosen to focus on clinical practice or seek careers outside of academia.

For PhD-trained medical school faculty in the basic sciences, the challenges are no less daunting—the extramural funding climate has been increasingly difficult in recent years. Until the American Recovery and Reinvestment Act was signed into law and made incremental funding for biomedical research available, funding from the National Institutes of Health had been flat for the preceding 3 to 4 years. When combined with inflationary increases, that stagnation led to a significant decrease in the purchasing power of grant funding. Simultaneously, the broader economic conditions have resulted in fewer funding opportunities from foundations and other philanthropic sources; faculty have spent significantly more time writing grant applications to keep their laboratory operations intact. Junior faculty facing promotion review frequently must choose between devoting precious time to writing grants or preparing manuscripts for publication, just one of several decisions that are pivotal early in one's career as a researcher; however, this is a decision that they may not have the experience or strategic planning skills to make at that point in their careers.

❖ Theory and Organizing Structure of Research Mentorship

In this challenging climate for academic medicine, the opportunity for junior faculty to learn from and be guided by a more experienced colleague can be the difference between whether or not they establish a successful research program and an upward career trajectory. Although more empirical evidence is needed to reach definitive conclusions about the characteristics of successful mentoring relationships in academic medicine (5), it is clear that mentees who report having successful mentoring relationships believe that these relationships profoundly affect their careers. Indeed, several studies have shown that a positive mentoring experience for junior faculty predicts their attainment of high levels of career development, as measured by publications, grant awards, academic rank, leadership positions, income, and career satisfaction (1–3, 5). Conversely, as Pololi and Knight (3) noted, lack of access to mentors has been associated with reduced scholarly productivity and lower levels of career satisfaction. It may also be linked to attrition from academic medicine.

Recent findings by Ries and coworkers from the University of California at San Diego suggest that an institutional faculty development and mentoring program can have positive effects on faculty retention (6). Moreover, an increase in faculty retention rates can provide financial benefit to an institution by obviating the need to replace faculty in whom significant resources have been invested.

Many of the same benefits accrue to the mentor. Satisfaction comes from assisting mentees in their development as the mentor's role evolves from coach to colleague. Ideally, as suggested by Ries and colleagues (6), the mentor experiences an expanded professional and social network, helps retain excellent colleagues, establishes and promotes collaborations, and helps enhance the quality of the department and the institution.

With the declining number of academicians available to serve as effective mentors (4), the tradition of informal mentoring as the primary mode of professional development in academic medicine must be augmented by a broader institutional strategy to ensure the scholarly success of junior colleagues. The highly successful mentoring program at the University of Wisconsin is based on the belief that reliance on informal relationships can limit access to mentoring opportunities. For as Pfund and colleagues (7) note, the mentored research experience is vital to the success of an academic research institution because it facilitates a host of developmental opportunities at the intersection of an institution's educational and research missions. Furthermore, they note that "the diversity of science is dependent on the quality of mentored research because this experience is a key to attracting underrepresented groups to science." With so much at stake, then, it is not surprising to see repeated calls from academic organizations and funding entities (8, 9) for institutions to develop comprehensive and integrated approaches to mentoring. These mentoring programs are needed to ensure, as Keyser and colleagues (1) described, "that emerging scientists acquire the norms and standards, values and attitudes, and knowledge, skills and behaviors to develop into successful independent researchers."

The classic definition of mentor involves an established academic professional providing a mentee with guidance, support, and instruction in order to enhance the mentee's career. Sackett (10) has further defined four elements of successful mentoring relationships for clinician-scientists: 1) the provision of resources to establish research programs (for example, space, equipment, and financial support); 2) opportunities, described as a mindset in which mentors review everything that comes across their desks for its ability to further a mentee's career development; 3) advice in the form of active listening, whereby the mentor challenges the mentee to think logically through key choices and opportunities; and 4) protection, both in terms of time to focus on the most salient issues associated with professional development (the mentee's research) and in helping mentees fend off more aggressive behavior from other established colleagues. These elements correlate well with the four realms identified by Rogers and colleagues (11) as experienced by mentees in successful medical faculty mentoring relationships: 1) personal exploration, the systematic reviewing of career goals and options; 2) practical guidance, the mentor's systematic assistance in evaluating objectives and plans; 3) mentor support, the mentor's sharing of personal experience, expressions of confidence in the mentee, and role as a "sounding board" when a mentee encounters difficult situations; and 4) mentor advice, through the communication of specific recommendations, tactics, and strategies.

❖ Domains of Research Mentorship

How does an institution best think about the design and implementation of mentoring programs that facilitate the key experiences of the research mentoring relationships? Keyser and colleagues (1) challenge us to consider five central domains described in the literature, beginning with the criteria for selecting mentors (Box 9-1).

Selecting an Effective Mentor

Selecting an effective mentor involves both the skills and experience of the proposed mentors and the process by which the institution selects and trains the mentors. As Sackett (10) has noted, effective mentors must themselves be competent, confident clinical investigators or basic scientists who can allow their mentees to assume primary roles in research projects and the resulting publications. Furthermore, effective mentors have the interpersonal skills necessary for these multifaceted relationships to flourish. Blixen and colleagues (4) have described the importance of the mentor's showing "fire in the belly" or a passion for research. Keyser and coworkers (1) have written that effective mentors engender trust, uphold integrity, practice patience, and are readily accessible to their mentees.

It is clear that mentees both perceive and experience these characteristics as being important in the success of their mentoring relationships. In a qualitative review of the mentoring program at the University of Pennsylvania School of Medicine, junior faculty who reported that they

---

Box 9-1. Domains for Successful Research Mentorship

1. Selecting an effective mentor
2. Creating a climate that encourages senior faculty to mentor
3. Promoting factors that facilitate successful mentoring relationships
4. Enhancing mentees' ability to compete successfully, ethically, and responsibly as independent investigators
5. Providing institutional support for the professional development of mentees and mentors

From Keyser DJ, Lakoski JM, Lara-Cinisomo S, Schultz D, Williams V, Zellers DF, Pincus HA. Advancing institutional efforts to support research mentorship: a conceptual framework and self-assessment tool. Acad Med. 2008;83:217-225.

were in a successful relationship commented that mentoring typically was offered "without fanfare or need for recognition." They noted that there was no expectation of quid pro quo for the mentor's contributions. Commenting on a specific—and valued—mentor, one mentee observed that "he [the mentor] honestly is interested in helping junior faculty succeed, even when they do not directly contribute to his own research." Another mentee, writing about his mentor, stated that "he has no ulterior motives in mentoring me. His goal is my success." Yet another said that "he does not make you feel that you are wasting his time, but rather that he is trying to make your time more valuable." The mentees recognized that the mentor was personally invested in their career development and success and that the mentor believed in them. Likewise, the mentors frequently conveyed how proud they were of the mentees' accomplishments, consistent with Rogers and colleagues' description of the importance of "mentor support" (11). The impact and influence of a mentor as a role model cannot be overstated. The legacy of the mentoring experience has been conveyed by mentees who report thinking, "What would [mentor] do?" when faced with challenging situations.

Mentor selection and training require an ongoing institutional commitment to the professional development of senior colleagues, that is, the mentors. For example, Pfund and coworkers (7) explained that the goals of the Wisconsin Mentoring Seminar are to "train mentors to communicate effectively, to consider issues of human diversity, to discuss mentoring approaches, and to apply a 'scientific teaching' approach to mentoring." Different methods can be used to design such programs, including both a didactic curriculum and case-based learning. These methods can focus solely on the mentor or include both mentor and mentee. Blixen and colleagues (4) used the latter approach to develop a mentorship program for clinical researchers at the Cleveland Clinic Foundation. Feldman and coworkers (12) recently described a novel Mentor Development Program at the University of California at San Francisco's Clinical and Translational Science Institute, which is geared toward midcareer and early senior clinical and translational researchers. After participating in the structured Mentor Development Program, faculty form peer mentoring networks. This method is recommended by Pololi and Knight (3) as an effective way to design and implement mentoring programs. A central component of effective mentor training involves providing mentors structured feedback so that, as Sackett (10) has described, they can evaluate performance, identify opportunities to improve skills, and, as their mentees continue to develop, make effective decisions about whether they should remain the mentor for that individual.

Creating a Climate That Encourages Senior Faculty to Mentor

According to Keyser and colleagues (1), a second primary domain of research mentorship involves ensuring that institutions motivate senior faculty to serve as effective mentors to their junior colleagues. This motivation can take many forms, such as a discussion during the annual review with the chair or division chief about a faculty member's performance as a mentor; scheduling "formal time" at the institutional level for mentoring activities, including mentoring activities in promotion reviews for faculty in senior ranks; or having a defined mechanism to recognize faculty deemed outstanding mentors. These and other related activities promote a culture of mentoring within an institution and help ensure that these values become embedded over time.

At the University of Pennsylvania, a special award was established for faculty mentoring, and is presented as one of several annual awards of the School of Medicine denoting excellence. The award recognizes a faculty member who has fostered the professional development of other faculty members by providing inspiring and effective counsel and opportunities for achievement. The outstanding mentor establishes a supportive and nurturing relationship with other faculty members and helps them to negotiate the complex demands of academic life, improve their skills and opportunities, and reconcile the competing claims of work and home life.

Since its inaugural year in 2004, nominations for this prestigious award significantly outnumber those submitted for any other School of Medicine Award of Excellence. In addition, several departments have recognized the value of acknowledging and rewarding mentoring excellence and have implemented their own award process locally.

Promoting Factors That Facilitate Successful Mentoring Relationships

The third important domain of research mentorship, as described by Keyser and colleagues (1), involves identifying and promoting the factors that facilitate the success of these mentoring relationships. One such factor is the method by which the mentor and mentee come to be paired. Active participation by the mentee is clearly important; as discussed by Straus and colleagues (13), mentors and mentees are concerned if they engage only in mentoring relationships assigned by the institution rather than one in which the mentee actively seeks a relationship on the basis of program interest and career aspiration. In a review of studies of mentoring across disciplines (both academic and corporate), Allen and coworkers (14) noted that the mentee's perceived input into mentor selection is associated with the overall success of the relationship. Ideally, then, mentees can select from an ongoing "menu" of mentoring choices, including one-to-one, mentoring committees, institutional workshops or seminars, and online resources. Accountability for mentoring is shared among institutional and departmental leaders and mentors and mentees. Inherent in this paradigm is senior faculty's responsibility to respond to mentoring requests and be attentive to potential mentoring needs among their junior colleagues. In addition, institutional leaders must embrace their responsibilities to make clear to junior faculty that they have a right to be mentored and need to actively seek out these mentoring relationships. Empowering junior faculty to assume control over their careers is a fundamental reason for mentoring.

Indeed, as Jackson and colleagues (15) and Wasserstein and coworkers (16) have described, mentees often seek and benefit from relationships with multiple mentors, each providing a distinct set of experiences and opportunities for growth. For example, a clinician-scientist at the University of Pennsylvania School of Medicine who was promoted in the tenure track reported that, "Officially, I had one mentor. Unofficially, I had many more." Accordingly, it is important for institutions to encourage and facilitate the development of multiple mentor contacts for junior faculty. In this paradigm, the initial assigned mentor provides opportunities for early connection with senior faculty so the mentee can readily identify other individuals with whom a mentoring relationship would be appropriate. Supporting the conclusions of Straus and colleagues (13) and those of Allen and coworkers (14), an analysis of the University of Pennsylvania's mentoring program suggests that the most effective mentoring experiences have arisen not from the assignment of mentors by the institution but largely through the less formal initiative of the mentees and the mentors themselves. Indeed, the theme of the National Leadership Workshop on Mentoring Women in Biomedical Careers (17) aptly captured the message: "Mentoring Is Everybody's Business."

To facilitate contact between junior and senior faculty, mentor–mentee pairing should begin as early as the initial faculty appointment. A mentor may be identified by the department chair during the negotiation process, and some larger departments may have a vice-chair whose responsibilities include oversight of mentoring and faculty professional development. In some cases, it may be preferable to identify a mentor outside the department, but one who may be closer to the new faculty member's area of research. This depends largely on the expectations of the role of the assigned mentor; will he or she be the primary academic mentor or perhaps the advisor who helps to facilitate a network of mentors? It may be valuable to assemble a mentoring committee at this early stage. The mentoring committee or team may be composed of faculty in different departments or even different schools of the university, but who have shared academic interests. Then, the institution needs to ensure that appropriate resources are provided, including formal coursework relating to success in science, writing, teaching, and career management, so that the mentoring relationship thrives not in isolation but within a culture devoted to faculty development.

An additional factor identified by Keyser and colleagues (1) that facilitates successful mentoring relationships is the communication of clear expectations for these relationships. In this vein, Blixen and colleagues (4) described the "Code of Mentorship" that was established as part of the clinical scientist mentoring program at the Cleveland Clinic Foundation. The Code makes explicit the expectations for both mentors and mentees and identifies the fundamentals on which successful mentoring relationships are built. The University of Pennsylvania School of Medicine has created a document titled "Shaping a Career in Academic Medicine: Guidelines for Mentor/Mentee Conversations." This is given to all junior faculty and their mentors and is an important resource in the development of their mentoring relationships. Written with input from senior faculty, the document addresses the keys to successful career development for basic science researchers, physician-scientists, and clinical investigators, as well as helpful guidelines and vignettes for how to discuss this information in the context of the mentoring relationship.

Enhancing Mentees' Ability to Compete Successfully, Ethically, and Responsibly as Independent Investigators

The fourth domain for institutional success in research mentorship concerns the ways in which mentoring can enhance a mentee's ability to conduct independent research in an ethical and responsible manner (1). This aspect of mentoring is central to the perceived success of the mentor–mentee relationship and the mentee's subsequent professional development (5, 13). Mentees will often indicate that the single most important skill of an effective mentor is his or her expertise as a grant and manuscript writer and editor. Nominees for the University of Pennsylvania's Award of Excellence for Mentoring were described as meticulous reviewers who give tough but constructive feedback. They were described as open to counterarguments and collegial exchanges of opinions and ideas. One mentee wrote that his mentor "expertly integrates constructive criticism with positive reinforcement and demonstrates that objectivity and compassion can peacefully exist." Another mentee stated that the mentor gave him a copy of a successful R01 application. He stated that "to this day, I keep a hard copy of this application in my desk as a template and refer to it regularly."

In addition to fundamentals of grant and manuscript writing, good mentors exhibit ethical behavior to be modeled in their everyday interactions. As Detsky and Baerlocher (18) describe, they assign appropriate weight to the contributions of mentees and colleagues in their collaborative research endeavors, never taking credit for the written work of others or artificially assigning primary authorship to junior colleagues to help advance their career. They openly discuss with mentees issues such as appropriate disclosure and disposition of conflicts of interest, and they impress upon the mentee that adherence to the highest ethical standards is fundamental to success as a researcher. Similarly, institutions reinforce the commitment to ethical standards through required ongoing training in institutional review board protocol, animal welfare, and other matters related to the conduct of laboratory operations.

Providing Institutional Support for the Professional Development of Mentees and Mentors

The final domain identified by Keyser and colleagues (1) involves institutional support of the factors that contribute to the professional development of both mentees and mentors. Faculty development courses were noted earlier. In addition, in the early stages of the mentoring relationship, a key element of institutional support involves structured opportunities for the socialization of new junior faculty members into their environment. This could include introducing them to colleagues, networking with other potential mentors, and sharing information about institutional culture so that they recognize the political idiosyncrasies of the institution and can begin to successfully negotiate the complex administrative structures that affect their research endeavors.

Effective mentors work diligently to provide networking opportunities beyond the institutional level, so that mentees can, as described by Jackson and coworkers (15), "gain access to otherwise closed important academic circles." Examples of this include arranging invitations to important national meetings; offering their mentee names for speaking engagements in high-profile national and international venues; nominating them for national committees and awards; arranging meetings with visiting professors; participating in media reviews that introduce the mentee to people who are important to know; and arranging for them to present at site visits, review manuscripts for high-impact journals, or write invited reviews and book chapters. These connections, when nurtured appropriately by mentees, provide unparalleled opportunity to showcase their work and build credibility and visibility within their disciplines. Institutions and mentors can also work in tandem to guide mentees on how to be effective self-promoters. Training on résumé organization, academic writing, and presentation skills is augmented by mentor instruction on understanding the "ground rules" within a discipline and guidance on navigating the politics associated with achieving career success.

As has been identified throughout this chapter, investment in the ongoing development of midcareer and senior faculty is an important component in the creation and sustainability of a broader mentoring environment, and the Mentor Development Program discussed by Feldman and colleagues (12) is an important example of this commitment. Institutionally supported faculty development programs, in tandem with mentoring programs, should include an emphasis on effective career management for more senior colleagues. This can and should include a leadership development curriculum focused on midcareer faculty, who are poised to assume positions of greater responsibility within the institution and within their respective disciplines. Such a program's curriculum should include introductory programs on management, conflict resolution, and negotiation for junior faculty colleagues.

Finally, as institutions move forward in nurturing existing mentoring programs or developing new ones, it is important to consider the important concerns associated with mentoring women and minority faculty. Diversity is an institutional goal; providing an intellectually and culturally rich academic environment can enhance retention, productivity, and satisfaction (19). To be at the forefront of academic medicine, all institutions must aspire to and work toward achieving a diverse, inclusive environment.

❖ Case Scenarios

The following real-life examples of situations encountered by faculty and leadership elucidate the common challenges involved with research mentoring. For each scenario, potentially helpful responses from the institution and for the faculty themselves are identified.

Case Scenario 1: Departure of Primary Mentor

The primary reason Dr. Greg Smith accepted the appointment as a physician-scientist/assistant professor in the tenure track was the opportunity to work with Dr. Susan Helms, whom he greatly admired and with whom he shared a research interest. Dr. Smith began a productive collaboration with Dr. Helms. Although she was not in the same department, she served as his primary mentor. This relationship was important to Dr. Smith because he and Dr. Helms worked in a new area of research, one with very few active investigators. Dr. Smith had just hired his first postdoctoral fellow when Dr. Helm, who had been a highly regarded senior investigator at the institution for many years, announced her decision to accept a position in industry.

Responses and Results
- Dr. Smith met with Dr. Helms, who offered to work with him to arrange for new mentors. Dr. Helms had a well-established research network in the home institution and around the world.
- Dr. Smith met with his department chair, faculty experts identified by his chair, and other faculty members in related research areas throughout the institution to seek advice, identify new mentors, and explore potential collaborations.
- Dr. Helms continued to serve as an outside mentor for Dr. Smith and facilitated introductions to additional faculty outside of the institution.
- Dr. Smith's quick and strategic response to reaching out to faculty experts within his institution resulted in a network of productive mentoring relationships and collaborative opportunities.
- Dr. Smith, now preparing for his promotion review, offers advice to fellows and new faculty on developing *multiple* productive mentoring relationships as early as possible.

Case Scenario 2: Establishing a Funding Portfolio

Dr. Ann Conway is an assistant professor, approximately halfway through her tenure probationary period, whose research is in a highly competitive field. Like many of her colleagues, she was struggling to obtain research funding. She occasionally met with her mentor, who had been assigned to her, but he did not seem too interested in her research or her career. Dr. Conway met informally with other senior faculty but had not established any formal mentoring relationships with any of them. She had completed a draft of a grant and needed more experienced researchers to review it.

Discussions and Decisions
- Dr. Conway decided that her chances for funding would be improved substantially with input from experienced researchers who had a successful history of grant funding. She contacted several senior faculty, three of whom agreed to serve as reviewers.
- Dr. Conway met with each faculty member to discuss her research and provided each with an electronic copy of the

grant. She also allowed sufficient time for them to review the grant and make suggestions for revision.

- Dr. Conway continued to meet with the reviewers as she continued her research. She also asked these new mentors to suggest others who may be helpful to her.
- Dr. Conway enrolled in the faculty professional development program on grant writing.
- Dr. Conway met with her department chair to explain her current situation and asked her to identify another senior faculty member as her primary mentor.

Case Scenario 3: Managing Competing Priorities

Dr. Brooks is a clinical investigator in a small division that has experienced recent turnover. As a result, Dr. Brooks, an assistant professor, has assumed administrative responsibilities while his department chair searches for a new division chief. Dr. Brooks enjoys the administrative work, but is finding it difficult to carve out time for clinical research and scholarship. He does not wish to admit to his chair, who also serves as his primary mentor, that he is struggling, but he is getting concerned that he will not be able to meet the requirements for promotion.

Issues and Analysis
- Although a department chair should always be accessible as a mentor, he or she should not serve as the primary mentor because of inherent conflicts of interest associated with the supervisory position.
- Dr. Brooks should seek mentoring from another senior faculty member, ideally several senior faculty members, for advice on academic issues and balancing his various roles.
- Dr. Brooks should seek advice from senior colleagues on strategies for a productive discussion with his chair about his schedule and his concerns about promotion. One of these more seasoned faculty members may serve as an advocate for Dr. Brooks with his department chair.
- Dr. Brooks should arrange a meeting with his faculty affairs office to review the promotion process so he is aware of the various policies, procedures, and deadlines. He should also meet with the chair of his department's promotion committee to obtain some feedback on his dossier and his likelihood of promotion if he continues his current responsibilities.

❖ Conclusion

Mentoring is a shared responsibility of all members of the academic community, and a shared investment by the institution and individual faculty members throughout a career. Institutions have an obligation to the current and future generation of scientists to ensure that mentoring is not viewed as a "hobby" (2, 10, 15) or gesture, but rather as a fundamental commitment and a rite of passage in the advance of basic and clinical science. In the current climate for academic medicine, the need for skilled mentors who can effectively shape and guide the development of the next generation of leaders is greater than ever. In the face of increased economic pressure and ever more complicated research milieu, the traditional career path for research faculty is at risk. A comprehensive mentoring program—one that is dynamic, flexible, and broad, encompassing and supporting the goals of individual faculty within the framework of both a department's and an institution's strategic mission—is critical to ensure the ongoing vitality of academic medicine's research mission.

REFERENCES

1. **Keyser DJ, Lakoski JM, Lara-Cinisomo S, Schultz DJ, Williams VL, Zellers DF, et al.** Advancing institutional efforts to support research mentorship: a conceptual framework and self-assessment tool. Acad Med. 2008;83:217-25.
2. **Zerzan JT, Hess R, Schur E, Phillips RS, Rigotti N.** Making the most of mentors: a guide for mentees. Acad Med. 2009;84:140-4.
3. **Pololi L, Knight S.** Mentoring faculty in academic medicine. A new paradigm? J Gen Intern Med. 2005;20:866-70.
4. **Blixen CE, Papp KK, Hull AL, Rudick RA, Bramstedt KA.** Developing a mentorship program for clinical researchers. J Contin Educ Health Prof. 2007;27:86-93
5. **Sambunjak D, Straus SE, Marusic A.** Mentoring in academic medicine: a systematic review. JAMA. 2006;296:1103-15.
6. **Ries A, Wingard D, Morgan C, Farrell E, Letter S, Reznik V.** Retention of junior faculty in academic medicine at the University of California, San Diego. Acad Med. 2009;84: 37-41.
7. **Pfund C, Maidl Pribbenow C, Branchaw J, Miller Lauffer S, Handelsman J.** Professional skills. The merits of training mentors. Science. 2006;311:473-4.
8. **Association of American Medical Colleges.** Compact Between Postdoctoral Appointees and Their Mentors. Washington, DC: Association of American Medical Colleges; 2006. Accessed at: https://services.aamc.org/publications/showfile.cfm?file=version76.pdf &prd_id=176&prv_id=210&pdf_id=76.
9. **National Institutes of Health.** NIH Roadmap Workshop: Clinical Research Training in Medical and Dental Schools. Bethesda, MD: National Institutes of Health; 2004. Accessed at http://nihroadmap.nih.gov/clinicalresearch/WorkshopReport-CRTraining-0504.pdf.
10. **Sackett DL.** On the determinants of academic success as a clinician-scientist. Clin Invest Med. 2001;24:94-100.

11. **Rogers J, Monteiro FM, Nora A.** Toward measuring the domains of mentoring. Fam Med. 2008;40:259-63.

12. **Feldman MD, Huang L, Guglielmo BJ, Jordan R, Kahn J, Creasman JM, et al.** Training the Next Generation of Research Mentors: The University of California, San Francisco, Clinical & Translational Science Institute Mentor Development Program. Clin Transl Sci. 2009;2:216-221.

13. **Straus SE, Chatur F, Taylor M.** Issues in the mentor-mentee relationship in academic medicine: a qualitative study. Acad Med. 2009;84:135-9.

14. **Allen TD, Eby LT, Lentz E.** Mentorship behaviors and mentorship quality associated with formal mentoring programs: closing the gap between research and practice. J Appl Psychol. 2006;91:567-78.

15. **Jackson VA, Palepu A, Szalacha L, Caswell C, Carr PL, Inui T.** "Having the right chemistry": a qualitative study of mentoring in academic medicine. Acad Med. 2003;78:328-34.

16. **Wasserstein AG, Quistberg DA, Shea JA.** Mentoring at the University of Pennsylvania: results of a faculty survey. J Gen Intern Med. 2007;22:210-4.

17. **Office of Research on Women's Health, National Institutes of Health.** National Leadership Workshop on Mentoring Women in Biomedical Careers. Bethesda, MD: National Institutes of Health; 2007. Available at: http://womeninscience.nih.gov/mentoring/documents/National_Leadership_Workshop_on_Mentoring_Women_in_Biomedical_Careers.pdf.

18. **Detsky AS, Baerlocher MO.** Academic mentoring—how to give it and how to get it. JAMA. 2007;297:2134-6.

19. **Nivet MA, Taylor VS, Butts GC, Strelnick AH, Herbert-Carter J, Fry-Johnson YW, et al.** Diversity in academic medicine no. 1 case for minority faculty development today. Mt Sinai J Med. 2008;75:491-8.

Section III
Mentoring Special Populations

10

Closing the Gap: Mentoring Women in Academic Internal Medicine

Holly J. Humphrey, MD, MACP

Kelly Smith, MPP

> If your success is not on your own terms, if it looks good to the world but does not feel good in your heart, it is not success at all (1).
>
> —*Anna Quindlen*

W omen are now entering medical schools and residency programs and joining academic medical faculties in larger numbers than ever before. Despite these gains, however, women continue to be underrepresented in senior faculty ranks and in leadership positions in academic medicine (2). Although women are disproportionately represented in primary care specialties, they are significantly underrepresented in some subspecialties, such as cardiology, gastroenterology, and pulmonary/critical care (3). Without a critical mass of women in leadership positions and in specific fields, isolation remains a significant issue that could affect career development and faculty well-being. Left unattended, the lack of critical mass creates a vicious cycle. Furthermore, women continue to be more likely than men to leave academic medicine (4).

While female faculty themselves will surely benefit by correcting the lagging rates of academic promotion, ascendence to leadership positions, and attaining more equal representation in the medical subspecialties, academic medical centers stand to benefit as well—perhaps even more. In general, women are natural collaborators, enjoy team-based work, and are less focused on power than men (5, 6). These attributes will prove critical to academic medical centers facing the tumult of the fractured health care environment. Diverse teams confer more stability and resilience to organizations than homogenous ones,

KEY POINTS

- Mentors need to acknowledge the struggle women face with the competing demands of work, study, and family, as well as the environmental issues that female physicians identify as hostile more often than male physicians do.

- In mentoring women, mentors should also address the following: scholarly interests, faculty development opportunities, career path choices (including promotion and tenure policies), resources, and personal guidance for balancing career and family.

- Female medical students and residents are at special risk for lack of mentorship. These groups continue to report significant rates of sexual harassment. Pregnant medical residents face particular challenges when the demands of residency collide with certification requirements, fellowship applications, and training.

- In the subspecialty fields undersubscribed by women, there is a significant need for mentors who will redouble their efforts to change the culture at their institutions; women in these fields report not only inadequate mentorship but increased rates of gender-based harassment and discrimination.

- For women who are physician-scientists, mentors must pay active attention to ensuring they have sufficient access to the resources that support achievements in research.

- Time alone is not sufficient to ensure that women rise to senior leadership positions in academic medicine; active steps must be taken to ensure that women have access to opportunities and support for preparing for leadership roles. These steps include advising search committees to seek and consider women in succession planning.

in part because they can more flexibly adapt to changing conditions (5). Clearly, academic medicine, science, and academic medical centers (and especially their patients) have much to gain by addressing career progression for women in medicine.

This chapter focuses on mentoring women for careers in academic medicine, including mentoring medical students and residents as well as faculty on various academic career paths; balancing work and family;

leadership positions in medicine; and managing complicated situations, such as bias, harassment, and hostile environments

❖ Special Considerations in Mentoring Women for Academic Careers

It's so much easier to write a resume than to craft a spirit (7).
—Anna Quindlen

Several common themes are worth exploring in mentoring women. Although these themes are important to explore regardless of gender, they take on specific resonance for women (Box 10-1).

While one individual may not have specific knowledge about all the issues listed, being aware of the themes and knowing where to direct the mentee for answers is a critical piece of successful mentorship. As important as having factual information is taking the opportunity to engage in conversations ranging from exploring career paths to advice about parental leave, working part-time, or sorting through new opportunities. Understanding institutional culture and helping a woman navigate the terrain is essential. For example, knowing which meetings and committee assignments are high-yield versus lower priority makes an important difference to junior female faculty who may have young children at home. Brainstorming about opportunities for scholarly pursuits in teaching, patient care, or research can be equally stimulating for the mentor and the mentee. Knowing whether the institution has a tenure clock with limits or provisions that allow faculty to stop the clock to attend to family issues is a concrete issue, but equally important is acknowledging the struggles of

---

Box 10-1. Special Themes to Consider When Mentoring Women

1. Scholarly interests
2. Mentorship options
3. Faculty development opportunities
4. Promotion and tenure policies
5. Resources (child care/maternity leave options, sexual harassment policies)
6. Balancing career and family (personal guidance and models for self-reflection)

the demands of work and family. One of the most important interventions for teachers and advisors of mentees is to actively acknowledge that women struggle with the competing demands of work, study, and family (8). When women feel this support, they are encouraged to strive for both personal and professional goals.

Encouraging Mentorship Regardless of Gender Lines

This support can be provided equally well by male or female mentors. Because women remain underrepresented in academic leadership positions, many women will largely continue to be mentored by men. Mentoring across gender lines can be extremely positive and should be encouraged. Indeed, the advancements that women have made in the past 20 years could be attributed in part to the exceptional mentorship and support that women have received from their male mentors. Mentoring across gender lines may require being sensitive to differences in perceptions and priorities, which will be explored in other sections of this chapter. However, these sensitivities should not discourage men from seeking women mentees and vice versa. Men can, and do, provide exceptional professional advice and mentorship to women. Studies highlighted in this chapter cite *lack* of mentorship as one of the problems that may be keeping women from advancing, not *who* is doing the mentoring.

Mentoring Medical Students and Residents

Encouraging mentorship is particularly pressing for female medical students and residents. Only one third of students and half of internal medicine residents report having a mentor (9, 10). The numbers are even lower for interns and underrepresented minority students and residents. These data are particularly troubling because female medical students and residents face many of the same issues that female faculty face. For example, common questions among students and residents might include the following:

- "I want to be successful in the lab, but the senior investigator gives all the best projects to his favorite medical student, who is 2 years behind me and a male. They attend all of the national and international meetings to present their work, while the rest of us keep generating the results in the lab that they present."
- "If I have a baby during residency, can I finish on time and start my fellowship?"
- "Is it realistic to consider a career as a cardiologist and still have time to raise my children?"
- "I am uncomfortable with the way Dr. X speaks about women."

This chapter explores strategies for addressing these questions, but it is important to acknowledge that medical students and residents are grappling with many of these issues at a time when they are particularly vulnerable. Students and residents need extra care and time to inculcate the values of the profession and the wisdom and history of medicine. The powerful effect of the hidden curriculum on students' professional behavior requires that role models and mentors help students and residents navigate medical school, residency, and junior faculty positions. When done well, careers are born; when done poorly or not at all, discouragement and dropout can follow. A recent study in *Academic Medicine* found that female medical students struggle to define their role on the wards and encounter a "gender learning curve" that influences their expectations of gender roles in medicine (11). Mentored residents were nearly twice as likely to describe having excellent career preparation as their nonmentored colleagues.

Among the many issues that female students and residents face are those related to pregnancy and their personal life. Residents, particularly women, have a tendency to feel increasingly isolated as they handle the demands of their grueling work schedule. Women without a family network often feel particularly isolated. Working intense hours in a new city and hospital severely limits their social networks and ability to balance work with a personal life. Married women, meanwhile, begin residency at the same time they are contemplating the appropriate timing for starting a family. These compelling personal questions coincide with the most demanding and relatively inflexible periods in the education and training of a doctor (12). Female residents contemplating a pregnancy have to balance their own personal and educational needs against the effect a pregnancy will have on the other residents in the program, who now work with more limited flexibility because of duty hours limits and program curricular requirements. The Accreditation Council for Graduate Medical Education now requires all programs to have maternity leave policies and to provide those policies to trainees. As any parent knows, however, the pregnancy and maternity leave are only the beginning of what becomes a wonderful but complicated journey of caring for a baby and raising a child. Doing this during residency or fellowship can be very difficult because it is not uncommon for women to face a lack of support from peers and from faculty related to their child care needs. Mentors can make a significant difference in this scenario by providing support and wisdom. Even if the mentor is not familiar with the detailed maternity leave policy and board certification requirements, supporting the resident in working with the program director and chief resident adds an important extra layer of guidance and encouragement.

Mentoring Female Clinician Educators

Female faculty report having fewer mentors than their male counterparts or having less effective mentoring (13, 14). Clinician-educators are also less likely to have mentors than their counterparts in traditional tenure tracks (15, 16). Therefore, female clinician-educators are at particular risk for inadequate mentorship. When clinician-educators do have a mentor, they indicate that this was the most positive aspect of their career development in medical education (17). Mentored clinician-educators also spend more time in scholarly activity than nonmentored clinician-educators (15). Thus, having a mentor for female clinician-educators might address the gender imbalance in senior positions in academic medicine by providing the support needed to help them rise through the ranks.

Female clinician educators may take advantage of networking with national organizations, such as the Society of General Internal Medicine (SGIM). Over the past several years, this organization has organized a One-On-One Mentoring Program for those interested in engaging in a mentoring relationship with a more senior person from another institution. SGIM also has an active Women's Caucus Interest Group that meets during regional and national meetings and that sponsors an online discussion group (18).

Many subspecialty organizations also offer networking opportunities or mentoring programs for women. Examples include the Women in Nephrology Group and the American Thoracic Society, which provides one-on-one career guidance and a Web site with extensive career development information (19, 20). These national societies provide a critical support network for female physicians practicing in subspecialties where women continue to be underrepresented.

Mentoring Women for Subspecialty Careers

Many of the subspecialties in internal medicine struggle to attract women to their field, in part because of perceptions of being family unfriendly compared with careers in other specialties (21, 22). A 2006 career and lifestyle survey by the American College of Cardiology found that female cardiologists were less likely to be married or to have children than male cardiologists (23). Despite significant societal shifts in attitudes toward career and family, discrimination based on gender and parenting was prevalent among the cardiologists surveyed. Most cardiologists reported not only having a mentor but having positive experiences regarding career development. These same mentors, mostly men, were viewed as very helpful with career development but not as personal role models—in fact, they actually had a negative influence regarding family issues. A longitudinal study of gastroenterology fellows reported that women were more likely to remain childless or to have fewer children at the end of training compared with their male counterparts (22). The female fellows in both cardiology and gastro-enterology also perceived significant levels of gender discrimination and harassment (22, 23).

Experience reported in the business literature sheds some light on why these issues are particularly prevalent in the medical subspecialties. Many men identify themselves as "career primary"; their career is the central focus of their lives. Women, meanwhile, often identify themselves as "career-and-family"; they want to pursue serious careers while also rearing children. "Career-primary" and "career-and-family" people may find it difficult to identify with each other, and simply may not have the tools or resources to support each other appropriately (24).

Therefore, in the subspecialty fields undersubscribed by women, there is a significant need for mentors who will redouble their efforts to not only support their mentees individually but to improve the culture at their institutions. Subspecialty organizations should continue to offer and highlight networking organizations specific to women who identify themselves as "career-and-family" physicians. Individual mentors should consider their own biases and assumptions and educate themselves regarding areas of mentoring with which they may be unfamiliar, such as family leave, child care, and other issues that may resonate more powerfully in women's career development. While the mentor does not need expertise with these issues, knowing where the resources exist is very helpful.

Because discrimination is strikingly prevalent in reports from both cardiology and gastroenterology fellows, mentors should be sensitive to practices and policies that may inadvertently discriminate against women in the workplace (22, 23). Raising questions in an empathetic manner will begin a dialogue to address some of the barriers that young women who have children or are contemplating having children might face. Women need easy access to receiving advice about timing of pregnancies, parental leave, possibilities of sharing a fellowship position, and the various career paths she might consider.

Mentoring Female Physician-Scientists

Many prominent groups in medicine and science have written about the leaky pipeline for female physician-scientists (25). While the biomedical pipeline is filled with good candidates, the National Institutes of Health reports that only 20% of their senior scientists are women. Women have high success rates for their first R01 applications, but lower success rates on their second or renewal grants. There are several potential explanations for this, including that female scientists produce fewer publications than men (26). The National Academies of Science 2007 report, "Beyond Bias and Barriers," indicated that women spend more time teaching and mentoring than men and have less access to graduate students and postdoctoral fellows (27).

The issues outlined in Box 10-2 are critically important to all young investigators pursuing the physician-scientist track, no less so men than women, and can be applied to junior faculty members (including, of course, women) on any academic track (28).

❖ Mentoring Women for Work and Family Balance

> We must be open to all points of the compass; husband, children, friends, home, community; stretched out, exposed, sensitive like a spider's web to each breeze that blows, to each call that comes. How difficult for us, then, to achieve a balance in the midst of these contradictory tensions, and yet how necessary for the proper functioning of our lives (29).
> —*Anne Morrow Lindbergh*

Institutional policies that make it difficult for women to balance their medical careers with family or that implicitly send the message that family time must be sacrificed to move along the academic track may contribute more to female faculty departing academic medicine than explicit acts of gender discrimination or harassment. For example, institutions lacking child care facilities and departmental meetings scheduled in early morning and late afternoons often create an untenable situation for women with children. Mentors' ability to help their mentees navigate the institutional culture and promotion tracks as they juggle demands of family and work are critical to helping women succeed and remain in academic medicine. Perspective pieces in medical journals often cite women's ongoing desire to want to better balance their careers with their family lives (30–32). Implicit in these articles is the worry that women in academia who have families, particularly large families, are perceived as less serious about their work than their colleagues (33). Studies confirm these anecdotal narratives that balancing work with family remains a paramount concern to female physicians.

Data from the Association of American Medical Colleges indicate that women's departure from academic medicine is disproportionately higher than that of their male counterparts (34). A University of Minnesota study found women in that institution were more likely than men to cite work–family conflicts as potential reasons for leaving academic medicine and that family-life factors serve as obstacles to their job satisfaction (35). Women in this study juggled more household duties than their male counterparts, spending an average of 31 hours per week on family and household chores

Box 10-2. Issues Important to Young Investigators (Women and Men) Pursuing the Physician-Scientist Track

Resources: The mentor may need to be an active advocate in helping the mentee secure laboratory space, secretarial and research support, and bridge funding. Encouraging medical and graduate students to work with the mentee is one simple way of providing research support.

Opportunities: The mentor should introduce mentees to opportunities that will enhance their research and writing portfolio. This could include giving the mentee opportunities to write commentaries or editorials, to present at scientific meetings, and to review grants and manuscripts. Young investigators should also be encouraged to join an ongoing research project while tackling a project of their own. Recommending the mentee to regional and national task forces can help the mentee make important contacts outside the institution and get a foothold in establishing their own personal network.

Scientific presentations: The mentor can play a key role in mentees' professional development by rehearsing their scientific presentations with them and teaching them how to field difficult questions before public presentations.

Managing clinical responsibilities: The mentor should help the mentee focus on high-quality patient care and teaching and provide guidance on time management for inpatient and outpatient responsibilities. Mentors may need to help mentees secure adequate support staff (nurses, research assistants, and administrative assistants) so that they have the time and energy to focus on their research pursuits.

Socialization: The mentor can ease the isolation that many young investigators face by extending invitations to dinner meetings and the social gatherings of the lab group.

Understanding the tenure clock: Mentors must be prepared to serve as an advocate for leaves of absence related to maternity and family issues, including understanding the criteria for promotion and whether the institution stops the tenure clock for maternity and family issues. Some National Institutes of

continued

> **Box 10-2. Issues Important to Young Investigators (Women and Men) Pursuing the Physician-Scientist Track (continued)**
>
> Health grants preclude junior faculty from working part-time, so having knowledge of available re-entry grants will be especially important to young investigators starting families. There is evidence that the NIH is beginning to reduce restrictions; it recently allowed K award recipients to request a reduction of their appointment to less than full-time (although not less than three-quarters time) (65).
>
> **Personal issues:** Mentees often depend on their mentors to provide guidance about how to balance work and family issues. Helping young investigators manage these stressors will encourage them to remain in the field.

compared with their male counterparts, who spent just 19 hours per week on such tasks. These women also had less help at home; 70% of female physicians surveyed had partners who were employed full-time, compared with 36% of men.

Clearly, a mentor cannot solve the institutional and life obstacles that make balancing a family and career difficult; however, having an understanding and empathetic mentor will allow women to tell their personal stories, receive feedback on how best to manage these challenges, and provide a support network to help them feel that they are a valuable and desired part of the profession. Mentors who have personal experience navigating this family–professional balance, even if the perspective is from a man's point of view, are valuable. Sharing stories can "validate and anchor the next generation of physicians and identify policies of change" (32).

It is possible that these issues may become gender-blind, as young physicians born in the X and Y generations continue to demand greater work–family balance (36). Much of this chapter has focused on how women with families achieve this balance, but it is also important to note that single women struggle equally with how to balance a career and personal life and may even feel more isolated than their married counterparts who have support at home. Mentors need to recognize the family and personal pressures that may make a resident or a junior faculty member question their career choice.

❖ Mentoring Women for Leadership

> The hardest times for me were not when people challenged what I said, but when I felt my voice was not heard (37).
>
> —*Carol Gilligan*

As academic medicine confronts challenges ranging from coping with intense financial pressure to concerns about institutional climate and the future of biomedical research, women's natural leadership attributes may be a significant asset as institutions transform to meet the needs of the 21st century. In oft-quoted descriptions of leadership styles, men are described as more likely to view leadership as a series of transactions with subordinates and to use their position in the hierarchy as well as the control of resources to motivate followers (5). Women are more likely to work to transform followers' self-interest into concern for the whole organization. Women more frequently use interpersonal skills to motivate others and encourage participation by sharing power and information that makes people feel important. Leadership styles vary considerably and are not gender-specific, but, as mentioned earlier in this chapter, organizations with a broad repertoire of leaders representing diverse groups increase the likelihood of surviving in a tumultuous and fast-changing environment (5). In addition, evidence suggests that gender diversity enhances corporate performance, including financial results and governance issues (38, 39).

Among women in the corporate world, helping one another succeed has notably improved. At one time, women in corporate America followed all of the entrenched rules to succeed, even being accused of the "queen bee syndrome," where ambitious women strove for the most powerful position in the workplace while excluding all rivals. Today, however, the emergence of women's networks to help the members advance and succeed are much more the norm (40). Because the demand for female talent is strong across industries, not only are women's networks helping women climb the corporate ladder, but companies are redoubling their effort to coach men on mentoring women. *The Wall Street Journal* reported Ernst and Young's efforts to help men become better mentors to women (41). Because 85% of senior leadership are men, women in senior leadership cannot be solely used to mentor other women (41). Some of the concerns men had in serving in a mentoring role to women included providing feedback to women on the need to dress more professionally, fearing that women will cry if given critical feedback, and not knowing how to help women build relationships to get ahead.

In a survey of deans of U.S. and Canadian medical schools, the deans perceived gender inequity based on the lack of appropriate representation of women in senior leadership positions and the persistence of a condescending attitude toward women on the part of some faculty. They felt that time alone is insufficient for women to move into leadership positions and felt the need to improve the work environment for women (42). Among the most important findings in this survey was that female deans reported using a broader range of practices to develop leadership among their faculty and many more strategies specifically to support female faculty. For example, female deans identified the following as being useful to supporting female faculty:

- Nominating women for leadership training outside the institution
- Mentoring female direct reports through regular contact
- Providing coaching by a designated internal coach
- Appointing women to high-level committees and task forces

The ELAM (Executive Leadership in Academic Medicine) program is one external intervention that several studies identify as effective in increasing senior female faculty's leadership knowledge and skills and helping them achieve leadership aspirations in the academic medical center (43). Another resource is "Advancing Your Career in Medicine" from the American Medical Women's Association (44). This tool asks women to articulate their goals, including why they want to be a leader, taking a leadership skills inventory, learning the strategies for leadership success, best practices for women business leaders in the U.S. health care industry, and behaviors for women to avoid. The Association of American Medical Colleges also sponsors 3-day professional development seminars for early and midcareer faculty members to help women build the skills they need to advance their careers (45).

For the tools outlined above to have a sustained impact, leaders within academic health centers need to publicly prioritize and value women's leadership. Senior leaders in academic medicine—both men and women—need to commit time and allocate resources to training junior faculty members on the skills they need to attain leadership positions. This includes charging search committees to actively seek out and consider women for leadership positions.

❖ Mentoring Women in Complicated Situations

Sure there's still discrimination, but women have to figure out a way to get around and beyond it (46).

—*Kay Koplovitz, CEO, Liz Claiborne Inc.*

Even today, women in medicine continue to report that episodes of gender bias, discrimination, and sexual harassment are common (47–50). Female physicians, more frequently than their male colleagues, identify their work environment as hostile (51). Despite multiple reports of discrimination and sexual harassment among medical students, residents, and faculty—both junior and senior—little evidence suggests that the workplace environment for women in medicine is changing (51). To provide a foundation for this discussion, the critical terminology is presented in Box 10-3 (52, 53).

Bias may underlie the appointment of women to the faculty and to leadership positions. In a recent report released by the National Research Council, women represented 45% of the PhDs in biology at research-intensive universities, but only 26% of applicants for tenure-track positions (54). The only strategy that increased the number of women in the applicant pool was having a woman serve as chair of the search committee and a high number of women on the committee. Meanwhile, at the Massachusetts Institute of Technology, following the release of an institutionally sponsored "Study of the Status of Women Scientists at MIT," the dean, Robert Birgeneau, launched a full-scale effort to increase the number of tenure-track female scientists (55). This meant that efforts to identify exceptionally talented women candidates had to move beyond the conventional manner of soliciting candidates and that search committees needed to redouble their efforts to find these talented women (56).

Box 10-3. Definitions of Terms

Bias: a preference, especially one that inhibits impartial judgment

Gender discrimination: unfair treatment of a person based on gender

Sexual harassment: sexual advances, requests for sexual favors, or sexually directed remarks or behavior that is unwelcome and continues despite its rejection.

Hostile work environment: a climate in which unwelcome comments or conduct based on sex, race, or other legally protected characteristics interfere with an employee's work performance or create an intimidating or offensive work environment

Although bias and discrimination may contribute to the leaky pipeline, sexual harassment is a serious issue potentially affecting not only the career advancement of women but also institutional climate and culture. Medical students, residents, and fellows continue to report a high prevalence of sexual harassment (50, 51). Some examples of sexual harassment may be regarded as relatively minor: unwelcome offensive flirtations, suggestive innuendoes or lewd comments, sexually suggestive screen savers, or gestures intending to be humorous. More serious offenses include unwanted contact, including touching, pinching, and propositions or pressure for sexual activity. There may be continued suggestions for social activity outside the workplace after it has been made clear that these invitations are unwelcome.

Hostile work environments are difficult to address in any workplace because they often involve differences in perceptions and, more important, power. A recent *Wall Street Journal* article humorously noted that touching in the workplace (hugging, patting the shoulder) is a sensitive issue that resonates across gender and industry (57). However, given the power differentials inherent in medicine, these minor offenses can take on unwanted meanings. A study published in the *New England Journal of Medicine* found that men in academic medicine tend to have less negative reactions to sexually harassing behavior than women (50). This discrepancy can be explained in part by the power deferential: Actions of people in power are more often perceived as threatening or hostile to those without power. A male faculty member may make an off-hand comment on rounds that he considers to be a meaningless joke. The female medical resident or intern may perceive the comment as demeaning or offensive, in part because of their difference in status. She may be reluctant to voice discomfort for fear of being considered "too sensitive" and that asserting herself will reflect poorly on her performance evaluation or on the attending physician's perception of her as a "team player."

Since men still dominate leadership positions within academic medicine, they may be unaware that comments they make can contribute to a hostile work environment, or they do not find it necessary to change their behavior because they are not challenged to do so. It is worth noting that as women become overrepresented in specific specialties, they must be particularly sensitive to the comments they make to male trainees for exactly the same reason. Indeed, men perceive a greater prevalence of gender discrimination and sexual harassment in pediatrics and obstetrics-gynecology than women do (51).

Mentors should be aware of these power differences so that they can support and validate mentees' concerns and complaints. Individual action by the woman is often the most effective way to stop inappropriate behavior in the workplace with a minimum of conflict when the objective is to stop the behavior, the offender is unaware that the behavior is offensive, or the behavior is at a comparatively low level of activity (58).

Table 10-1 shows a template for saying "no" to unwanted behavior. The language in the table is useful because it provides specific suggestions for what many female medical students and residents feel but may not be able to articulate when they are subjected to inappropriate comments. If the offensive comments are made by faculty who are in the position of evaluating the clinical performance of trainees, the situation must be handled carefully. Rather than confronting the faculty member individually, the mentor may want to advise the mentee to discuss the situation with an ombudsmen, dean, or chief resident. Mentors should be familiar with institutional resources and policies on sexual harassment and hostile work environments so that they can provide mentees with options to consider, including the resources to file formal complaints if necessary.

❖ Case Studies

The studies and benchmarking reports cited previously document that issues of work–family balance, gender discrimination, and sexual harassment continue to raise challenges for women in academic medicine and

Table 10-1. A Template for Saying "No" to Unwanted Behavior

When you... (Describe the behavior you do not like)	I feel... (Describe your feelings)	Because... (Say why the behavior bothers you)	Please... (Request the behavior you want)
• call me "dear" • touch me • joke about my appearance • speak disparagingly about my ethnic group • comment insensitively about religion	• embarrassed • angry • uncomfortable • demeaned	• I want to be taken seriously • I want to be treated as a professional • I want to be respected	• call me by my name • don't tell offensive jokes • don't touch me

Reproduced with permission from: Gender and Diversity: A Program of the Consultative Group on International Agricultural Research. A Victim's Guide for Dealing With Sexual Harassment. www.genderdiversity.cgiar.org/inclusiveworkplace/dignity/harassment/intro.htm.

make this area a more hostile environment for women than men. The fact that these issues remain despite the influx of women into medical schools can be attributed in part to the difficulty that chairs, mentors, and senior faculty members have in openly discussing sensitive topics. It is not easy to discuss topics that delve into personal areas, such as maintaining work and family balance or being subjected to offensive comments and behavior. The following cases show how mentors may help their mentees address these specific concerns:

Case Scenario 1: Hostile Environment

During a monthly mentoring meeting, a female medical student mentions that she is beginning to question why she entered medicine in the first place. She feels disillusioned about the field. When asked why she feels this way, she say that an attending (she does not give a name) makes inappropriate comments about the female members on his team, including comments about their legs and guessing chest sizes.

Useful Strategies
- Acknowledge that the faculty member's comments are inappropriate, unprofessional, and not in keeping with the ideals of either the profession or the institution.
- While the student can be counseled to discuss her discomfort directly with the attending physician, his role as the "evaluator," together with the significant power differential, make this option uncomfortable and generally not viable.
- If these comments are made in the presence of more senior members of the team, including residents, the mentor can suggest that the residents and the student discuss their concerns with someone they trust (perhaps a chief resident) who can approach the faculty member not on behalf of the student but on behalf of the entire team. Depending on the team members' preferences, the discussion may occur during their working assignment or once that assignment has finished. Whatever course is followed, the student and other team members need feedback on the follow-up.
- Let the student (and other team members if applicable) know that institutional policies are in place to protect her. Sexual harassment is characterized as "sexually directed remarks or behavior that is unwelcome and continues despite its rejection." If Dr. X continues with his unwanted comments, the student

has the right to file a formal complaint. Give her a copy of the university's or medical school's harassment policies and encourage her to speak with the appropriate person in the medical school (for example, the dean of students).

- The student may be reluctant to report the physician's actions to the institution for fear of retribution. Many medical schools have anonymous reporting mechanisms in place or an ombudsman available to handle complaints. If appropriate, volunteer to discuss the issue with the medical school dean, the chair of the department, or the appropriate individual. Again, this could be done to protect the student's privacy; for example:

"A student expressed concern that one of our faculty members is making inappropriate comments to women on the team. While she was not willing to give me the name, I wanted to let you know in case you get other complaints. I think it might be time to offer some kind of sexual harassment or diversity training to address these issues."

- Work with the student to learn skills on how to manage such situations should they occur in the future. For example:

"When you make references to my dress, it makes me uncomfortable. I would rather focus on discussing our patient's treatment."

Scenario 2: Handling Pregnancy in the Workplace

An intern approaches you visibly stressed and anxious. She and her husband have just learned that they are expecting their first child. They are very excited about the news, but the pregnancy was not planned and she does not know how to broach the subject with her colleagues or the program director. She realizes that the news will create a shift in resident schedules and could create resentment among house staff. Her larger concern is that time away will negatively affect her career.

Assurances and Information
- Assure the intern that her news—while unexpected—is indeed exciting and will affect her life in many ways that she cannot entirely anticipate. Assure her that she is not the first intern to have gone through this. Often there will be a more senior resident, a chief resident, or a faculty member who was once in a similar situation. These individuals can be enormously comforting and helpful.

- Acknowledge her concern about her career and the impact her news may have on the residency program. Remind her that this is an important time for her to take one step at a time and protect her health and the health of her baby. Notifying the chief resident and program director sooner rather than later is generally a good practice. This way they have ample time to adjust rotation assignments and call schedules. Following is an example of how to broach the conversation:

"I am pregnant and expecting a baby on this date. I would like to discuss the implications for my schedule and for finishing the residency in time to apply for fellowships. I know that I may have to extend my residency, and I want to be sure that I understand the best options. I also know that this has an impact on the other interns and I want to do whatever I can to minimize the disruption to them. I am really excited to be a parent but equally committed to my career."

- Generally the details about maternity leave can be found on the hospital intranet or Web site but are best discussed with a chief resident or program director. In many institutions, the intern may not qualify for paid maternity leave and also does not qualify for the 12 weeks of unpaid leave through the Family and Medical Leave Act because she has not been employed for at least a year.
- In the case of internal medicine, any disruption in training of the 36 total months (allowing 3 for vacation) will require the residency time to extend, as noted in the sample conversation above. These details are on the American Board of Internal Medicine's Web site (www.abim.org).

Scenario 3: Maintaining Work–Family Balance: Part-Time Work

A junior faculty member expresses concerns that she will no longer be able to handle the stresses of full-time work and her family. Her husband is a lawyer who also has an unpredictable work schedule, and they have two young children. Neither the hospital nor her husband's firm provides on-site child care. They have had difficulty finding appropriate child care. She is considering switching to a part-time position and would like to know what the implications of this would be.

Encouraging Reflection, Weighing Pros and Cons
- Encourage the faculty member to go through an inventory of personal and career goals. Faculty find part-time work more beneficial when they have first undergone significant self-reflection about the decision and what its long-term implications may be (59). The application for the SGIM's Horn Scholars Program provides a useful model for questions faculty should consider before deciding to move to part-time work (60). The program is a 3-year career development award intended to foster a career track for physicians that focuses on balancing career, family, and social responsibilities (60) (Table 10-2).

Table 10-2. Examples of Horn Scholarship Application Questions

Work, family, and social responsibilities

Describe your current life roles, including how you have chosen to prioritize them. What are the challenges and rewards in your various roles?

Career goals/aspirations

Describe your professional interests, strengths, limitations, and aspirations

Which of these would you be willing to give up or accomplish over a longer timeframe for you to fulfill *all* of your lifetime goals and commitments?

Current educational role

Describe current involvement in the education of medical students, residents, and fellows and indicate how this role would change for you if you were to spend 20–25 hours per week in career activities

Current clinical responsibilities

Describe the time currently devoted to patient care. Indicate the size and nature of the patient population for which primary direct care is assumed.

Perceived barriers and support for half of a full-time position

Describe how you believe your colleagues, chief, and administrators will facilitate or hinder the success of your future career in a half-time position

Reproduced with permission from Harrison RA, Gregg JL. A time for change: an exploration of attitudes toward part-time work in academia among women internists and their division chiefs. Acad Med. 2009;84:80-6.

- The faculty member should consider the pros and cons of part-time work and the potential implications on her career. The University of Minnesota summarizes the pros and cons of part-time work, based on a survey of faculty members who chose to pursue part-time work and division chiefs who supported their decision from an administrative perspective (9) (Tables 10-3 and 10-4).
- In this example, it is important for the mentor to evaluate whether the career change is part of a long-term career strategy or a short-term response to frustration with her current child care situation. Before deciding to pursue a part-time career, the faculty member may benefit from sharing her child care concerns with other members of the team or administrative staff for recommendations of other child care providers.

❖ Conclusion

As a group, women in medicine represent a talent pool of as-yet unrealized potential. While large in number, they have yet to attain the same levels of seniority and leadership in academic medicine as men. Institutions stand to benefit enormously from capitalizing on the innate skills of their team-

Table 10-3. Positive Consequences of Part-time Work

Career Benefits	Personal Benefits
More research time	Greater quantity and quality of family time
Enabled worker to focus on career goals	Ability to participate in children's activities, parent groups
Worker as role model to others	Increased time for school and community involvement
Transition from clinician-educator to clinician-investigator	Time for journaling/creative writing
Ability to pursue new scholarship	Time for spirituality
Ability to pursue advanced degree	Time for exercise and self-care

Reproduced with permission from Harrison RA, Gregg JL. A time for change: an exploration of attitudes toward part-time work in academia among women internists and their division chiefs. Acad Med. 2009;84:80-6.

Table 10-4. Negative Consequences of Part-time Work

Faculty Participants	Division Chief View
Less pay and loss of benefits	Lower pay
More work than full-time equivalents	Fewer or no benefits and health insurance
Slow to promotion/overlooked for career opportunities	Less protected time per full-time equivalent
Less desirable work	Potential to be viewed as less committed worker
Institutional culture not supporting part-time/lack of leadership support	
Lack of support from colleagues	Not fully integrated into the division
Being marginalized within the division	

Reproduced with permission from Harrison RA, Gregg JL. A time for change: an exploration of attitudes toward part-time work in academia among women internists and their division chiefs. Acad Med. 2009;84:80-6.

based approaches to work and a style of building relationships rather than hierarchies. One of the ways that departments of medicine and academic medical centers can help improve both the climate and the career trajectories for their female faculty is to develop and support high-quality, sustainable mentoring programs (61–63). The recipients of the Association of American Medical College's Women in Medicine Leadership Development Award are an outstanding sample of successful faculty development programs (64). Some of the features these programs have in common include having a dedicated funding stream and staff support from the dean's office. The programs all also provide a regularly scheduled seminar or lunch series and encourage the advancement of women through mentorship and leadership awards.

Mentoring women in academic medicine calls for general guidance in scholarship, career paths (including promotion and tenure), and work–family balance, as well as a willingness on the part of mentors and institutions to confront issues ranging from gender bias to overt harassment. Mentors should feel empowered to work within the system to shape and revise policies and always press for a more favorable institutional climate for women. To the extent that the profession is willing to take on this challenge, academic medical centers, science, patients, and society at large all stand to benefit.

I want ... to be at peace with myself. I want a singleness of eye, a purity of intention, a central core to my life that will enable me to carry out these obligations and activities as well as I can. I want, in fact ... to live 'in grace' as much of the time as possible (30).

—Anne Morrow Lindbergh

Acknowledgments: The authors would like to thank Dana Levinson, MPH for her assistance editing this article and Drs. Vineet Arora, Halina Brukner, and Deborah Burnet for their guidance.

REFERENCES

1. **Quindlen A.** Mount Holyoke College. Anna Quindlen's commencement speech. Mount Holyoke College. Published May 23, 1999. Accessed at: http://mtholyoke.edu/offices/comm/oped/Quindlen.shtml.
2. **Association of American Medical Colleges.** Women in US Academic Medicine Statistics and Benchmarking Report, 2007-2008. Washington, DC: Association of American Medical Colleges. Accessed at www.aamc.org/members/gwims/statistics/stats08/start.htm.
3. AMA Masterfile. Chicago: American Medical Association; January 2008.
4. **Lowenstein SR, Fernandez G, Crane LA.** Medical school faculty discontent: prevalence and predictors of intent to leave academic careers. BMC Med Educ. 2007;7:37.
5. **Eagly A, Carli L.** Women and the labyrinth of leadership. Harvard Business Review. 2007;September:63-71.
6. **Rosener JB.** Ways Women Lead. Harvard Business Review. 1990;68:119-25.
7. **Quindlen A.** A Short Guide to a Happy Life. New York: Random House; 2000.
8. **Merriam SB, Clark MC.** Lifelines: Patterns of Work, Love, and Learning in Adulthood. San Francisco: Jossey-Bass; 1991.
9. **Aagaard EM, Hauer KE.** A cross-sectional descriptive study of mentoring relationships formed by medical students. J Gen Intern Med. 2003;18:298-302.
10. **Ramanan RA, Taylor WC, Davis RB, Phillips RS.** Mentoring matters. Mentoring and career preparation in internal medicine residency training. J Gen Intern Med. 2006; 21:340-5.
11. **Babaria P, Abedin S, Nunez-Smith M.** The effect of gender on the clinical clerkship experiences of female medical students: results from a qualitative study. Acad Med. 2009;84:859-66.
12. **Jagsi R, Tarbell NJ, Weinstein DF.** Becoming a doctor, starting a family—leaves of absence from graduate medical education. N Engl J Med. 2007;357:1889-91.
13. **Yedidia MJ, Bickel J.** Why aren't there more women leaders in academic medicine? The views of clinical department chairs. Acad Med. 2001;76:453-65.
14. **Fried LP, Francomano CA, MacDonald SM, Wagner EM, Stokes EJ, Carbone KM, et al.** Career development for women in academic medicine: Multiple interventions in a department of medicine. JAMA. 1996;276:898-905.
15. **Wasserstein AG, Quistberg DA, Shea JA.** Mentoring at the University of Pennsylvania: results of a faculty survey. J Gen Intern Med. 2007;22:210-4.
16. **Chew LD, Watanabe JM, Buchwald D, Lessler DS.** Junior faculty's perspectives on mentoring. Acad Med. 2003;78:652.

17. **Marks MB.** Academic careers in medical education: perceptions of the effects of a faculty development program. Acad Med. 1999;74:S72-4.
18. **Society of General Internal Medicine.** Women's Caucus Interest Group. Accessed at www.sgim.org/index.cfm?pageId=592.
19. **Women in Nephrology.** Accessed at www.womeninnephrology.org/aboutus.htm.
20. Women's mentoring program offers networking and career guidance. American Thoracic Society News. 2002; 28.
21. **Saxon LA, Rao AK, Klarich KW.** Shortage of female cardiologists: exploring the issues. Mayo Clin Proc. 2008;83:1022-5.
22. **Arlow FL, Raymond PL, Karlstadt RG, Croitoru R, Rybicki BA, Sastri SV.** Gastroenterology training and career choices: a prospective longitudinal study of the impact of gender and of managed care. Am J Gastroenterol. 2002;97:459-69.
23. **Poppas A, Cummings J, Dorbala S, Douglas PS, Foster E, Limacher MC.** Survey results: a decade of change in professional life in cardiology: a 2008 report of the ACC women in cardiology council. J Am Coll Cardiol. 2008;52:2215-26.
24. **Harvard Business Essentials.** Women and minorities: special mentoring challenges. In: Coaching and Mentoring: How to Develop Top Talent and Achieve Stronger Performance. Boston: Harvard Business School Pr; 2006.
25. **Leboy P.** Fixing the leaky pipeline: Why aren't there many women in the top spots in academia? The Scientist. Accessed at www.thescientist.com/article/print/54076.
26. **Ledin A, Bornmann L, Gannon F, Wallon G.** A persistent problem. Traditional gender roles hold back female scientists. EMBO Rep. 2007;8:982-7.
27. **Committee on Maximizing the Potential of Women in Academic Science and Engineering, Committee on Science, Engineering and Public Policy.** Beyond Bias and Barriers: Fulfilling the Potential of Women in Academic Science and Engineering. Washington, DC: National Academies P; 2007.
28. **Sackett DL.** On the determinants of academic success as a clinician-scientist. Clin Invest Med. 2001;24:94-100.
29. **Lindberg AM.** Gifts from the Sea. New York: Pantheon; 1955.
30. **Andrews NC.** Climbing through medicine's glass ceiling. N Engl J Med. 2007;357:1887-9.
31. **Harrison R.** Evolving trends in balancing work and family for future academic physicians: a role for personal stories. Med Teach. 2008;30:316-8.
32. **Klass P.** So where's my medal? N Engl J Med. 2005;353:2107-9.
33. **Wilson R.** Is having more than 2 children an unspoken taboo? Chronicle of Higher Education. July 10, 2009. Accessed at http://chronicle.com/article/Is-Having-More-Than-2-Child/47015/.
34. **Association of American Medical Colleges.** The long-term retention and attribution of U.S. medical school faculty. Analysis in Brief. 2008;8:1-2.
35. **Shollen SL, Bland CJ, Finstad DA, Taylor AL.** Organizational climate and family life: how these factors affect the status of women faculty at one medical school. Acad Med. 2009;84:87-94.
36. **Bickel J, Brown AJ.** Generation X: implications for faculty recruitment and development in academic health centers. Acad Med. 2005;80:205-10.
37. **Wylie MS.** The untold story: an interview with Carol Gilligan. Psychotherapy Networker – Washington. 2002; Nov/Dec.
38. The Bottom Line: Connecting Corporate Performance and Gender Diversity. New York: Catalyst; 2004.

39. **Kramer V, Konrad A, Erkut S.** Critical mass on corporate boards: why three or more women enhance governance: Executive Summary. Wellesley Center for Women. Accessed at www.wcwonline.org/content/view/585/208.

40. **Hymowitz C.** Women get better at forming networks to help their climb. Wall Street Journal. November 19, 2007.

41. **Hymowitz C.** Coaching men on mentoring women is Ernst & Young partner's mission. Wall Street Journal. June 14, 2007. Accessed at http://online.wsj.com/article/SB118167178575132768.html.

42. **Dannels S, McLaughlin J, Gleason KA, McDade SA, Richman R, Morahan PS.** Medical school deans' perceptions of organizational climate: useful indicators for advancement of women faculty and evaluation of a leadership program's impact. Acad Med. 2009; 84:67-79.

43. **Dannels SA, Yamagata H, McDade SA, Chuang YC, Gleason KA, McLaughlin JM, et al.** Evaluating a leadership program: a comparative, longitudinal study to assess the impact of the Executive Leadership in Academic Medicine (ELAM) Program for Women. Acad Med. 2008;83:488-95.

44. **American Medical Women's Association.** AMWA Online CME Series: Advancing your career in medicine: women as medical leaders. Accessed at www.amwa-doc.org.

45. **Association of American Medical Colleges.** Women in Medicine Professional Development Seminars. Washington, DC: Association of American Medical Colleges.

46. **Koplovitz K.** Bold Women, Big Ideas: Learning to Play the High-Risk Entrepreneurial Game. New York: PublicAffairs; 2002.

47. **Witte FM, Stratton TD, Nora LM.** Stories from the field: students' descriptions of gender discrimination and sexual harassment during medical school. Acad Med. 2006; 81:648-54.

48. **Carr PL, Ash AS, Friedman RH, Szalacha L, Barnett RC, Palepu A, et al.** Faculty perceptions of gender discrimination and sexual harassment in academic medicine. Ann Intern Med. 2000;132:889-96.

49. **Komaromy M, Bindman AB, Haber RJ, Sande MA.** Sexual harassment in medical training. N Engl J Med. 1993;328:322-6.

50. **Nora LM, McLaughlin MA, Fosson SE, Stratton TD, Murphy-Spencer A, Fincher RM, et al.** Gender discrimination and sexual harassment in medical education: perspectives gained by a 14-school study. Acad Med. 2002;77:1226-34.

51. **Schiffman M, Frank E.** Harassment of women physicians. J Am Med Womens Assoc. 1995;50:207-11.

52. **Merriam-Webster Online.** Accessed at www.merriam-webster.com.

53. **University of Chicago.** Unlawful harassment: a guide for faculty, staff, and students 2008-2009. Accessed at http://csl.uchicago.edu/pdfs/unlawfulharassment08.pdf.

54. **Committee on Gender Differences in the Careers of Science, Engineering, and Mathematics Faculty; Committee on Women in Science, Engineering, and Medicine; National Research Council.** Gender Differences at Critical Transitions in the Careers of Science, Engineering, and Mathematics Faculty. Washington, DC: National Academies Pr; 2009.

55. **Massachusetts Institute of Technology Committee on Women Faculty.** A study on the status of women faculty in science at MIT. The MIT Faculty Newsletter. 1999;11.

56. **Lawler A.** Tenured women battle to make it less lonely at the top. Science. 1999;286: 1272-78.

57. **Bernstein E.** Touching me, touching you—at work. Wall Street Journal. July 9, 2009:D6.

58. Gender and Diversity: A Program of the Consultative Group on International Agricultural Research. A victim's guide for dealing with sexual harassment. Gender and Diversity. Accessed at www.genderdiversity.cgiar.org/inclusiveworkplace/dignity/harassment/intro.htm.

59. **Harrison RA, Gregg JL.** A time for change: an exploration of attitudes toward part-time work in academia among women internists and their division chiefs. Acad Med. 2009; 84:80-6.

60. **Society of General Internal Medicine.** Mary O'Flaherty Horn scholars in general internal medicine. Accessed at www.sgim.org/index.cfm?pageId=670.

61. **Georgetown University School of Medicine.** Georgetown Women in Medicine. Accessed at http://gwim.georgetown.edu/support.htm.

62. **Washington University School of Medicine.** Academic Women's Network. Accessed at http://awn.wustl.edu.

63. **University of Pennsylvania School of Medicine.** Focus on Health & Leadership for Women. Accessed at www.med.upenn.edu/focus.

64. **Association of American Medical Colleges.** Women in Leadership Development Award. Accessed at www.aamc.org/members/gwims/award.htm

65. **Linzer M, Warde C, Volberding PA, Kerr E, O'Hara J.** ASP Contributes to new NIH policy on part-time careers. Academic Internal Medicine Insight. 2009;7:2.

11

Mentoring Underrepresented Minority Students, Residents, and Faculty: Insights, Challenges, and Strategies

Clarence H. Braddock III, MD, MPH, FACP
Ian L. Tong, MD

In the late 1960s and early 1970s, the civil rights movement, affirmative action programs, and national initiatives led to significant progress in bringing more students from minority backgrounds into medicine. Medical school enrollment of underrepresented-in-medicine (URM) minority students as a percentage of all entrants more than tripled: from 3% in 1968 to 10% in 1974 (1). Despite this initially impressive gain, efforts to increase this percentage further so that the physician workforce would reflect the racial and ethnic diversity of the U.S. population have stalled.

The Association of American Medical Colleges (AAMC) defines "underrepresented in medicine" to include "those racial and ethnic populations that are underrepresented in the medical profession relative to their numbers in the general population." This definition is an important a departure from the traditional designation of blacks, Mexican-Americans, Native Americans (that is, American Indians, Alaska Natives, and Native Hawaiians), and mainland Puerto Ricans as representing the full spectrum of those who would be termed "URM." It has refocused the lens to a broader and more dynamic definition of diversity that would evolve with changing demographics (2). This chapter uses the term "URM" in the same way as the AAMC definition.

Recent data underscore how few URM students are matriculating in medical schools in the United States. As recently as 2008, the per-

KEY POINTS

- URM students and trainees continue to face unique challenges that call for unique approaches to mentorship.
- Institutions need to adopt proactive practices to develop a mentorship infrastructure that can address the needs of URM trainees.
- Recruitment and retention of URM faculty are critical elements to the success of mentorship to URM trainees, even if these faculty are not the primary mentors.
- Numerous national resources can help programs establish or expand their URM mentorship activities.
- Effective mentorship with URM trainees begins with understanding some unique aspects of their lived experience, finding formal and informal ways to demonstrate specific awareness to and empathy for those stressors, and recognizing that URM mentorship exists in the larger milieu of academic institutions whose very lack of diversity can hamper these efforts.
- A strong commitment to work on diversity and a celebration thereof can have a huge impact on the culture of the institution. It can effectively cultivate a new legacy of embracing diversity.
- Institutions can improve the success of URM trainees through the appointment of diversity managers, task forces, and mentoring programs.

centage of black and Latino medical school graduates remains only 14% (Figure 11-1). This is in contrast to the U.S. general population, in which black and Latino persons account for over 25%. Among academic medicine faculty, the results of efforts over the past 30 years are even more disappointing, with those same minority groups accounting for only up to 7% of the total (1) (Figure 11-2). Many commentators have highlighted the vicious cycle that this has created: Without minority role models and mentors, few URM medical students enter academic medicine; and with so few URM students entering academic careers, the percentage of URM faculty will remain disappointingly stagnant.

These trends indicate the significant challenge for recruiting and retaining URM students in medicine. This challenge underscores the need to provide support and mentorship to URM students, residents, and faculty.

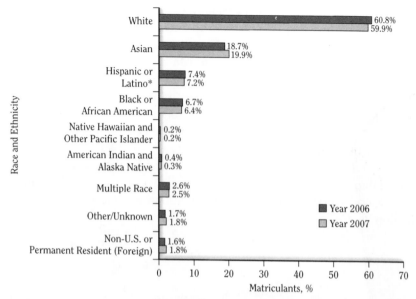

Figure 11-1 Percentage of U.S. medical school matriculants by race and ethnicity, 2006–2007. Note: Categories are non-Hispanic, with the exception of Hispanics and foreign/unknown citizenship. Since 2002, individuals have the option of reporting both their race and ethnicity alone or in combination with some other race or ethnicity. In this figure, numbers are reported for race alone; those that reported more than one race are included under Multiple Race. *Includes Cuban, Mexican American, Puerto Rican, Other Hispanic, and Multiple Hispanic. ©2008 Association of American Medical Colleges. All rights reserved. Reproduced with permission.

This chapter outlines some unique challenges of mentorship, outlines a framework for mentorship that can support growth of URM students and residents and ensure success of URM faculty, and includes perspectives from the literature as well as the authors' personal observations over many years of working with URM students and residents.

❖ Unique Challenges Faced by URM Students and Residents

All students and faculty can benefit from the personal support and guidance of a mentor. Mentorship provides guidance through the socialization process in the profession; advice for career choices, such as specialty and type of practice; and a caring and nurturing personal relationship. Many of the mentorship needs of URM students and residents are thus similar to the general need for mentorship, as are the challenges of providing a robust system that guarantees excellent mentorship for all trainees. In corporate America, mentorship has been shown to outperform other programmatic efforts to end workplace inequality (3). Figure 11-3 shows Equal Employment Opportunity Commission data collected by Dobbin and colleagues on 829 private companies with 100 employees over a 31-year period. Their study sought to specifically measure the effect of different types of diversity programs. They found that mentorship programs have the most significant and far-reaching impact. Beyond the general positive effects of strong mentorship for all trainees, there are unique issues of importance to URM trainees and specific challenges to meeting these needs through mentorship. Similarly, the needs of and challenges faced by URM trainees have evolved over generations, creating additional complexity for providing mentorship (4).

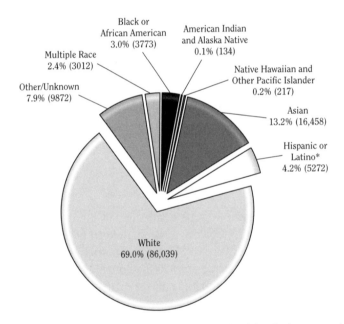

Figure 11-2 Percentage and number of U.S. medical school faculty by race and ethnicity, 2007. The race and ethnicity categories in this figure reflect how the data have been collected since 2002. Individuals have the option of reporting both their race and ethnicity alone or in combination with some other race or ethnicity. In this figure, numbers are reported for race alone; those that reported more than one race and ethnicity are included under Multiple Race. *Includes Mexican American, Puerto Rican, Cuban, Other Hispanic or Latino, and Multiple Hispanic. ©2008 Association of American Medical Colleges. All rights reserved. Reproduced with permission.

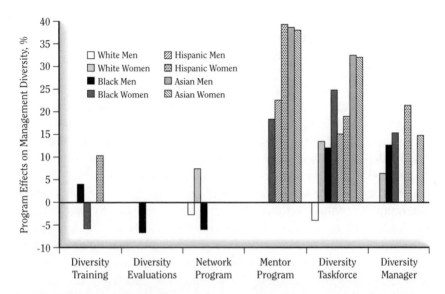

Figure 11-3 Percentage change in the proportion of managers. Reproduced with permission from University of California Press. Dobbin F, Kalev A, Kelly E. Diversity management in corporate America. Contexts American Sociological Association. 2007;4:21-27.

Generational Changes in Issues for URM Trainees

In the early days of affirmative action, still in the shadow of "separate but equal" education, URM students often entered medical school not having received the same level of preparation (1). Beyond the obvious comparisons of public education versus private, premedical preparation, the overall academic credentials for these minority students often presaged the difficulty that some would have navigating the challenging preclerkship curriculum in medical school. As a result, medical school URM mentorship focused on academic support and tutoring. In addition, the very existence of formal affirmative action programs created an occasionally hostile learning environment for these students—some fellow students openly labeled them as "affirmative action" students. Furthermore, hospital segregation was still present in the mid-1960s and was still a strong memory in the 1970s. As a result, it was very common for minority residents to encounter prejudice from patients, hospital staff, and faculty (1).

In more recent years, the challenges faced by URM students and residents have evolved. With the growth of affluence in minority communities, many more URM students and residents come from families of means, many more have parents who are themselves professionals, and far more have therefore enjoyed the same rigorous academic preparation as their majority colleagues. Similarly, the "affirmative action" taunts and overt expressions of racism from patients and health professionals of yesteryear are less common for contemporary URM students and residents (5).

Although to the outside observer this evolution might be assumed to reduce or eliminate the tension of race in contemporary medical education, bias and prejudice against contemporary URM students are now paradoxically just as strong, and perhaps more insidious. These attitudes continue to exist but may just be more subtly conveyed. Some writers have drawn parallels with the physical comparison between severe acute pain and a chronic dull ache; the latter may be less severe, but its ongoing nature makes the cumulative impact often unbearable (6).

With the need to address insufficient preparation for the rigors of medical training and the specter of affirmative action receding to issues of lesser significance to current URM students and residents, two domains of their experience have taken on more importance: 1) obtaining psychosocial support for the lived experience of being a minority in medicine and 2) gaining insights into navigating the world inside academic medicine. The following section describes concerns frequently expressed and problems frequently encountered by URM students and residents. These findings are drawn from the authors' collective experiences, augmented by data from semi-structured interviews with URM students and residents.

Conducted over a 2-year period, these focus groups were opportunities for internal medicine residents and medical students to discuss issues concerning the experiences of URM students and residents related to race, gender, sexual orientation, and ethnicity. These focus groups were part of an initiative to enhance URM recruitment and retention. The authors used the results of these focus groups, and Association of Professors of Medicine Diversity Task Force recommendations (7), to collaborate with program directors to create a noon conference series titled "Diversity in Medicine"; established a URM recruitment subcommittee; and trained committee members to participate in URM recruitment (Tong I, Braddock, C. Focus group

Table 11-1. Recruitment of Underrepresented-in-Medicine Residents to the Stanford Internal Medicine Residency Program

Year	Invited to Interview, n	Interviewed, n	Matched, n (%)
2005	21	17	1 (2.6)
2006	31	28	1 (2.5)
2007	54	32	3 (7.5)
2008	52	34	8 (16)
2009	67	35	8 (16)

Data obtained from Stanford Internal Medicine Residency Program.

discussions. Unpublished data; 2005–2007). The authors also established a data collection system to track URM applicants and program performance in the area of recruitment. Table 11-1 shows some results of these efforts.

The explanations for the increase in URM matriculants into this residency program are multifactorial and require further study. However, the creation of focus groups and provision of identifiable mentors to discuss issues of diversity within the program were probably major factors. Recruiting URM trainees in the preceding example may be a downstream result or even side effect of peer-to-peer mentoring among faculty. However, peer-to-peer mentoring at the faculty level cannot directly address the challenges facing students and residents.

Common Concerns of URM Students and Residents

The focus group data were analyzed for dominant themes among URM students and residents. These themes are presented as a framework for understanding the unique issues in this cohort.

Fitting in

Learning the rules of social engagement in a new environment can be especially challenging for URM students. These rules are not commonly "written down" anywhere, but rather are communicated informally through networks of close social connection. These networks often revolve around co-membership or shared lineage or stem from natural bonds that form between people—initially strangers—who perceive that they share some common characteristic. In describing Implicit Association Tests in his book *Blink*, Malcolm Gladwell lays out the unconscious attitudes that will at least partially inform how "you behave in the presence of a black person" (8). URM trainees often can identify interactions where they may have been victims of implicit association.

An inappropriate but not uncommon scenario on a medical service revolves around the assignment of "scut" work to a URM student. Most students in this scenario, non-URM and URM alike, begin to feel singled out as the "low man on the totem pole." However, URM students, if racially, culturally, or ethnically disparate from their supervising physicians, must contend with the additional layer of race as the motivation for being singled out. Research in interpersonal communication has revealed that an interaction between two racially similar strangers is frequently more extensive than between racially discordant strangers. For example, studies of doctor–patient communication have shown that conversations between white physicians and black patients are more likely to be dominated by biomedical subject matter, whereas racially concordant visits show a more balanced conversation, including social interactions (9). This subconscious barrier to open sharing of informal "rules of the game" can lead URM learners to miss some key information, leaving them frustrated as they attempt to navigate their new world. Further, with fewer racially concordant faculty members and thinner social networks in academic medical centers, fewer opportunities for spontaneous "reaching out" based on shared identity are available to URM students.

Social Isolation and Lack of a Support Network

In an episode of the television show "Hill Street Blues," an African-American police precinct captain takes one of his white subordinates to a restaurant where almost all the patrons are black. As they walk through the door, the din of conversation lessens, further heightening the tension that the white officer is already feeling. The captain asks the officer, "What's wrong?" The officer murmurs, "You must be kidding. I'm sure you realize how uncomfortable I feel—I'm the only white person here!" The captain replies, "Welcome to how I feel every day."

Because there are often so few other URM students and residents (or faculty) around them, these individuals are often struggling with a debilitating feeling of visibility: "Will a patient make a comment?" "Is that person looking at me because I look different?" This theme has been explored in literature, most notably in Ralph Ellison's *Invisible Man* (10) and Ellis Cose's *Rage of a Privileged Class* (11). Lack of mentors, especially in high-ranking medical schools and residencies, leaves students of color feeling as if they are on the outside. They are looking for people who they feel have shared their experience or who have some interest in connecting to them and their experience. Several recent studies have shown that URM students look for mentors of all types (7). These mentors do not have to be people of color, but must have shown students that they are interested in guiding URM students specifically. Students and residents know that not all people of color are a perfect match. The URM student finds himself or herself with fewer choices and cannot decode which non-URM faculty would be open to mentoring him or her.

The most easily identified group of potential mentors is the few URM faculty members in their institution. However, the targeted faculty members are not always up to the task, and students suspect this. Trainees are aware of the many demands on URM faculty and witness how they often work harder for less pay, less respect, and less promotion. A recent study measuring the effects of race and gender on physician compensation showed that black, Asian, and Latino female doctors earned on average approximately 25% less than their white male counterparts (Figure 11-4) (12).

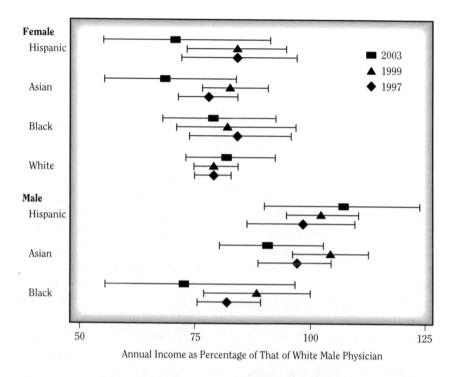

Figure 11-4 Adjusted incomes for internal medicine physicians, by sex and race. Symbols represent point estimates, and error bars represent 95% confidence intervals.

Being a Stranger

Team dynamics during internship and third-year clerkships pose a unique challenge for the URM team member. From an attending to a third-year clerkship student, it is often the interaction of team members that determines whether a tough month can be considered a success or a failure. Therein lies the critical importance of interpersonal skills for the URM student, intern, or resident. Their success is directly related to their ability to assimilate into the culture in which they are immersed.

Depending on the level of cultural competence among non-URM team members, the URM intern or student must put the team "at ease." He or she does this by penetrating the team culture with a balance of humor, academic excellence, hard work, and cultural understanding that often must exceed that of the other team members. Rudyard Kipling's poem "If" summarizes this well: "and yet don't look too good or sound too wise" (13). It is true that most URM students, interns, and residents have already mastered this challenge to a measurable degree—otherwise they would not have gotten this far. The active work that the URM trainee must do is above and beyond what it takes to merely perform at a level commensurate with the goals and expectations set forth for them.

There are other challenges, however, that border on cultural, may touch on socioeconomic background, or could simply bubble up from the same tradition of hatred and fear that has long haunted America's national psyche. Racism still exists, and there is little to no protection for the minority team member. Should the Latino student always be the default team interpreter for Spanish-speaking patients? What if he or she does not speak Spanish? Does the non-URM remainder of the team then question his or her minority status? How should a student respond if the team says, "Maybe you can talk to this family since you're black [as they are]?" Jerome Groopman's book *How Doctors Think* and his discussion of how doctors approach the process of framing patients show an interesting parallel process (14). Do doctors frame students and categorize them just as they do patients?

Another dimension of self-doubt, particularly for mixed-race URM students, is the double-edged sword of figuring out their own identity. The black student who is told by classmates, "You're not really black; you don't talk like a black person," is both offended and confused. What determines identity? Is it skin color? A manner of speaking? A profession?

Self-Doubt
Despite their success, URM students, interns, and residents question their skills and talents, and the acceptance of their colleagues. Self-doubt and feelings of inadequacy are not unique to the URM physician. However, URM students and residents live with the worry that others around them will make comparisons with the unflattering stereotypes of their racial or ethnic identity rather than seeing a person. Too often this concern affects URM trainee performance through a phenomenon known as "stereotype threat," introduced and elegantly described in the research of Claude Steele and Joshua Aronson at Stanford University (15). Their study showed that black students may score lower on standardized tests if they feel the test measures their intellectual ability. It is in this context that URM trainees in the medical field face the unforgiving rigor of the MCAT (Medical College Admissions Test); USMLE (U.S. Medical Licensing Examination) steps I, II, and III; and board certification examinations to further their training. URM students and residents worry that non-URM faculty may also assume that URM somehow equals compromised quality. For some this is a powerful motivator; for others it can undermine confidence.

Walking on Water

Even when a URM student or resident has found a URM faculty to work with, he or she has not necessarily found a mentor. URM students, interns, and residents often subconsciously seek out faculty who are approachable and maybe even vulnerable. URM students have a hard time connecting to faculty who are extremely successful and gifted if they believe that faculty member is assessing them (16). The doubt mentioned above often tells URM trainees that they cannot achieve the same level of success as outstanding URM faculty. They think such faculty "walk on water" or are super-human. Conversely, trainees may fail to bond interpersonally with powerful high-level faculty and feel abused when placed in hierarchical mentoring relationships (17).

❖ Strategies for Mentoring URM Students and Residents

There is no magic formula for mentoring URM students. The challenges they face are unique, yet their personal mentoring needs are similar to those of any students or residents. At the same time, strategies can ease barriers to finding effective mentors, and that can mitigate the forces that hinder the creation of a nurturing learning environment.

Exploring the Person Within

URM medical students probably have more similarities with their majority classmates than differences. Rather than a reliance on assumptions about the URM student's or resident's life experience, an explicit exploration can be particularly meaningful in this context. One approach can be found in the basic principles described by Daniel Pink, author of *A Whole New Mind* (18).

- *Empathy:* URM students will benefit from the mentor's effort and interest in their experiences. Asking questions that inform knowledge of the students' specific challenges and triumphs will allow the students to convey their feelings and emotions. Students will know that the mentor has an interest in their experiences and values these experiences as unique examples of their skills and talents. Many URM medical students will provide a narrative that reveals a journey best described as "distance traveled." Some will be the family's first college graduate, others have overcome academic challenges, and most have dealt with some form of discrimination. Each of these challenges provides an opportunity for the mentor to learn about the student in a celebration of his or her success.

- *Humor:* Mentors often display a cloak of professionalism for students. In early medical school education, this cloak models for students the behaviors that define the physician identity (see chapter 1 of this book). However, URM students will discredit physicians who cannot laugh at themselves. As these students mature and take on clinical responsibilities, they welcome and value the opportunity to remove their own cloaks: to laugh, to acknowledge vulnerability, and to connect with their mentors. Mentors will gain students' respect if they model not only credibility but also authenticity.

- *Meaning:* Students have embarked on a search for meaning. Medicine provides URM students with a path to find meaning in what they do every day, but it does not always link what they do to who they are. Without diminishing the inherent importance in what students do, it is who they are that differentiates them from their majority counterparts. It is important for mentors to recognize that who URM students are is just as important as what they do. URM students often see themselves as representatives of their families, their communities, and the vast and often unrealized potential of other people just like them. The trajectory of their success establishes them as leaders and role models for their peers. Part of the responsibility of mentors is to maintain awareness of this very important role and responsibility filled by their URM students. Mentors must accept a portion of this responsibility as they guide, educate, and secure the success of their minority students.

Increasing Diversity Among Faculty and Medical School Leaders

Any discussion of mentoring for URM students and residents should make the connection between the lived experience of these trainees and the need to increase diversity among faculty in academic medical centers. Nationally, only 3% of medical school faculty members are African-American (2). An even smaller percentage of URM faculty are in positions of leadership, such as deans or department chairs. Until medical school faculty and academic medical leaders reflect the diversity of the United States, the profession will struggle with all the challenges outlined above.

When faced with the shame of having no black head coaches, the National Football League developed a policy that any team with a head coaching vacancy had to interview at least one black candidate, the so-called "Rooney Rule" (19). In a few short years, the result has been that a black head coach in the NFL is no longer rare. There is now a network of peer support among these coaches, such that young football coaches can more easily aspire to this career pinnacle. Can one imagine such a rule in a medical school? For any open chair, the search committee would have to interview at least one minority candidate (and one female candidate [since the same glass ceiling persists for women in medicine]). The point here is that the success of mentoring of URM students and residents will always be limited by the embarrassingly few minority role models they see, and their experience will remain stressful so long as they cannot look around and see others with whom they can identify. Increasing diversity in academic medicine is a critical precondition to creating the climate in which mentorship can have its maximum effect.

Fostering Social Networks

Creating a nurturing environment for URM students and residents often requires more specific attention to creation of social networks. As trainees with shared experiences get caught up in running from one task to another and from one rotation to another, the sense of social isolation can increase. For the reasons discussed earlier, many URM students are not (or at least do not feel) embraced by the rest of their clinical team. Institutions should consider supporting these trainees as they seek to create social networks. Such networks can take many shapes, but may include minority discussion groups, meet-the-professor sessions, or even social events. The intent is not to force URM trainees to participate, nor to assume that these trainees only want to participate in such activities; rather, it is for leaders and institutions to be aware and supportive of requests from trainees for this kind of social networking.

This same phenomenon often arises in the context of recruitment of URM student and residents into training programs. Many URM students, particularly those who come from geographic areas with demographic profiles that have minimized their sense of social isolation, are hesitant to come to a new place if they cannot see evidence of support for or the existence of social networks. For example, Stanford University found that minority residency applicants often welcomed a chance to attend a dinner with their future minority peers and mentors, in part because it helps them to imagine a future in which they are supported and free from isolation. With a modest investment from a department chair, it was possible to hold several of these dinners during residency recruitment. Stanford University has seen a remarkable increase in interest among minority applicants in its programs (see Table 11-1).

Shared Journeys

Another strategy for fostering a nurturing environment for URM students and residents is to develop sessions in which they can hear narratives of the life journey of faculty and senior peers, or even of one another. As noted earlier, many URM students have difficulty identifying the source for their feelings of inadequacy: "Is it because I am black, or am I just not good enough?" Hearing narratives of how others with whom they can identify discuss similar feelings and describe how they were able to overcome such feelings can be incredibly empowering for URM trainees.

Such sessions do not have to be only with URM participants; there are many faculty who have faced obstacles created by having a single parent, being poor, being disabled, and the like. What people share is the experience of feeling different, and how to reconceptualize that feeling into a strength, and source of pride, rather than as a constant weight and reminder of their feelings of inadequacy.

❖ Developing a URM Mentorship Program

To develop a systematic approach to providing mentorship to URM students and residents, the following initial steps are recommended (Box 11-1).

Conduct Interviews or Focus Groups With URM Faculty and Trainees

There is a twofold benefit to gathering these kind of qualitative data. First, one can begin to gain insight into the unique institutional barriers and negative forces of URM trainees' experience, and understand the resources that may exist but are off the radar screen of official institutional leader-

---

Box 11-1. Five Key Steps to Establishing a Minority Mentorship Program

1. Initiate focus groups of faculty and trainees
2. Use national (AAMC) and regional organizational resources
3. Develop strategic plan for minority faculty recruitment
4. Recruit, support, and encourage faculty interested in URM recruitment
5. Adopt best practices of successful departments within institution and regionally

Table 11-2. National Societies and Student Groups

Organization	Web Address
American Association of American Medical Colleges	www.aamc.org
American Medical Students Association	www.amsa.org
American Medical Women's Association	www.amwa-doc.org
Gay and Lesbian Medical Association	www.glma.org
Latino Medical Student Association	http://lmsa.net
National Medical Association	www.nmanet.org
U.S. Department of Veterans Affairs Office of Diversity and Inclusion	www.diversity.hr.va.gov
Student National Medical Association	www.snma.org

ship. Second, the participants in this qualitative inquiry themselves will be grateful for the interest in their lived experience.

Reach Out to National or Regional Organizations With Experience in Minority Affairs

Organizations such as the AAMC have online data, reports, and monographs that can help inform and educate faculty leaders about issues important to minorities in medicine. Many specialty societies similarly have initiatives that can be a great resource for ideas and specific interventions. The Student National Medical Association (SNMA) and Latino Medical Student Association (LMSA) are national student groups that have tremendous networks of premed and medical student leaders who can be great sources of ideas. They also can provide venues to help enhance recruitment of underrepresented minorities (Table 11-2).

Develop an Institutional Strategy to Increase Faculty Diversity

As noted earlier, faculty diversity can help or hinder efforts to provide mentorship to URM students. If qualitative study reveals that lack of diversity is a major theme, arising often enough in focus groups or other inquiry to suggest a significant problem, then the institution should begin a specific initiative to increase recruitment and retention of minority faculty. While the specific best practices in this area are beyond the scope of this chapter, they include inclusion of minority members to search committees, requiring search committees to interview minority candidates (medicine's "Rooney Rule"), and development of mentorship programs for minority junior faculty.

Recruit Faculty Interested in Minority Recruitment and Retention to the Effort

One common error that institutions make in this area is assuming that *only* minority faculty will be interested. This is greatly limiting; efforts to find the "great mentors" can identify individuals with extraordinary talent and commitment to mentorship in general, and these individuals can be invaluable in shaping a superb program, including mentorship for URM faculty and trainees.

Formal Sharing of Ideas Between Programs

Most institutions that explore minority mentorship programs will find pockets of success within their midst. A particular residency program or postdoctoral program may have years of successful experience. It is critical to find these areas of excellence and share both their specific strategies and their moral energy and commitment with other departments and programs. Academic medical center leadership can further elevate these efforts by formal recognition and celebration, which often increases the visibility of programs that otherwise might remain off the radar screen of institutional training programs.

❖ Case Studies

Case Scenario 1: Identifying a Mentor for a URM Fellow

Dr. Hightower is a non-URM director of a well-respected cardiology fellowship program on the East Coast. He is struggling with how to approach one of his female fellows, Dr. Theresa Munoz. Dr. Munoz is a Latina physician in a subspecialty with few URM or female faculty and trainees. Dr. Hightower has had little contact with her, but would like to ensure that all his residents are properly mentored. He is concerned that he cannot easily identify a mentor for Dr. Munoz and would like to speak with her. However, he does not wish to single her out or imply that she needs help. He has identified the three following options:

1. Call the only Latino faculty member in his department to suggest that he mentor her, even though that faculty member has shown little interest in the resident training program.

2. Follow the normal practice and wait to see if Dr. Munoz can establish her own mentor within the department.

3. Call Dr. Munoz into his office and discuss his desire to help her find a mentor.

Recommended Response

Although there is no correct answer for Dr. Hightower, a reasonable approach would be the third one, if not some combination of all of the above. Dr. Hightower is right to give this issue special attention, and involving Dr. Munoz in the process is probably the most thoughtful and respectful way to proceed. Rather than seeing Dr. Munoz as a problem or dilemma that he is ill-equipped to deal with, he can empower her to engage in the process while expressing his interest in her future success. For many of the reasons discussed in this chapter, it is possible that Dr. Munoz has some trepidation about this process as both a woman and Latina in a white male-dominated subspecialty. In their discussion, Dr. Hightower can offer to suggest a mentor for Dr. Munoz or listen to her interests and ask if she has identified anyone that she is interested in working with. He will discover whether she wishes to work with the Latino male faculty member and can facilitate an introduction. Dr. Hightower can also offer to mentor Dr. Munoz himself until either of them identifies a more suitable mentor.

Another strategy is to evoke the "Rooney Rule" discussed earlier. In Dr. Munoz's case, this would mean that Dr. Hightower will consider her when new clinical or research opportunities arise within the program. It does not imply that Dr. Munoz should get preference for all of these opportunities, but it can help to ensure that she does not become neglected or avoided because her superiors are reluctant to approach her.

Dr. Hightower would be advised to avoid common pitfalls that can thwart provision of mentoring by non-URM faculty to URM trainees. First, many non-URM faculty falsely presume that only a URM faculty member can mentor these individuals. While certainly the co-membership of similar ethnic background can be common ground for mentoring relationships, it is neither necessary nor sufficient for an effective mentoring relationship. It is far preferable to find a faculty member with compatible interests and skills of effective mentorship. A second pitfall is to make unwarranted assumptions about an individual's career path or personal experiences. For example, it would be a mistake to assume anything about the Latina fellow's background merely on the basis of her surname. Just as in clinical practice, open-ended questions showing genuine curiosity about the student's life journey are far more effective; the curiosity shown may allay the sense of isolation. Simple questions such as, "I like to learn something about my fellows; tell me about your family," or "How did you first get interested in medicine?" can be wonderful ways to open conversations.

Case Scenario 2: Providing Culturally Sensitive Mentoring to a URM Student

Jennifer Day is a third-year Native American medical student in a prominent academic medical school. While on her medicine clerkship, her resident evaluates her as detached and disengaged. She is called in by the clerkship director, Dr. Jones. In their meeting, Dr. Jones asks Jennifer about her performance:

"Jennifer, your latest evaluation came to my attention because it seems inconsistent with your performance in other clerkships. I wanted to ask you if everything is all right."

"Is there something wrong with my evaluation?" Jennifer wants to know.

Dr. Jones reassures Jennifer. "Your resident felt you were distracted. There are many reasons one might be distracted and I wanted to see if you felt that was an accurate assessment before I make any judgment on the evaluation. More important, if there are any specific challenges facing you, I wanted you to know that you are supported by me and the medical school."

Jennifer goes on to explain that her brother, recently returned from serving in Iraq, is suffering from posttraumatic stress disorder. Jennifer's family relies heavily on her for guidance. They are pressuring her to return home because her first duty is to her family and community.

Recommended Response

Dr. Jones handled this situation well from the start. Before accepting the resident's feedback in a vacuum, she researched Jennifer's past performance in other rotations. Most URM medical students already have a track record of success that has qualified them for medical school and advancement. Rather than directly confronting Jennifer with a "bad" evaluation, Dr. Jones frames the feedback as an anomaly; suggesting she already knows Jennifer is a good student. She also points out that there are legitimate reasons for being distracted and asks for Jennifer's own assessment. By giving Jennifer equal footing with the resident, Dr. Jones manages not to place Jennifer on the defensive. Finally, she stresses that she is offering Jennifer support if it is needed. The outcome for Jennifer's brother is uncertain, but for Jennifer it will probably be a good outcome. Dr. Jones created a safe, nonjudgmental environment for Jennifer. The context for Jennifer's performance was revealed, and Dr. Jones can consider this when summarizing Jennifer's overall clerkship performance. URM trainees are often relied upon heavily by their families and communities. Mentors cannot be expected to solve challenges like the one facing Jennifer, but they can maintain an awareness for such issues before making judgments on trainee performance.

Case Scenario 3: Finding a Mentor for a URM Faculty Member

As noted, only 7% of medical school faculty are black or Hispanic. This fact highlights the difficulty junior URM faculty face in locating a URM faculty mentor. It also foreshadows the critical role non-URM senior faculty must assume until the pipeline of URM faculty mentors is better supplied. Many senior non-URM faculty members have accepted this role gladly, as evidenced in the following exchange between Dr. Marion, a non-URM senior faculty PhD, and Dr. Leigh, a junior African-American internal medicine faculty member, as they pass each other in the hall:

Dr. Marion recognizes Dr. Leigh. "You're Dr. Leigh, aren't you?"

"Yes, hi!" says Dr. Leigh. They shake hands.

"I'm Leslie Marion. Rhonda Jackson told me you wanted to do some clinical research with health care access?"

"Yeah, I was hoping to get started on some projects this summer, but..."

Dr. Marion interrupts. "You know, I have mentored a lot of people in this area, and I really like the work you are doing. Would you like to meet with me?"

"How about later this month? Should I e-mail you to set it up?" Dr. Leigh asks.

"Yes, okay, just let me know when you are available after next week. I am going to my son's graduation."

"Congratulations, I'll e-mail you when you get back" says Dr. Leigh.

"Okay, great! Looking forward to talking to you!"

Recommended Response
Unfortunately, this does not happen every day, and might seem like a superficial exchange. However, some of the subtleties should be examined more thoroughly because they can assure the non-URM faculty just how simple it is to engage URM faculty. What the dialogue does not convey is the enthusiasm present in the smile of Dr. Marion. Throughout this entire interaction, which took only seconds while the two passed in a curving stairway going in opposite directions, she maintained eye contact and conveyed a genuine enthusiasm for what Dr. Leigh had to say. In a few quick

sentences, Dr. Marion established her track record of successfully mentoring people in their shared field of interest, invited Dr. Leigh to work with her, and complimented the work Dr. Leigh has done in the area already.

In the authors' experience, Dr. Marion has communicated key elements of an effective faculty mentor that outweigh the importance of being URM faculty. She has a shared field of interest that provides the potential for a productive collaboration. Dr. Marion feels confident that she has time, energy, and expertise, which she will apply to making Dr. Leigh an academic success.

❖ Conclusion

Mentoring URM students, residents, and faculty for success in academic medicine presents unique challenges, not least of which is the dearth of available racially concordant mentors. Nevertheless, implementing a framework for mentorship that can support growth of URM students, residents, and faculty is an important, necessary step if the percentage of URM in the physician workforce is to reflect the racial and ethnic diversity of the U.S. population. This step is also needed to address the too few numbers of URM among faculty at academic medical centers. Drawing upon national resources, using best practices in implementing mentoring programs, and tapping the skills and strengths of non-URM faculty as potential mentors are crucial strategies. Disseminating a broader understanding of the specific challenges that URM students, residents, and faculty face is another key step in ensuring that institutions and faculty implement appropriately supportive programs. Finally, mentors can play a key role in developing an institutional strategy to increase diversity.

REFERENCES

1. **Ludmerer KM.** Time to Heal: American Medical Education from the Turn of the Century to the Era of Managed Care. New York: Oxford Univ Pr; 1999.
2. **Association of American Medical Colleges.** Diversity in Medical Education Facts and Figures. Washington, DC: Association of American Medical Colleges; 2008.
3. **Dobbin F, Kalev A, Kelly E.** Best practices or best guesses? Diversity management and the remediation of inequality. American Sociological Review. 2006;71:589-617.
4. **Jeste DV, Twamley EW, Cardenas V, Lebowitz B, Reynolds CF 3rd.** A call for training the trainers: focus on mentoring to enhance diversity in mental health research. Am J Public Health. 2009;99 Suppl 1:S31-7.
5. **Elam CL, Johnson MM, Wiggs JS, Messmer JM, Brown PI, Hinkley R.** Diversity in medical school: perceptions of first-year students at four southeastern U.S. medical schools. Acad Med. 2001;76:60-5.
6. **Graham J.** A Chicago doctor talks about racism. Chicagotribune.com. July 10, 2008. Accessed at http://newsblogs.chicagotribune.com/triage/2008/07/a-chicago-docto.html.

7. **Wesson DE, King TE Jr, Todd RF, Torres EA, Hellmann DB, Flack JM, et al.** Achieving diversity in academic internal medicine: recommendations for leaders. Am J Med. 2006; 119:76-81.

8. **Gladwell M.** Blink. New York: Little, Brown; 2005.

9. **Roter DL, Hall JA, Katz NR.** Patient-physician communication: a descriptive summary of the literature. Patient Educ Couns. 1988;12:99-119.

10. **Ellison R.** Invisible Man. New York: Random House; 1952.

11. **Cose E.** The Rage of a Privileged Class. New York: HarperCollins; 1993.

12. **Weeks WB, Wallace TA, Wallace AE.** How do race and sex affect the earnings of primary care physicians? Health Aff (Millwood). 2009;28:557-66.

13. **Kipling R.** If. In: Rewards and Fairies. 1909.

14. **Groopman J.** How Doctors Think. Boston: Houghton Mifflin; 2007.

15. **Steele CM, Aronson J.** Stereotype threat and the intellectual test performance of African Americans. J Pers Soc Psychol. 1995;69:797-811.

16. **Okereke CD.** Mentoring—the trainee's perspective. J Accid Emerg Med. 2000;17:133-5.

17. **Bussey-Jones J, Bernstein L, Higgins S, Malebranche D, Paranjape A, Genao I, et al.** Repaving the road to academic success: the IMeRGE approach to peer mentoring. Acad Med. 2006;81:674-9.

18. **Pink D.** A Whole New Mind. New York: Riverhead Books; 2005.

19. **Collins B.** Tackling unconscious bias in hiring practices: the plight of the Rooney Rule. New York University Law Review. 2007;82:870-912.

12

Mentoring a Vulnerable Cohort for Success: The Special Case of the Foreign Medical Graduate

Steven F. Reichert, MD, FACP
Abey K. Thomas, MD

Programs that train international medical graduates (IMGs) encounter a variety of challenges in helping these individuals adapt to the living and working environments in the United States. Although many of these challenges are well known and much experience has been gained over the years, few studies have addressed these issues in a rigorous, data-driven way. Several attempts have been made to develop a curriculum that addresses the needs of IMGs, but no widespread or standardized approaches have been adopted. Understanding the needs of this specific group of physicians-in-training, who represent no small percentage of all residents training in the United States, and developing effective strategies for supporting them in their medical education and future careers are essential to their successful integration into the U.S. medical culture.

❖ Definitions and Demographics

It is useful to begin with a definition of what is meant by international medical graduate. An IMG is a graduate of any medical school around the globe, with the exception of schools in the United States, Puerto Rico, and Canada (which are accredited by the Liaison Committee for Medical Education or the American Osteopathic Association). IMGs can then be further differentiated into two distinct subgroups:

KEY POINTS

- International medical graduates (IMGs) are a heterogeneous group of learners whose backgrounds and training are highly varied.
- Among IMGs, foreign medical graduates (FMGs) in particular will require significant acclimatization to the U.S. health care system because they may be unaware of U.S. terminology, hospital practices, health care delivery systems, documentation practices, malpractice concerns, and day-to-day responsibilities of a house officer.
- Some IMGs, especially FMGs, require significant cultural acclimatization and may face increased pressure from social isolation and adaptation to a new living environment.
- FMGs training under visas require services of an immigration lawyer as well as guidance from a faculty member knowledgeable of the restrictions in training, fellowship, and job procurement imposed by the particular visa.
- FMGs may face increased scrutiny or be subject to perceived discrimination because of their status as a foreign graduate and immigrant.
- A successful mentor for FMGs must carefully consider all factors that arise in training of any house officer, while giving attention to issues that are unique to the experience of the IMG.

- A *USIMG* is a U.S. citizen who graduated from a foreign medical school. Most have participated in clinical rotations in the United States and are familiar with the workings of U.S. hospitals.
- An *FMG (foreign medical graduate)* is a citizen of a foreign country trained in a school not accredited by the Liaison Committee on Medical Education or American Osteopathic Association. Most have not had experiences in clinical settings in the United States while in medical school.

The bulk of this chapter focuses on the FMG, whose needs tend to be more challenging and complex than those of USIMGs.

International medical graduates account for a growing number of physicians in the United States. Overall, IMGs account for 26% of the overall physician work force, with internal medicine the chosen specialty of the largest group of IMGs (Tables 12-1 and 12-2). Applications of FMGs to the National Resident Matching Program (NRMP) in particular have risen sharply over the past few years, from 8943 applicants in 2005 to 11,467 in 2009 (1). The number of FMGs seeking training in internal medicine is disproportionately high when compared with other specialties. In the 2009 NRMP match, FMGs filled 1335, or 28%, of the 4853 categorical internal medicine positions in the match. In terms of percentages, this is closely followed by the field of family medicine, in which FMGs filled 21% of the 2296 family medicine positions in the match (1). It is important that leaders in academic medicine understand the impact of the unique challenges these residents face, particularly those in internal medicine.

Looking beyond training, it is important as well to note the differences in practice patterns that distinguish IMGs from U.S. medical graduates (USMGs). On average, IMGs are older and further out from their year of graduation, fewer are board-certified, and they are more likely than USMGs to be employed by the government (2) (Table 12-3).

❖ Characteristics of the FMG

The transition from medical student to resident is one of the most significant challenges a physician will face. The learning curve of an intern is steep, and the adjustment is not always an easy one. The FMG, however, faces other hurdles, both in the clinical setting and in the socioeconomic

Table 12-1. Physician Characteristics and Distribution in the United States

Physicians, n	921,904
IMG physicians, n	236,669 (from 127 countries)
IMG physicians in United States, %	26
IMGs in residency programs, %	12
IMGs in primary care, %	37
USIMGs in primary care, %	33
IMGs in patient care, %	78
IMGs in academics, %	16

Data obtained from Physician Characteristics and Distribution in the United States. Chicago: American Medical Association; 2008.

IMG = international medical graduate; USIMG = U.S. citizen who graduated from a foreign medical school.

Table 12-2. Number of Practicing Primary Care Physicians in the United States, 2000*

Physician Specialty	USMG	IMG	USIMG	FMG
Total physicians, n	410,684	113,720	15,678	91,885
Primary care physicians, n	140,587	45,043	6764	34,987
Percentage of total	34.2	39.6	43.1	38.1
Family practice physicians, n	53,346	8786	2115	6151
Percentage of total	13.0	7.7	13.5	6.7
Percentage of primary care	37.9	19.5	31.3	17.6
General practice physicians, n	12,239	4220	449	3707
Percentage of total	3.0	3.7	2.9	4.0
Percentage of primary care	8.7	9.4	6.6	10.6
Internal medicine physicians, n	48,263	21,204	3185	16,083
Percentage of total	11.8	18.6	20.3	17.5
Percentage of primary care	34.3	47.1	47.1	46.0
Pediatric medicine physicians, n	26,739	10,833	1015	9046
Percentage of total	6.5	9.5	6.5	9.8
Percentage of primary care	19.0	24.1	15.0	25.9

Reproduced with permission from Fink KS, Phillips RL Jr, Fryer GE, Koehn N. International medical graduates and the primary care workforce for rural underserved areas. Health Aff (Millwood). 2003;22:255-62.

FMG = foreign medical graduate; IMG = international medical graduate; USIMG = U.S. citizen who graduated from a foreign medical school; USMG = U.S. citizen who graduated from a U.S. medical school.

*Nonfederal allopathic and osteopathic physicians who had completed residency training and were involved in direct patient care. Except for the difference between the percentage of primary care physicians for USIMGs and FMGs in internal medicine ($P = 0.09$), all differences between USMGs and IMGs and between USIMGs and FMGs were statistically significant at $P < 0.01$.

environment, that the USMG or even the USIMG does not. This adds pressure and presents mentors of FMG residents with additional challenges.

As a group, FMGs are extremely varied in their cultural backgrounds, training, and experience. The largest single subgroup comes from South Asia (predominantly India, Pakistan, and Bangladesh), followed by significant numbers from African nations, East Asia, the Middle East, the Caribbean, and Europe (both eastern and western) (3).

Most medical schools outside the United States and Canada have a 5.5- to 6-year training structure. Candidates are generally eligible to apply for admission to medical school immediately after completing high school. The admission procedure often includes highly competitive entrance examina-

Table 12-3. Characteristics of International Medical Graduates and U.S. Medical Graduates Practicing in the United States

Characteristic	IMGs (n = 1000)	USMGs (n = 1000)	P Value*
Mean age, y (SD)	50.5 (13.3)	47.6 (13.4)	<0.001
Mean time since graduation, y (SD)	23.4 (13.0)	18.2 (13.0)	<0.001
Women, %	30.0	26.1	0.05
Practice specialty, %†			<0.001
Family practice	8.3	12.1	
Internal medicine	21.9	12.0	
Pediatrics	8.7	7.5	
Obstetrics-gynecology	4.1	5.5	
General surgery	3.3	4.6	
Board certification, %‡	72.6	81.1	<0.001
Practice type, %§			0.72
Resident	13.4	13.8	
Direct patient care	83.2	79.6	
Administration	1.0	1.6	
Medical teaching	1.3	1.2	
Medical research	1.2	1.1	
Practice location, %‖			0.60
Urban	89.2	88.0	
Large rural	5.6	6.8	
Small rural	1.7	2.2	
Isolated small rural	0.8	0.8	
Primary employer, %¶			<0.001
Government	6.4	4.6	
Solo practice	19.9	13.4	
Two-physician practice	2.6	3.3	
Group practice	20.8	31.2	
Health maintenance organization	0.5	0.3	
Medical school	2.9	2.8	
Nongovernment hospital	16.3	17.2	

Reproduced with permission from Akl EA, Mustafa R, Bdair F, Schünemann HJ. The United States physician workforce and international medical graduates: trends and characteristics. J Gen Intern Med. 2007;22:264-8. ©Society of General Internal Medicine 2007.
IMG = international medical graduate; USMG = U.S. citizen who graduated from a U.S. medical school.
*Based on t-tests for interval variables (age, time since graduation) and chi-square tests for categorical variables.
†Only primary care specialties are listed.
‡Residents excluded from denominator.
§Only relevant categories are listed; data missing for n = 91.
‖Data missing for n = 49.
¶Only relevant categories are listed.

tions. Undergraduate medical education courses typically last 4.5 years, followed by a period of clinical medical training. This may include a year of rotating clinical internship, during which medical students undergo training in surgery, internal medicine, obstetrics-gynecology, pediatrics, and other disciplines. The completion of this training confers eligibility for licensing and practice as a general practitioner or for further postgraduate training.

Medical education in different countries varies significantly in focus and quality (4). Because of resource limitations, clinical curricula in many schools, especially in developing countries, place greater emphasis on thorough history-taking and physical examination than on use of costly tests. Even a diagnostic test used routinely in the United States may be out of reach for medical schools in some countries. Hence, students who receive their medical education in these countries may be relatively less experienced with newer technologies available in the United States. It is also possible that students who complete medical education in more conservative societies may not have the breadth of experience with patients that is considered routine in the United States. For example, some societies or cultures may require that only female physicians examine women and only male physicians examine men, resulting in difficulties when these students are later expected to examine and care for patients of the opposite sex as residents in the United States (5).

Further, the hierarchy of relationships in foreign medical schools and hospitals is usually quite different from what is prevalent in the United States. Interactions with faculty are usually very formal, and interactions with nursing and other ancillary staff are rarely collegial. The concept of "team care" of patients might be quite alien to someone whose experience has been in such settings. Even the practice of medicine itself might appear to be comparatively paternalistic because patient autonomy, privacy, end-of-life care, and involvement in decisions are not viewed as they are in the United States (6).

It is understandable that graduates of such programs may have limited practice-based and systems-based management skills, which are essential for working in U.S. medical environments. Added to these professional hurdles are cultural and socioeconomic challenges that most immigrant physicians face. Many are away from familiar environments, friends, and families. The struggle to adapt to an alien culture and deal with separation from loved ones can affect work. To adjust to life in this society and to practice medicine in United States, FMGs need to not only be familiar with U.S. culture but also understand its nuances. This is not easily attained while also functioning as a house officer.

❖ Case Studies and Mentorship Strategies for FMG Residents

Mentors working with FMGs may encounter the aforementioned and other challenges. These include acclimation to a new system of medical practice, a new culture, and issues related to immigration and visas. Other issues faced by FMGs include the effect of discrimination and prejudice and special challenges and obstacles for career counseling. Foreign medical graduates may face inordinate obstacles in obtaining fellowships and perceive (appropriately or inappropriately) that their career options are relatively limited.

The next section presents four sample cases with background, along with descriptions of potential strategies or best practices that mentors might use to help FMGs resident overcome obstacles and move forward successfully in their medical education.

Case Scenario 1: Acclimating to the System

As an associate program director you have been asked by the program director and the departmental clinical competency committee to mentor Dr. A, a struggling trainee 4 months into her internship. Dr. A is a graduate of a top medical school in South Asia who spent 5 years in bench research before joining your program. Although her references and research accomplishments are impeccable, her board scores were just above passing and she has struggled in her first months as an intern. Evaluations from attending physicians and her supervising residents describe her as inefficient, lacking initiative, and passive. Her fund of knowledge appears weak, her notes are disorganized and incomplete, and her diagnostic plans are superficial. Concurrently, she has received multiple complaints from nursing staff and case managers that she is aloof, unapproachable, and at times condescending. You personally witnessed a very disturbing incident where her treatment of an elderly woman with advanced cancer and depression appeared to be disdainful and dismissive. Your program director has asked you to provide guidance.

Background

Before the mentor provides any advice, the underperforming intern's performance should be fully evaluated to determine the nature of the problem. It is the mentor's obligation to gather supporting data to rule out common secondary causes of poor performance. Five common domains (the five Ds: depression, distraction, deprivation, drugs, and disordered personality) are frequently cited as secondary causes of poor resident performance (Table 12-4) (7).

Table 12-4. The "Five Ds" of Secondary Causes of Poor Performance

Depression	Major, minor, adjustment reactions
Distraction	Concerns about children, relationships; need to manage family or personal illness
Deprivation	Sleep, food, social interaction
Drugs	Alcohol, prescription drugs, illicit drugs
Disordered personality	Any nonaffective personality disorder

If issues within these domains are suspected, the mentor must enlist the expertise of a professional who is skilled in the diagnosis and management of such problems and collaborate with the mentee and the clinical evaluation committee to provide appropriate support. If these factors are excluded, the mentor must then probe the house officer for other potential distracting factors. If the mentor is not personally an FMG or has little experience working with FMGs, it is important that the mentor understand the unique challenges these residents face.

Perhaps the greatest challenge for the FMG is acclimating to what is often a very different health care environment compared to what they experienced as medical students. Along with the adjustments during internship to which all residents are subjected—no matter where they went to medical school—FMGs face numerous specific challenges, including the hospital structure, documentation requirements, interactions with nursing staff, and unclear expectations of the role of supporting staff in providing patient care (8). Foreign medical graduate residents have typically not experienced collegial interaction with nursing or other ancillary staff. Nurses practicing in other countries may not have the high level of training of, and educational expectations that are placed on, nurses in the United States. Staff such as social workers, case managers, physical therapists, and occupational therapists are uncommon in resource-poor countries. Previous inexperience in interacting with the other members of the health care team may lead to a deficit in the systems-based practice skills required of a successful intern.

Expectations for authority in the learning environment result in different approaches to teaching and learning (9). In their native countries, FMGs may be expected to be modest and unassuming in the educational environment. Interactions with faculty in medical school frequently occur in a formal, rigid, and hierarchical manner (10). This deferential approach can be mistaken for passivity. Because the deferential resident is unaccustomed to speaking out in the presence of authority, these residents are at risk for inaccurate assessments of their knowledge (11).

Communication issues, either with patients or team members, are another commonly cited challenge for the FMG (12). Mentors and programs must be aware that FMGs often need to develop communication skills, including the subtle and pragmatic aspects of language interactions. Others' use of body language, posture, physical contact, or slang may place the FMG at a significant disadvantage. Mentors must understand and recognize these concerns in the FMG (13). Of note, while program directors identify communication issues as the main challenges faced by FMGs, foreign residents themselves identified more structural factors, such as knowledge of pharmaceuticals and hospital formularies and knowledge of the hospital system, as their most significant challenges to adapting to a new medical system (14, 15). The FMGs will have little, if any, awareness of the systems of Medicare, Medicaid, or managed care. In addition, their hospital experiences may not have given them sufficient experience with the advanced technology and diagnostic testing and treatments now available to them. Moreover, in the case of Dr. A, the problem resident at hand, her marginal performance on standardized testing and lack of recent clinical experience suggest that she is at risk for struggling during residency (16).

Mentorship Strategies

This resident presents a significant challenge for a mentor. Once the five Ds of underperformance have been eliminated (see Table 12-4), the mentor must still determine whether the resident is facing any or all of the above-described barriers. To be effective, the mentor must first understand these barriers and assess their effect on the resident's performance through personal observation and open, effective communications with the mentee. The relationship must be cultivated, including aspects that must come from the mentee (17). This may be a particular challenge for the FMG who is used to a strict hierarchy, yet this boundary must be addressed openly to form an effective and honest relationship. Once this issue of collaboration and shared responsibility for the relationship has been addressed, setting goals and expectations, providing feedback, and establishing priorities can begin.

Effective mentoring for Dr. A required a multistage approach. While a degree of depression related to difficulties in adjustment did emerge during one-on-one advising sessions with the program director, depression alone did not account for the poor clinical performance and perceived aloof attitude. It was clear that the gap in training left her unprepared for internship. She also failed to understand how she was perceived by nursing staff and patients. Dr. A was assigned to a chief resident, who shadowed her clinical performance on the wards and provided individual guidance with note-writing and day-to-day organization. Along with these sessions, the program director used 360° evaluations from nursing staff, while social workers provided additional insight for Dr. A and allowed her to improve her working relationship with hospital staff and her interactions with patients.

Case Scenario 2: Cultural Acclimation

Dr. B is a recent graduate from India who flourished in the first 4 months of internship. However, this was followed by poor performance. After 3 months and a formal academic warning, you approach her as program director. Although reticent at first, Dr. B eventually discloses that she has been under tremendous family pressure after her recent arranged marriage. During her month in the medical intensive care unit, the first rotation during which her performance eroded, she was informed of her arranged marriage and given the burden of arranging the ceremony on only several weeks' notice. Since being married, her spouse, who lives in another city, has placed unexpected demands on her that require frequent travel to his home. He has recently asked her to move to be with him, going back on a promise he had made before marriage that she could finish her residency first, then move. Her parents and siblings are overseas and provide little social support.

Background

Along with the significant challenges of conforming to the U.S. health care system, the FMG faces significant personal and cultural adjustment issues. While internship is a challenge to every resident's sense of confidence and security, the added strain of bridging cultures and adjusting to multiple losses presents the FMG with additional challenges. The degree of cultural loss varies. A Hispanic resident training in Miami or an Indian resident training in New York will face less isolation than the FMG who trains in a city with less ethnic diversity (10). The FMG is at increased risk for social isolation, given the loss of culture, country, accessibility to family and friends, and lifestyle. Unlike their American peers, FMGs leave the hospital to engage with a community whose culture is complex, foreign, and potentially overwhelming, and in which they must learn to live and work on daily basis (8).

Life cycle considerations are of particular importance (18). Whether they are an unattached young adult or are part of a young couple without children, a couple with young children, or a family with older children, all residents faces challenges in coping with these different phases of the life cycle while completing a rigorous residency program. The FMG may be less equipped to manage changes while also adjusting to a new culture and serving as a resident (10). Dr. B in case scenario 2 requires a mentor who will understand the impact of the social mores with which she was raised and recognize the specific challenges she faces.

Mentorship Strategies
Mentorship for this resident first involved assessing the cause of her problems. Discussion with Dr. B revealed both distraction and depression given her family pressures and desire to meet the expectations of her new husband. Because Dr. B was facing possible termination from the program, she was mentored by the program director, who first reiterated her obligations to the program. As it became clearer that she could not meet the expectations of both the program and her husband, she decided to complete the year and transfer to another program. She had no further difficulties in her second placement once this decision was made.

Case Scenario 3: Communication and Socialization Issues

Just 3 months into internship, Dr. C is struggling greatly. Attendings, supervising residents, nurses, and even patients complain that he is cold and distant and communicates poorly. This is not surprising—although his spoken English is passable, when he is under stress his language becomes broken and, at times, unintelligible. Your own conversations with Dr. C are frustrating because he has a difficult time expressing himself and understanding the nuance of language. In addition, staff have complained that his personal hygiene is lacking.

Background
Dr. C demonstrates that even with the preresidency screening and accreditation process, which includes passing the U.S. Medical Licensing Examination (USMLE) step 2 (Clinical Skills), FMGs frequently lack language and communication skills (11). The failure to master competency in interpersonal skills and communication impairs the resident's overall performance. Poor communicators are perceived as lacking knowledge or being poor members of a health care team. In particular, FMGs have been noted to be less likely to recognize depression in themselves or in their patients; this phenomenon has been attributed to cultural differences and poor communication skills (19). It is also possible that an FMG may be unaccustomed to personal hygiene habits (bathing, dental hygiene, use of deodorants) that are common in the United States. FMGs who present themselves as olfactory affronts to patients and staff may lose respect before being given the opportunity to prove themselves as clinicians.

Successful mentorship of these house officers requires that the mentor anticipate the problems and needs of their trainee. This degree of cultural sensitivity is similar to the skills required to care for patients from diverse cultural backgrounds. While the mentor may not recognize the specific cultural nuances of each individual trainee, mentors can demonstrate the open communication and consideration for the significant cultural adjustments faced by the FMG.

Mentorship Strategies
Dr. C's problems illustrated the difficulty in acculturation many FMGs face. Options for mentorship include an acculturation program during orientation. However, because this resource was not available at that time, a chief resident who was also an FMG was assigned as a mentor. Dr. C was encouraged to immerse himself in the language and culture of the area, including speaking English at all times, even with family and friends. Although a sensitive topic, the resident's hygiene was addressed in a specific mentorship session with both the chief resident and the program director. In time, as Dr. C became more acculturated, his clinical performance improved.

Case Scenario 4: Immigration, Visas, and Fellowships

> *Dr. D is a postgraduate year 3 resident training under an H-1B visa who is struggling to obtain a fellowship in cardiology. Although he holds an advanced degree in cardiology from Egypt, where he completed a residency and fellowship, served for 4 years as faculty member at a major medical center in Cairo, and has numerous publications (including two first-author papers completed during his current residency and three abstracts presented at national meetings), he received only five interviews at fellowship programs. Compounding his problems, after his vacation in Egypt, Dr. D was denied a return to the United States because of a delay in security clearance. He could not return for 3 months and must now delay completion of his residency. This delay also meant that he missed the window for fellowship interviews.*

Background
Although many residents face challenges with adapting to new hospitals and even new cultural milieus (if, for example, they have moved to a new region of the country), the most distinct and unique challenge faced by the FMG compared to the USMG or the USIMG is the work visa. The FMG who does not possess a green card presents a unique challenge to a mentor and necessitates an understanding of the visa process.

FMGs may train in the United States under the H-1B or the J-1 visa. Previously, the J-1 visa was the dominant visa used by FMGs who trained in the United States (20). However, in October 2000, President Clinton raised the cap limits for H-1B visas and provided an exemption for nonprofit organizations or institutions of higher education that allowed trainees at many hospitals to train under the H-1B visa. Currently, resident visas are almost equally divided between the H-1B and J-1 visa. To provide mentorship to either the prospective intern or the resident already in your program on a visa, it is important to understand the distinctions between the two visas (Table 12-5).

The J-1 visa is a student visa sponsored by the Educational Commission for Foreign Medical Graduates (ECFMG). It permits the resident to train in the United States for up to 7 years in a residency or fellowship position. Qualifications for the J-1 include ECFMG certification and passage of USMLE

Table 12-5. Comparison of J-1 and H-1B Visas

Type of Visa	Advantages	Disadvantages
J-1 visa	Requires passage of USMLE steps 1 and 2 only	Limited to 7 years of training
	Short processing times	2-year rule (trainee must return to home country for 2 years at end of visa)
	Low cost	
	2-year rule can be waived if employed in underserved area after training (J-1 waiver job)	Not sponsored by some fellowships
		Cannot be converted to green card without waiver job
H-1B visa	Can be converted to green card	Limited to 6 years
	No 2-year rule	Requires passage of USMLE step 3
	Can be rapidly processed (for premium processing fee)	Expensive
		Long waiting times (unless premium processing fees paid)
		Not sponsored by some fellowships

USMLE = U.S. Medical Licensing Examination.

step 1 and step 2, including the clinical skills examination. The J-1 visa may not be used for research training or as a portal for permanent entry into the United States—trainees are required to return to their home country for at least 2 years before returning to work in the United States. This home country requirement may be waived after residency only if residents obtainn J-1 waiver positions in an underserved community or if they can prove that return to their home country presents a significant hardship to their family.

The H-1B visa is an employer-sponsored visa that allows the resident to train in the United States for up to 6 years in a residency or fellowship position. Qualifications for the H-1B are similar to those for the J-1 but also require passing USMLE step 3. Because it is sponsored by the employer, this visa depends on the prospective employer to sponsor the resident and participate in the application process, which is more complex for resident and employer alike than obtaining a J-1 visa. Unlike the J-1, the H-1B visa does not require a return to home country for 2 years. Instead, the H-1B can be converted to permanent residency via green card status (if sponsored). This has made the H-1B visa a popular option for resident trainees who do not desire to return to their home country. However, the H-1B visa carries several potential problems for the program applicant or the resident in training. First, the H-1B carries significant expense (approximately $2500 at inception of visa), which the employer is expected to pay. Second, many fellowship programs chose to sponsor the J-1 but not the H-1B visa because the federal government does not reimburse fellowship programs for fellows on H-1B visas. Finally, while the H-1B visa may be converted to a green card, and permanent resident status, the resident must find an employer who is willing to undertake this process.

FMGs on J-1 visas are often seen to be less desirable by fellowship programs because many leave fellowships, particularly when a J-1 waiver job becomes available. The J-1 waiver job, which must be government approved and provide care to a designated underserved population, allows the resident working under a J-1 waiver to continue to work in the United States and, more important, eliminates the requirement of returning to the resident's home country at the end of the visa. This allows residents who wish to apply for permanent residency status a clearer path to work in the United States permanently. While some FMGs enter the United States with a clear goal of returning home, many have no desire to return to their home country. Thus, fellows may chose a waiver job over their current fellowship and opt out of the program, clearing their way for permanent employment in the United States but abandoning the fellowship program.

Since the September 11, 2001, attacks, obtaining security clearances has become an increasing problem for FMGs. Matched residents immigrating to start training, as well as residents enrolled in residency programs who travel home for vacation, face the potential for security delays. Countries/territories that present potential security issues include Pakistan, Syria, the Philippines, Haiti, Israel, the West Bank, Gaza, Sri Lanka, Georgia, Nigeria, Nepal, Kenya, Yemen, Iran, Lebanon, Afghanistan, Colombia, Saudi Arabia, and Iraq. Residents from these countries may face barriers to travel, which may interrupt or delay their training (21).

Of note, the resident in case 4, like so many of his colleagues, hopes to obtain a fellowship. Perhaps the most frequent challenge faced by a mentor is providing mentees with effective career guidance; for internal medicine residents this frequently means helping them with decisions regarding fellowship. Residents in internal medicine, for example, quickly realize that their decision to choose a residency has narrowed their career paths only modestly. The options for careers in internal medicine are broad, from specialization to primary care, and from private practice to public health. All residents need mentorship to help with their career decisions. As previously noted, unique issues faced by FMGs include limitation of fellowship options due to visa status. The failure to obtain a fellowship may be particularly troubling for FMGs, many of whom place a high value on obtaining a fellowship and see one as crucial to their future success in medicine (22).

Mentorship Strategies
Mentoring Dr. D in case scenario 4 will first require an understanding of the limited options available to him. His options for fellowship are limited because of his visa status, and his delay in obtaining security clearance has further compounded his dilemma—he will now have to delay finishing his residency. The mentor must guide the resident through his emotional reactions regarding his future prospects. While Dr. D should be encouraged to persevere, he must also be cautioned not to panic and make rash judgments. The strength of his academic preparation and research achievements will almost certainly secure him a fellowship; however, Dr. D may have to work to change his visa status to appeal to additional programs that do not sponsor the H-1B.

❖ Issues Related to Bias

Bias is an unfortunate fact of life, and FMGs are at a higher risk for encountering such behavior, both subtle and explicit. Being different is often perceived as being inferior. This could lead to situations in which FMGs experience racial and cultural prejudice and discrimination from patients, other staff, and possibly colleagues (23, 24). Prejudicial behavior can have an impact at every stage, from medical school through residency (10, 11). Medical students are less likely to develop professional and personal bonds with FMG residents and hence may view their rotation less positively. Popular residency selection guides advise U.S. medical students to avoid residency programs that have a large proportion of IMGs in their numbers, and U.S. graduates may be reluctant to interact with FMG residents at the same hospitals (25).

Residents not fluent in English or those who speak with an accent may be seen as "slow" and less than competent. Patients and their families may feel that such residents do not comprehend their needs and hence may be less accepting of care from FMGs. Attending physicians may be less willing to have FMGs participate in the care of their patients; similar concerns may be raised by hospital administration. The FMGs report struggles for acceptance, fear of rejection, and fear of disappointing patients that can lead to fear of punishment for committing an error (26).

Such sentiments may seriously affect the confidence of vulnerable FMGs in their own capacity to care for patients in U.S. health system and may adversely affect their work. It is important for the program administration and department chair to publicly support their international house staff. Adopting measures to help FMGs function effectively within the system is essential.

The mentor must be prepared to work with the resident who faces possible discrimination. Extreme sensitivity is required because the FMG may feel as if she or he has no recourse. The mentor should work with the FMG to achieve open communication and build trust so that the mentor can assess the true extent of the problem. If overt discrimination is found, the mentor is obligated to share this information with the program director, chair, and head of graduate medical education or human resources to defend the rights of the resident. Programs can prepare their trainee FMGs better by addressing these disturbing experiences and acknowledging the existence of this prejudice during orientation programs and through regular meetings for feedback with the resident. They can also help residents develop comfortable responses to be used in situations where FMG residents are faced with prejudice. Role-playing can be used to rehearse possible responses. All residents can profit from these discussions because there are multiple parallels that they may encounter in their own careers.

The mentor must understand the perceived loss of status in residents if a fellowship cannot be secured. However, the mentor must also help the resident understand that fellowship for the sake of specialization may lead to career dissatisfaction. The resident should also realize that the failure to specialize is not a failure at all but instead a positive and vital career option.

With the decrease in interest nationwide in primary care, the FMG will probably find increased opportunity for job placement in a primary care position.

Mentors should also be aware that there are a great variety of ethnic medical societies at the state and national level, which may be of great assistance in job placement for the FMG (Table 12-6).

❖ Summary

Even with the tremendous growth in the presence of FMGs in internal medicine training, widespread programs to help FMGs acclimate are lacking. Educators have called for academic leadership to take responsibility in supporting IMGs and disseminating a better understanding of the unique challenges these residents face (11). Residency program directors believe that an assigned mentor with structured supervision is one of the most successful interventions to assist problem residents (27). However, mentors and international medical graduates entering residency programs

Table 12-6. Ethnic Medical Societies

National Arab American Medical Association
National American Taiwan Medical Association
Philippine American Medical Society
Romanian Medical Society of New York
Salvadoran American Medical Society
Serbian-American Medical Society
Thai Physicians Association of America
Ukrainian Medical Association of North America
Venezuelan American Medical Association
National Hispanic Medical Association
Peruvian American Medical Society
Polish-American Medical Society
Russian American Medical Association
Semmelwies Scientific Society
Spanish-American Medical Society
Turkish American Physicians Association
United States Colombian Medical Association
Vietnamese Medical Association of the USA

need resources and support in understanding the subtleties of their situation. Both the ECFMG and the American College of Physicians offer Web-based reference materials for trainees and faculty to draw upon. Examples of successful acculturation programs during residency have been described in surgical, psychiatric, family medicine, and internal medicine residency programs (9, 28–30). Unfortunately, these programs are isolated and require significant educational resources; this makes their replication at other sites more challenging. Increasing awareness and education of the obstacles faced by FMGs present an opportunity for continued dissemination of new educational methods at local and national levels. While the growth of these resources will assist in the process, the successes in mentorship of the FMG will still rely on the commitment of individual trainees and academic physicians.

Acknowledgment: The authors would like to thank Stephen Perlitsh, JD, for his assistance.

REFERENCES

1. **National Residency Matching Program.** Results and Data: 2009 Main Residency Match. Accessed at www.nrmp.org/data/resultsanddata2009.pdf.
2. **Akl EA, Mustafa R, Bdair F, Schünemann HJ.** The United States physician workforce and international medical graduates: trends and characteristics. J Gen Intern Med. 2007;22:264-8.
3. **Fink KS, Phillips RL Jr, Fryer GE, Koehn N.** International medical graduates and the primary care workforce for rural underserved areas. Health Aff (Millwood). 2003; 22:255-62.
4. **Porter JL, Townley T, Huggett K, Warrier R.** An acculturization curriculum: orienting international medical graduates to an internal medicine residency program. Teach Learn Med. 2008;20:37-43.
5. **Gawande A.** Naked. N Engl J Med. 2005;353:645-8.
6. **Searight H, Gafford J, Mohan V.** Training of international medical graduates. In: Feldmand, M, Christenen J, eds. Behavioral Medicine: A Guide for Clinical Practice. 3rd ed. New YorkL McGraw-Hill/Lange; 2007:440-1.
7. **Reichert S, Beliveau M.** Spanning the Cultural Divide: Case Studies of Chief Residents and IMGs. A Toolkit for Today's Chief Medical Resident. 16th ed. Washington, DC: Association of Program Directors in Internal Medicine; 2008:23-8.
8. **Whelan GP.** Commentary: Coming to America: the integration of international medical graduates into the American medical culture. Acad Med. 2006;81:176-8.
9. **Porter JL, Townley T, Huggett K, Warrier R.** An acculturization curriculum: orienting international medical graduates to an internal medicine residency program. Teach Learn Med. 2008;20:37-43.
10. **Cole-Kelly K.** Cultures engaging cultures: international medical graduates training in the United States. Fam Med. 1994;26:618-24.

11. **Schuster BL.** Strengths and weaknesses of international medical graduates in U.S. programs: a chairperson's perspective. Accessed at www.acponline.org/about_acp/international/graduates/training_in_us/shuster.htm.

12. **Viner E, Joshi AS, Porter BA, Rajput V, Alguire PC, Cavanaugh SK, et al.** Understanding the American medical system. In: Alguire PC, Whelan GP, Rajput V, eds. The International Medical Graduate's Guide to US Medicine and Residency Training. Philadelphia: ACP Pr; 2009:162.

13. **Pilotto LS, Duncan GF, Anderson-Wurf J.** Issues for clinicians training international medical graduates: a systematic review. Med J Aust. 2007;187:225-8.

14. **Zulla R, Baerlocher MO, Verma S.** International medical graduates (IMGs) needs assessment study: comparison between current IMG trainees and program directors. BMC Med Educ. 2008;8:42. IMGs

15. **McMahon GT.** Coming to America—international medical graduates in the United States. N Engl J Med. 2004;350:2435-7.

16. **Part HM, Markert RJ.** Predicting the first-year performances of international medical graduates in an internal medicine residency. Acad Med. 1993;68:856-8.

17. **Zerzan JT, Hess R, Schur E, Phillips RS, Rigotti N.** Making the most of mentors: a guide for mentees. Acad Med. 2009;84:140-4.

18. **Whelan G.** Living in America: popular culture. In: Alguire PC, Whelan GP, Rajput V, eds. The International Medical Graduate's Guide to US Medicine and Residency Training. Philadelphia: ACP Pr; 2009:188-99.

19. **Searight HR, Gafford J.** Behavioral science education and the international medical graduate. Acad Med. 2006;81:164-70.

20. **Mullan F, Politzer RM, Davis CH.** Medical migration and the physician workforce. International medical graduates and American medicine. JAMA. 1995;273:1521-7.

21. **Fitzpatrick E, Wallowicz T.** Transitioning to the United States. In: Alguire PC, Whelan GP, Rajput V, eds. The International Medical Graduate's Guide to US Medicine and Residency Training. Philadelphia: ACP Pr; 2009:58-63.

22. **Khan FA.** International medical graduates. Finished your residency—what's next? American College of Physicians. Accessed at www.acponline.org/about_acp/international/graduates/practicing_in_us/khan.htm.

23. **Gelb AM, Cassell E.** Approaches to the training of foreign medical graduates. J Med Educ. 1972;47:429-33.

24. **Haveliwala YA.** Problems of foreign born psychiatrists. Psychiatr Q. 1979;51:307-11.

25. **Steward DE; Association of Professors of Medicine.** The internal medicine workforce, international medical graduates, and medical school departments of medicine. Am J Med. 2003;115:80-4.

26. **Fiscella K, Roman-Diaz M, Lue BH, Botelho R, Frankel R.** 'Being a foreigner, I may be punished if I make a small mistake': assessing transcultural experiences in caring for patients. Fam Pract. 1997;14:112-6.

27. **Yao DC, Wright SM.** National survey of internal medicine residency program directors regarding problem residents. JAMA. 2000;284:1099-104.

28. **Curran V, Hollett A, Hann S, Bradbury C.** A qualitative study of the international medical graduate and the orientation process. Can J Rural Med. 2008;13:163-9.

29. **Kramer M.** Educational challenges of international medical graduates in psychiatric residencies. J Am Acad Psychoanal Dyn Psychiatry. 2006;34:163-71.

30. **Horvath K, Coluccio G, Foy H, Pellegrini C.** A program for successful integration of international medical graduates (IMGs) into U.S. surgical residency training. Curr Surg. 2004;61:492-8.

Epilogue

Lessons From My Mentor: Advice for Living and Learning in Academic Medicine

Holly J. Humphrey, MD, MACP

This book has explored mentoring from several different points of view and considered professional development for students, residents, and faculty. One key aspect of mentoring, however, may be difficult to convey in a book: namely, the powerful lessons learned from a mentoring experience and the way in which a mentor can shape and guide the course of a protégé's career, providing fulfillment for a lifetime.

Over the course of a dozen years at the very beginning of my career as a student, resident, chief resident, and program director, I personally experienced one of life's greatest gifts—a transformative mentoring experience. From my mentor, I learned many powerful lessons that continue to resonate and serve me well, even today. These lessons provide a valuable framework for anyone serious about mentoring the next generation of leaders in academic medicine. Moving beyond the principles and best practices discussed in this book, I will share a sample of the hundreds of lessons I learned from my mentor. Many of these lessons came from watching my mentor, then a department chair, engage on a deep, personal level with students, residents, and faculty in a manner that never felt like an unwelcome intrusion or an incursion on my role as program director; rather, his approach felt additive and deeply synergistic. My hope is that these lessons will not only prove valuable to readers in and of themselves but also convey the way in which personal interactions and guiding principles can indelibly shape an individual's day-to-day experience and future life.

❖ Lesson 1: The Secret of the Care of the Resident Is in Caring for the Resident

This paraphrase of the oft-quoted words of Dr. Francis Peabody ("The secret of the care of the patient is in caring for the patient"), who was referring to patients being the center of a physician's attention and deep concern, apply well to the relationship of faculty and department leaders to their residents. One cannot fully teach or supervise residents unless one truly cares about each resident as a person. Departments of medicine have long treasured their residency and fellowship programs, but no form of departmental support or educational curriculum can replace the personal interest in residents as people who are learning medicine at a time in their lives when they experience constant challenges on both a personal and a professional level. Residents face an enormous burden as they confront the multiple stresses of being on the front lines of patient care and learning many skills for the first time, combined with the stress of educational debt and personal obligations to a spouse and children or aging parents.

One summer shortly after the new interns arrived on campus, an intern leaving the hospital encountered our department chair, who inquired how the first month of internship was going. The young intern mentioned that his patients were doing well and that his resident was very helpful. The intern also disclosed that the new bicycle he was using to get back and forth to the hospital had been stolen. The chair shared his disappointment about the theft; the next day, he called the chief resident to his office and asked the chief to deliver a personal check to that intern. The chair gave the chief resident specific instructions to let the intern know that the money was to replace the stolen bicycle and was being paid from "a special fund" in the department.

On more than one occasion in my role as program director, I was asked by chief residents whether the department really had a "special fund." While never explicitly addressed, we all came to know that the "special fund" was in fact, the personal fund of the department chair and his wife. This level of personal care for the intern spoke volumes not only about our department chair's generosity but also his concern for the life of a new intern navigating the terrain of internship and life in a new city.

❖ Lesson 2: Confront the Uncomfortable

It is not uncommon for leaders in academic medicine to be confronted with painful choices and unpopular decisions. The manner in which leaders manage this process can often be the difference between the success and failure of a plan, almost irrespective of the plan's merits or flaws. Managing uncomfortable situations and dealing openly, sensitively, and charitably with those who are unhappy with the choices and direction of a department or institution can be a leader's greatest challenge.

Early in my tenure as program director, we faced the question of whether we should continue an "open" intensive care unit (ICU) structure or create a "closed" ICU in which primary physicians from general medicine and subspecialty services would transfer their patients' care to the critical care team. Contemplating this change struck deeply at the core of how our faculty saw the department's mission and purpose. The department chair, rather than issue a directive or manage in a top-down manner, organized a committee process whereby dissenting opinions could be part of the conversation. Appointments to the committee, in addition to subspecialty and general medicine faculty and residents, included ethicists, social scientists, and health outcomes scholars. In this way, the decision-making process drew on the strength of an academic department: The discussion was scholarly, focused on sharing data openly, and explored discrepancies in order to reach the most robust conclusion. In fact, in the end, the department not only changed its clinical operations and structure but published a paper in the *Journal of the American Medical Association* on its work (1). Although some disagreed with the choice, no one doubted the necessity. The process may have seemed unnecessarily time-consuming at the front end, but once there was agreement about what should happen, the faculty and house staff in the department united to bring about the necessary change. Ultimately, this process designed to garner broad-based opinions and ideas and to evolve and explain decisions openly and carefully proved a most effective path forward.

❖ Lesson 3: Correct Misbehavior Promptly and Decisively

Sometimes when department chairs manage the volume of issues referred to their office, they are tempted to ignore the "minor" events and stay focused on the big picture issues that could reach the ears of the dean, university president, trustees, or local newspaper. Nevertheless, it is the accumulation of incidents in daily life that create our working and educational environment. It is a mistake to assume that an issue is "small" on the basis of the stature of the individuals involved. On one occasion, a resident was in tears after a section chief humiliated her for not leaving her own clinic and her patients to tend to the section chief's patient. When news of the incident reached the chair, he promptly picked up the telephone and calmly reminded his section chief that the resident was with us for the purpose of her education, not to immediately join him in clinic with his patient. In a polite tone, the chair told the section chief that his behavior was like "a bull in a china shop" and that he needed to respect the resident's competing priorities. The chair asked the section chief to apologize to the resident, and once that happened, all were able to move forward with confidence that similar interactions would not recur.

❖ Lesson 4: Don't Take Credit for Other People's Work

Conflicts arising from failing to properly credit or attribute work are as old as medicine itself. While clear guidance may be given in some areas, such as journals that provide very specific expectations for authors, in many situations in academic medicine clarity regarding attribution is unclear. In these instances, decisions are based on the personal practice of right and wrong.

The year was 1989; I had just completed my fellowship and was the newly appointed program director for the internal medicine residency. Six months earlier, our major teaching affiliate announced plans for a disaffiliation. Because many of our fellowship programs were integrated and, in fact, sponsored by the major teaching affiliate, we needed a prompt accreditation review of our residency and all 11 subspecialty fellowship programs. This would happen within 60 days of my taking over as program director. On the eve of our site visit, I sat with my chair in his office trying to persuade him that we should go into the site visit with me as the associate director and with him as the director. I was 30 years old, newly appointed to the faculty, and it made sense to me that we would be in a much better position with him in the "official" position. With that suggestion he said, "You have done all of the work—if I were to take credit for your work, it would be against everything I believe in. We are going forward into this site visit with you as program director." Although this was a significant risk on his part, he empowered me to begin my career as a program director from a position of confidence and strength.

Today, when I find myself working with junior colleagues, and recognize how much pleasure I take in their accomplishments, I often reflect on how my mentor displayed both integrity and confidence in me at the very beginning of my career. This reinforces the spirit of generosity I wish to share as broadly as my influence extends.

❖ Lesson 5: Motivate Followers and Create a Team

While the professional members of an academic department of medicine are intrinsically a highly motivated group, they need direction to use their motivation to become part of a team that rows their oars in the same direction. From my mentor, I learned three basic principles for accomplishing this goal. First, spend time with your team. Second, care about people beyond their contribution to the department. Get to know them as people. Learn about their family and their life outside the hospital. Finally, have a sense of humor when motivating people to do unpleasant work.

Dictating medical records falls in the realm of unpleasant but necessary work. Our hospital president published a weekly report on the number of undicated medical records; because our department admitted the most patients, our numbers stood out quite starkly. Instead of sending a stern memo to the chief residents and program director, our chairman drew caricatures of himself smiling or crying on the weekly report. If we saw a "smiley face," we knew that we had done well. If we saw large tears drawn on his face, we were inspired by his humor to try harder. Because he had made such an effort to know the residents on a personal level—attending their social events, organizing dinners, and taking the time to stop and talk—the residents were motivated to help and support him. Even the lightest, and the most light-hearted, sign of his disappointment gained attention and spurred a positive and constructive response.

❖ Lesson 6: Show Respect and Kindness—For All

Each of us interacts with a variety of people throughout each day. We engage frequently with some individuals because of the nature of our work. With others we interact only rarely. Some of these people are our bosses and some are our colleagues. It is not uncommon to meet people who have a different demeanor depending on whom they are with. We all remember the resident who impressed the attending physician but who let the intern stumble and the students struggle. There are department chairs who meet the expectations of the dean and the hospital president but may not know the names of the chief residents. The dean may spend most of each day tending to relationships with members of the board of trustees but spend little if any energy with department chairs, faculty, residents, or students.

One of the lessons our residents learned from our department chair is that there is no room in the life of a physician for arrogance. While our chair often shared this lesson in the context of working with patients and other members of the health care team, it was also a lesson applicable to multiple other domains. One of the most poignant examples occurred in his interactions with the middle-aged, crippled woman who cleaned his office. When he saw her, the chair invariably greeted her by name, inquired about her children, asked about her pain, and asked if there was anything she needed or that he could help with. It was clear that the woman cleaning his office was as important to him as the faculty, the residents and students, a member of the board of trustees, the university president, or one of his patients. The genuine respect and kindness shown to this woman who struggled to walk was a powerful demonstration of his authenticity as a man and an inspiring example of how to recognize the important contribution that so many different people play in our lives.

❖ Lesson 7: Choose Your Words Carefully and Tend to the Barometric Pressure

Admonitions about the power of the tongue or the wrath caused by misuse of words are as ancient as time. Psychiatrists and psychologists spend years in training to find just the right words at the right time to help patients therapeutically. Much is written about effective speaking, and courses promise to transform anyone with interest into an excellent communicator. Little attention, if any, is given to the preparation necessary when speaking informally to groups of colleagues. These hundreds of interactions that occur every day create the atmosphere—the barometric pressure—of the environment in which we work and learn.

One tradition in our residency program is a weekly lunchtime gathering of all the residents for socialization, program-related announcements, and occasional celebrations of a special accomplishment by one or more of the residents. The gathering, known as House Staff Lunch, is highly informal and is led by the chief residents. On the eve of starting my year as the chief resident, I received some surprising advice from the department chair: "Your year will rest on the tone that you set at House Staff Lunch." He went on to describe that when the house staff were gathered as a group and needed to follow the direction of the chief resident, they would base their decision on how they were spoken to and whether the tone that the chief resident set was one that they wanted to buy into! He made me aware that my comments, no matter how informal, would have a powerful impact on creating positive or negative energy among the residents.

Over the years I came to appreciate that this was advice he followed himself. He came to House Staff Lunch several times a year to bring the residents up to date on major new strategic directions of the department or to consult with the house staff about adding a new hospital affiliation to our residency program. Whenever he came, he was always prepared. This usually meant that the evening before, he took a pad of paper and hand-wrote the comments he planned to make. This was never an outline, but always comments written in full sentences and complete paragraphs. The next morning he gave me the several pages of handwritten remarks and asked me to critique them for content and for tone. The advice he gave me years earlier was now playing out but reciprocally.

It still amazes me that a busy department chair cared enough to establish the right tone with the house staff that he penned his comments by hand every time. Sometimes he spoke directly from his pages of notes and other times he spoke conversationally—but every single time, the words spoken were preceded by a handwritten account. By choosing his words carefully and by engaging with his department at all levels, he tended to the barometric pressure of the environment. He ensured that the atmosphere was a nurturing and supportive one and that residents were learning in a climate of mutual respect and collegiality.

Today, when I find myself standing in front of large groups of students or residents, I recall my mentor's very careful preparation for even informal meetings with our house staff. When my interaction with these groups goes well, I know that I prepared sufficiently. When it does not go as I had hoped, I know that I conducted the session without adequate preparation or consideration for how the audience would hear and understand my words and message.

❖ Lesson 8: Know What To Do When a Colleague Dies

Death is always difficult. Physicians are trained to understand the pathophysiology of the primary diseases leading to death and the subsequent hemodynamic collapse that ensues. Medical students are instructed in the methods of delivering bad news, and residents generally practice this skill far more often than they wish. But how are physicians taught to manage a death when it is one of their own—a trusted colleague, a friend, a contemporary?

My mentor taught our residents how to manage this tragedy when a senior resident died unexpectedly at the end of the summer. This tragedy occurred during the chair's vacation. When he learned the news, he immediately returned to the hospital and met with all of the residents at their morning report conference, where he compassionately addressed their shock and pain. He talked them through the steps that the program needed to take in response to this tragedy, but perhaps more powerfully, he talked about the steps they needed to take as individuals. Everyone is uncomfortable with death, he explained, but the discomfort cannot inhibit us from doing the right thing. The first and most important step is to reach out to the family. As much as the residents themselves are in pain, the family's pain is worse. He told the residents that they needed to reach out to the family—comfort them, sit with them, pledge to stay close to them.

The compassion and empathy, including the tearful exchange and emotional intensity in the conference room, imprinted the hearts and minds of the residents present. The ripple effect continues today. In the room that day was a chief resident who 7 years in the future would lose her husband in a tragic car accident, leaving her a widow with two young children and pregnant with their third child. That woman remembers the indelible lesson from her department chair.

Not in the room that day, however, was the program director. Quite unexpectedly, the program director's younger sister died the same day as the resident. I am that program director, now a dean. In the more than a decade since those simultaneous deaths, I have had the experience of reaching out to comfort families grieving the unexpected death of their children who were our students and residents. When this happens, I reflect back on the painful lesson learned in the context of grief and loss.

❖ Lesson 9: Manage Faculty—Their Coming and Their Going

One need spend only a brief time in academic medicine before understanding how much of a chair's job relates to retaining their star faculty. Throughout his time as chair, my mentor made extraordinary efforts to retain faculty members. More often than not, these efforts involved a significant investment of his personal time and attention. He was almost always successful. If in the end, however, he could not retain the faculty member, then he immediately shifted his focus into supporting their leaving, congratulating them, and wishing them well.

My mentor taught me the ultimate lesson when I watched as he was successfully recruited to the East Coast and left the university after 30 years. When this happened, he took many steps to leave the department in good order. There were special notes written to files, promotions of staff and faculty taken care of, an interim chair named, and the implementation of a process of preparing for a transition. First, he shared the news with his executive team, then with the residents at House Staff Lunch, then with the faculty and staff, and finally, week after week, with his patients. He wanted to personally tell each one of his patients about his impending departure, some of whom had been patients for 30 years. Although I tried to hold onto the idea that he would stay, I had been taught well: I supported his leaving, offered congratulations, wished him well, and have subsequently been delighted to see him flourish and imprint his legacy on another institution.

❖ Lesson 10: Remember the Primacy of Family

Over the many years of working with my mentor, it was clear that nothing was more important to him than family. Not only was this obvious from how he lived his life, but nearly every conversation that he had with students, residents, faculty, staff, or patients would mention their families. Family was an organizing principle of his life.

This principle was first apparent to me when I was a medical student in the "couples match" and he was a newly appointed department chair. When I sought his counsel about where I should pursue residency training, his advice was distinctly different from every other faculty member who advised me. To a person, everyone advised that I must do what was best for my career and then try to end up in the same city with my husband. My mentor's advice was that I would be very well educated in any of a large number of internal medicine programs and that I should concentrate on what is best for my family: my new husband, parents, and siblings. If I kept my priorities straight, then I would be able to perform at a high level knowing that my life was integrated and not one-dimensional. Not only did this advice provide the foundation for both my career and my family, but it is the advice I have shared with the hundreds of students and residents who have sought my counsel in the decades since.

Imagine how helpful and powerful this was to me as a young woman. He mentored me through the stages of being single as a medical student, married as a resident, a new mother as his chief resident, and ultimately a mother of three as one of his faculty members. Being nurtured both personally and professionally in this environment is one of life's greatest gifts, a gift that I hope to pass on to the next generation.

Equally important, my personal recounting of the lessons from my mentor speaks entirely to what I learned by working with him in his role as department chair. Others could articulate the lessons learned from his mentorship as a scientist in the laboratory where he made fundamental observations in his field. Still others could share lessons from his mentorship in clinical medicine where he took care of complicated patients. One dedicated mentor can broadly impact science, clinical medicine, education, and leadership extending to the next generation. In so doing, the next generation is inculcated with the values and ideals of the true professional.

> I want to be thoroughly used up when I die, for the harder I work the more I love. I rejoice in life for its own sake. Life is no brief candle to me; it is a sort of splendid torch which I've got a hold of for the moment and I want to make it burn as brightly as possible before handing it on to future generations.
> —*George Bernard Shaw*

REFERENCE

1. **Carson SS, Stocking C, Podsadecki T, Christenson J, Pohlman A, MacRae S, et al.** Effects of organizational change in the medical intensive care unit of a teaching hospital: a comparison of 'open' and 'closed' formats. JAMA. 1996;276:322-8.

Index